Swingland

Between the Sheets of the Secretive,
Sometimes Messy,
but Always Adventurous Swinging Lifestyle

DANIEL STERN

A TOUCHSTONE BOOK
Published by Simon & Schuster
New York London Toronto Sydney New Delhi

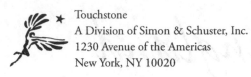
Touchstone
A Division of Simon & Schuster, Inc.
1230 Avenue of the Americas
New York, NY 10020

First Touchstone hardcover edition October 2013

TOUCHSTONE and colophon are registered trademarks of Simon & Schuster, Inc.

For information about special discounts for bulk purchases, please contact Simon & Schuster Special Sales at 1-866-506-1949 or business@simonandschuster.com.

The Simon & Schuster Speakers Bureau can bring authors to your live event. For more information or to book an event contact the Simon & Schuster Speakers Bureau at 866-248-3049 or visit our website at www.simonspeakers.com.

Designed by Aline C. Pace

Manufactured in the United States of America

10 9 8 7 6 5 4 3 2 1

Library of Congress Cataloging-in-Publication Data
    Stern, Daniel.
    Swingland : between the sheets of the secretive, sometimes messy, but always adventurous swinging lifestyle / Daniel Stern.
        pages   cm
    "A Touchstone Book."
    1. Group sex. I. Title.
    HQ23.G73 2000
    306.77—dc23
                                                                                    2013005231

ISBN 978-1-4767-3254-1

While the stories that follow are based on actual events and real people, names and locations have been changed to ensure discretion.

But most of us don't use our real names, so it doesn't really matter.

However, in the event that by changing your "name" I have given you your real name, know that it was purely coincidental.

The Lifestyle

NOUN. A global community whose members (swingers) engage in sexual relations as recreational or social activity.

Vanilla

ADJECTIVE. *Lifestyle slang.* NOT of or in the Lifestyle.

Contents

Between the Sheets   1

Author Disclaimer   11

Flirting

My Sort of Sex Education   19

My Quest Begins   27

Swing and a Miss   33

Lesson 1: The Lifestyle and the Single Male   43

Lesson 2: Pre-swing Considerations   49

Lesson 3: The Swing Commandments   61

Foreplay

The Deep End   69

A Threesome and Steven Seagal   79

Tamer Waters   87

Lesson 4: Gearing Up   99

Lesson 5: The Hunt   107

Lesson 6: Courting   115

Contents

Intercourse

Synthesis	123
Vanilla Reprieve	129
Same Book. Dusty Cover.	147
Lesson 7: Know Your Couple	155
Lesson 8: Meet 'n' Greet	165
Lesson 9: The Club Scene . . . Grudgingly	171

Orgasm

Poker Night	179
A Day in the Lives	195
So That Happened	209
Lesson 10: Playtime	219
Lesson 11: Party Primer	225
Lesson 12: When Fit Hits the Shan	231

The Morning After

Student Became Teacher Becomes Student	237
When It Rains	249
Full Circle	265
Lesson 13: Downtime	269

Little Black Book

Bonus Lesson: So You Wanna Host . . .	275
Acknowledgments	289
Glossary	291

Swingland

Between the Sheets

The first car arrived. From it emerged a husband toting a small gym bag and a wife bundled in a full-length raincoat buttoned to the top with just a flash of fishnet escaping at the hem. They scurried up the walk to the house that was every other house on every other suburban street, slipped through the front door, and shut it quickly behind them. Another car arrived. Then another. One by one they parked and two by two their occupants dashed inside with equal parts urgency to avoid detection and eagerness to escape the outside world and dwell, if only for a little, in the one inside.

I, too, walked up the path and knocked on the door on the designated night at the designated time as a month prior while cooling down post-play at a GB that ended up MFM, Gerard, the other M, extended a rare invitation to a couples house party.[1]

---

1 The GB (Gang Bang) ended up MFM (Male-Female-Male threesome) due to two flakes, a newbie who bailed between the hotel lounge and suite, and a self-professed Lifestyle veteran who "mysteriously" contracted a case of performance anxiety. *(Most Lifestyle terminology is self-explanatory, but for swing lingo virgins, there's a handy-dandy glossary at the back of the book.)*

"Respectful single males are insanely hard to find," he admitted.

"And skilled ones all but impossible." Rose, Gerard's wife and the star of our MFM sexual sandwich, winked.

I thanked them for the compliments and gratefully accepted their invitation. However, I knew the odds of a single male receiving a legit invite to a couples party. Slimmer chances have been overcome, I suppose. Like winning the lottery twice or experiencing spontaneous stage five cancer remission, but that's about it.

Three weeks later, I received the email, downloaded the attached file, and clicked play to view an animated pinup girl reclining atop a martini glass kicking her stilettoed foot into the air. Bannered overhead in red balloon letters:

Lionel & Sarah's
7th Annual
Anything Goes Party!

Arrival: 7:00
Dinner: 7:30
Playtime: 7:31

That instant, everything became about preparation. Diet, grooming, lighter workouts to preserve energy. Regimented, early bedtimes for proper rest. Suspension of all playtime and masturbation to charge my libido. There was no way I wasn't going to be able to perform.

As Sarah pulled back the door, she informed me that Rose and Gerard were running late. "But they said feel free to start without them."

In black nylons, heels, and a bustier one deep breath from exploding, Sarah belonged on the fuselage of a World War I bomber. Along with her red lips, talcum powder skin, and Bettie Page bangs.

"How's about the tour, sweetie?"

Like the home's outer facade, its living room was standard suburbia, except the furniture was moved to the walls to clear space for a jigsaw of sheeted sleeping pads that stretched to the far wall. Everyday life pushed aside for tonight.

"Here we have the group area."

Having shed their raincoats, wives floated around in rainbows of lingerie trailing exotic fragrances and clutching wineglasses with tips of brightly colored nails. Husbands reclined in baggy shorts and Tommy Bahamas, taking in the view. On every flat surface candy dishes teeming with condoms twinkled in the candlelight.

"Back here's the dining room."

A constellation of a chandelier hovered over a dining table offering two rows of silver chafing dishes. Beside it, a fully stocked bar glistened like a resevoir of liquid courage. Scattered nearby were chairs and fold-out tables arranged in groups accommodating four, perfect for intimate conversation.

"Private rooms are this way . . ."

A short hall let out at a pair of bedrooms, each with a bed stripped to its fitted sheet. Wall-mounted flat screens broadcasted muted porn, the light from which painted the mattresses like the adrenaline-producing lead-up to a wrestling match's main event. Folded washcloths and bottled waters perched on nightstands, waiting dutifully to serve.

"And, finally, the restroom."

A basket of rolled hand towels rested on the lip of a deep-soak tub across from a vanity sink circled by an impressive offering of single-serving toiletries. Mouthwash, breath mints, floss, individually wrapped toothbrushes, nail clippers . . . A tuxedoed bathroom attendant wouldn't have seemed the least bit out of place.

Every single male in the Lifestyle has heard countless myths of these parties, but only a chosen few can claim to have witnessed one.

"Oh," Sarah chirped. "I almost forgot the hot tub."

I was one of the chosen.

Before playtime commenced, everyone did their homework. Huddled on couches, crowded around tables, and clustered in corners, guests discovered who the voyeurs, cuckolds, the soft swappers and hard swappers were . . . which couples were after threesomes, foursomes, or moresomes. STI results were exchanged like business cards.[2]

I was partaking of the buffet when a stegosaurian-size shadow laid claim to me.[3] I looked up, way up, across the table and up still more where, behind the rising plumes of chafing-dish steam, materializing like a pagan god, a face perched atop an Everest of man smiled down at me.

"I'm Bob," the goliath identified itself, then inserted what looked to be half a barbecued chicken into its oral cavity.

Graft one of those Easter Island heads to a body of proportional size and that was Bob. A horizon of shoulder the width of my field of vision. Arms strataed with petrified muscle. Torso thick as a continental plate. And draped over it all was a tarp of a red silk kimono that was probably meant to diffuse Bob's level of physical intimidation, but instead detailed every peak and valley of muscular topography.

"I'm a boring, straight male" was how I introduced myself to Bob. It's how I always introduce myself because it usually gets a laugh and lightens the mood, the ideal atmosphere when trying to sleep with another man's wife.

Bob removed the flesh-stripped skeleton from his jaws and I thought I heard him chuckle at my "boring, straight male" comment.

---

2 *STI (Sexually Transmitted Infection)*—If you don't know this one, then you're part of the problem and I, as well as the community as a whole, would greatly appreciate that you study up on STIs before venturing into our world.

3 *Buffet*—A meal consisting of several dishes from which guests serve themselves. Not Lifestyle specific, I know, but here's your first lesson in swing culture: Buffets, quite good ones, are a common party offering. Why in God's name, you ask, would a host lay out a spread at an orgy? Could anything be less appetizing? Well, first off, it's polite. Second, food brings people together. Go all the way back to cavemen and you'll see it. Lastly, who doesn't love a free meal?

But his response was at most a slight grunt, so it may have just been a gob of meat detouring down the wrong pipe.

"Want to grab a table?" he commanded more than asked me.

We sat across from each other with the intensity of competitive chess players and, within minutes, Bob had queried about my turn-ons and turn-offs, fantasies, and experience. The only information he betrayed was his name. His first name. None of us have last names in the Lifestyle, when we have names at all.

"Limits?" Bob asked as he tore into another hunk of dead bird.

"No kids. No animals. Nothing toilet related." Those first two are given, but that last one . . . If I've learned anything in the Lifestyle, it's that it's better to be safe than sorry.

"What about condoms?"

The questions are always the same: Condoms or bareback? Favorite positions? What's the body hair situation?

I told Bob yes to condoms.

"That negotiable?"

I told Bob it was not.

Bob swigged some lemonade. "Same with us."

With the broad brushstrokes of our sexual proclivities aligned, it was what was *behind* our conversation that would decide things that night.[4] Strip away the words and my talk with Bob had really been:

> "Should I allow you to have sex with my wife?"
> "Yes, please."
> "Convince me."

---

4 Matching kink is easy—don't pair a foot fetishist with a water sports aficionado, or an average Joe with a size queen; put two subs together and you're in for a whole lot of inactivity—but if swinging were only about sex, there'd be no need for an insightful, informative, and entertaining book such as this. You're welcome.

And there was the rub. No man would pass into Bob's wife without first passing through Bob. Make no mistake; Bob may have allowed others to enjoy his betrothed, but that didn't mean he didn't love her. In fact, the skill with which he gauged my reactions, weighed my answers, and dissected every molecule of my being was nothing short of a Jedi's.

"What about oral?"

Case in point. On the surface, Bob's question seemed simple. Only it wasn't. Bob didn't ask about *my* fondness for oral sex, did he? Just oral sex. In the abstract. It was a slick bit of subterfuge to check if I was selfish, one of the worst qualities a single male can possess. Swingers find selfishness so despicable that a morbidly obese man with full-body acne, halitosis, dandruff, and malignant body odor gets laid in the Lifestyle before a selfish male. Fully aware of this irrefutable and depressing fact, I parried Bob's verbal joust with my patented "I prefer to give as much as receive."

Bob's jaw froze mid-chew. Its muscles inflated, expanded, and hardened like quick-dry cement. Barbecue sauce lavaed over the ridge of his pinkie, paused, then plummeted onto the plate. Eyes still locked on his partially ravaged feast, he asked, "How about kissing?" and resumed masticating.

The selection process is simple. Hubby exhausts every ploy in his psychological arsenal to filter out the liars, fakes, and undesirables. (If only every husband were so devoted . . .) Me, I try to prove that I'm not the stereotypical single male. That I'm in the Lifestyle for the right reasons. That I'm courteous and respectful. All of which are true, but the burden of proof is on me. It always is. And especially that night with Bob, as his wife was by far the most sought-after guest—evidenced by her fan club in constant orbit around her. I estimated thirty minutes of chitchat with Big Bob before I could even hope for the possibility of playtime to surface on the horizon. And even then my efforts could still have been for naught. Things with Bob could have gone a million different ways at any moment. But I'd been in that exact position too many times, so I wasn't sweating it.

"Kissing's not a problem," I assured Bob.

"But do you *like* to kiss?"

"Like" meant Bob's wife was big on kissing. And Bob stressing it meant he wanted me to know it. Problem was, Bob's "hint" raised a red flag, as it wasn't a hint so much as the most obvious gimme of all time lobbed into the heart of my strike zone—anyone's strike zone. So, with a guaranteed grand slam levitating before me, I was wondering why—when the night had just begun, and with a roster of eager suitors for his wife, and with his Jedi skills—was Bob rushing things?

Bob's mound of chicken had evaporated to a mass grave, so maybe he just wanted seconds. Then the first grunts and moans drifted in from the group area and I thought he might just want his wife to join. Whatever his reason, my Spidey sense had been triggered.

"I do like to kiss. Very much."

"Any good?"

And there it was. Any single male who knows anything about the Lifestyle knows arrogance ranks just below selfishness. Single men convinced they're sex gods are dismissed faster than they can mumble "blue balls" on their way home for yet another round of self-release.

Well played, Jedi Bob! Well played.

"Am I good?" I repeated Bob's question in a failed attempt to sidestep it. "That's pretty subjective, wouldn't you say?" Bob didn't, so I added, "Well, I haven't been told otherwise."

And for the first time since we sat, Bob looked up. His eyes, faded blue icebergs, locked onto mine. I could feel his sight enter me and search, looking for something, anything reason enough to deny me. I watched the machinery in his mind work, and, after what felt like a lifetime but was probably only seconds, he cracked a smile, which I took as acknowledgment that there might very well have been *two* Jedis dining at that table.

"What about down below?" Bob asked, laying down his final test. While it was void of subterfuge and straightforward, it was by far the most vital. So much so that should I have failed this final assessment, I would have undone everything.

See, far above arrogance and selfishness on the rankings of undesirable Lifestyle traits, topping the lengthy list of carnal sins, occupying its very own stratosphere of unforgivable reprehensibility, is lying. Without question, fibbing is the fastest way to secure a one-way trip to blackball status in the swing community. So assured is a liar's exile from the Lifestyle that should a perjurer come clean about a material untruth and *still* secure playtime, that individual will have rewritten the entire swing rulebook. And no matter how enticing it may be to rewrite history, I do not recommend attempting it. Not unless you're lusting after a celibate existence.

Back to Bob's query: I could have embellished, tried to wow. But where would I have been when the clothes came off? Mumbling "blue balls" on my schlep home, that's where. Which is exactly why I leveled with Bob. "If you're looking for size, I'm not your guy. No complaints, but I'm average."

"I meant do you trim?"

"Oh. Sorry. Yes."

"Balls?"

"Shaved."

"Good man."

Bob pushed aside his plate, leaned his inhuman bulk back in the plastic chair that groaned under his mass, and let me know, "I watch."

So Big Bob was a voyeur? I'd had him pegged Dom. But, frankly, I was relieved to have been mistaken. Now that Bob wouldn't be playing second playmate to his wife, I wouldn't have to negotiate his bulk. Nor would suffocation under his weight be of concern should his wife desire the more involved positions.

"Is watching a problem for you?" Bob asked.

I had progressed this far with Bob because I knew fucking Bob's wife was the same as fucking Bob. For who knew how many nights Bob had fallen asleep next to and just as many mornings woken up beside his wife. Maybe they had kids, a mortgage, car payments. You know, real-life stuff. Inviting a stranger into their bed was not a decision rushed into. Informing me that he'd watch, that he'd always be within arm's reach, that he'd chaperone every second of playtime, Bob was educating me regarding this very real, very nonnegotiable fact. So, yes, my cock might only be in Bob's wife, but I would definitely, oh so very definitely, be fucking Bob, too.

"Not a problem," I assured Bob. "Not at all."

So there I was, sliced open, psyche peeled back for Bob to probe[5]—a small price to pay to fuck another man's wife when you think about it. All that remained was Bob's verdict.

"All right, then," Bob said, more to himself than me. "Honey?" he bellowed while keeping his eyes trained on mine.

The doting crush parted and released Bob's wife. Gift-wrapped in black silk, with tresses of auburn hair that exist only in shampoo commercials, she drifted toward us and docked at Bob's side. Onto his cliff of a shoulder she slid a hand—a hand sporting a ring with a rock big enough to skip across a lake. Given the exhaustive vetting to which Bob had subjected me, I couldn't help but see the diamond as emblematic of the size and depth of their love, a sentiment which relieved me to no

---

5 *Probe* is perhaps not the best term, given the situation. *Investigate* might be more appropriate.

end. Bob was not a person with whom I'd like to tangle over a pang of jealousy.

Bob's wife's jade eyes once-overed me before the corners of her lips curled into a hint of smile.

"Honey," said Bob. "Say hi to . . . What did you say your name was?"

Author Disclaimer

I didn't throw you into the belly of the beast for shock value. Anyone can titillate with a lurid sex story. I did so because it's best you know from word one what you're getting into. I've diluted nothing. Not one drop. Which means you shouldn't expect that romanticized sexual utopia the movies, TV, and especially porn have dreamed up and continue to propagate. Like everything else, the Lifestyle has its pros and cons, and all of them are here. Most important, I make it plain that swinging isn't for everyone. But let's not get ahead of ourselves.

I've written for those who want to learn, *truly* learn, about a community with which they aren't familiar. Or for those who have preconceptions but can admit they may not be entirely accurate (and, in some cases, that they are completely wrong). This means my reader must possess an open mind and a certain level of curiosity. If that's you, proceed to checkout. An uncensored glimpse behind the curtain, hairy backs and all, awaits.

But maybe it's not the Lifestyle that interests you. Just sex. Well, you're also in luck. Plenty of tales of sex and debauchery are here for your—ahem—pleasure.

Finally, I suspect some of you cracked this spine because you have an itch tickling your libido. Rest assured, grasshopper, you, too, have chosen wisely. If it's a Lifestyle guide you seek, budding kinksters, follow me! Not only have I detailed my journey into the swing sub-culture, but I've also outlined how you, too, can explore the coital landscape.

Alls I'm saying is, use this book however you want. Indulge in the sex and skip the lessons. Or bypass the tales and cut right to the tutelage. Hell, if you want, read it all. I'm extending a helping hand; but only you know how best to use that hand (pun partially intended).

But before you rev up your libido, know this: Swingers are a unique breed. Not everyone is emotionally capable of having, much less enjoying, casual sex with a multitude of strangers. Even rarer is the mental and emotional fortitude necessary to devote hours, days, months, even years to a fruitless search that hacks away at your self-esteem one rejection after another and pile-drives you into a black hole of depression where you'll wallow convinced you're fated a eunuch. However, enough of us possess the constitutional moxie to comprise a highly active community. So, though odds dictate you aren't cut from the Lifestyle (loin) cloth, there's the slimmest chance you are. And this book might just help you figure that out.

Now, as a book of this nature cannot *not* appeal to a testosterone-inclined readership, a word with the single men. No doubt some of you (perhaps most) are reading to realize a backlog of sexual fantasies and orchestrate a life of orgasmic bliss. No one argues your motives are anything but normal (as far as male "normal" goes), but I don't want to set false expectations. So, in the interest of full disclosure:

First, these pages do not contain sorcery, trickery, or shortcuts to getting laid. For "proven methods" such as those, I suggest scouring late-night TV for some instructional DVDs available to you in three easy monthly payments.

Second, this book isn't a plush red carpet leading up to the Lifestyle doors. Even if it was, those doors have been purposely locked, dead-bolted, and all but hermetically sealed to you for good reason, something I'll soon address. Like it or not, there's one road into the Lifestyle, and it's long and arduous and requires nothing less than the hardest of work and most ardent of dedication, both of which, if applied unceasingly for who knows how long, may earn you a remote chance at Lifestyle acceptance. And that's your best-case scenario.

Now, men, despite my off-putting admissions, I actually do want you to read this book. With all my heart and soul, I do. But first you must know on which link of the Lifestyle food chain you reside. At the very top, ruling the sexual ecosystem, are couples. Just below couples are single women, whom we often refer to as "unicorns" for their rare and mythical existence.[1] Lastly, below the couples and unicorns, way, way down, pinned beneath the weight of the entire chain crushing their tracheas, struggling to be included somewhere, *anywhere* in the carnal caste system, are single males. It ain't pretty, guys, but the reality is we will never, *ever* be close to equal to couples. The ugly truth is this: a penis without accompanying vagina is a nonentity in the Lifestyle. The sooner you accept this fact, the faster you can make the best of it.

I'm not counting you out, gents. The fact that I, a single male, have written this book proves there's hope. Just as the lowliest plankton serves an integral function in the survival of every species on the planet,

---

1   Admittedly, there are differing schools of thought on the etymology of *unicorn*. Some use the term to denote a single female in the Lifestyle. Others use it in reference to a single, *bi* female, which I've also heard called a *golden unicorn*. Still others reserve the term for single, bi, *attractive* women, the Holy Grail of the unicorn species, whom I personally term *golden, rainbow unicorns*.

single men play a crucial Lifestyle role. And it can be a wildly enjoyable role—if you know and follow the rules.

So, fellas, understand things from the vantage of couples and women. Then accept my literary protein shot to your cortex, rehabilitate, and spread word to your horny brethren. You'll be pleased with the results. I promise.

Now, back to the reader at large: Some of you (perhaps many) feel I'm betraying the swingers' code of discretion—our ethical backbone—by not only recounting my sexual exploits, but by also opening doors for others wishing to join. To those who think that, know that I've changed names, altered identifying characteristics, relocated settings, and gone to staggering lengths to protect privacy. But even then there's my tutorial inclusion of the single male, which you may deem punishable by no less than castration. Before you excommunicate me, though, consider the wisdom of countering single male bad behavior with knowledge. 'Twas Nelson Mandela who said, "Education is the most powerful weapon we can use to change the world." And while it's probably safe to assume Mandela didn't have the Lifestyle in mind when he birthed that maxim, do you really possess the cojones to argue with Nelson Mandela?

Even still, some will hold that the smallest divulgence of swing activity to non-swingers is treason. Well, to those puritanical swingers I can only offer that my perceived betrayal is the unavoidable consequence of my grander purpose, one of community betterment. My intent isn't to let everyone *in*, but rather to let *out* our process, rules, and etiquette so those new to our ways can stop spoiling the fun for the rest of us. It's not unconditional inclusion I want, but universal understanding.

Far worse than the consequences I may face in the Lifestyle is the possibility that this book may lose me friends. Some of my most near and dear friends are swingers, many of whom appear in the pages that follow. I debated long and hard whether to endanger friendships and, in the end, was guided by the wisdom of Dr. Seuss: "Those who mind don't matter; and those who matter don't mind."[2]

I'm no expert, no natural-born talent, definitely no guru. As you'll soon learn, only through a colossal experiment in trial and error did I reach the sexual summit. Although I own up to having worn a cape in a few intimate scenarios, I don't possess supernatural powers of any kind. Perhaps my IQ is slightly above average, but Mensa isn't busting down my door. If pressed to define myself, I'd say I'm Horatio Alger between the sheets: a self-made swinging single male . . . with a hefty dose of Buster Keaton mixed in.

What I claim is extensive experience and a solid record of Lifestyle success. I have standing invitations to large events, house parties, group functions, and bedrooms of women and couples. I claim normalcy, every-man status, ordinary looks (at best), and an average cock size (also at best). I carry a few extra pounds, have a gap between my front teeth, and stand below average height. I have a soft (sometimes double) chin, and even after a decent number of laser treatments, my back remains a work in progress. Nothing abnormally tragic has befallen me. I have a phenomenal circle of Vanilla friends, and, all in all, I can't complain about my life.

I'm a regular guy. Granted, a regular guy who's had one-on-ones, MFMs, FMFs, foursomes, moresomes, gang bangs, orgies, phone sex, text sex, car sex, and public sex. I've played with white women, black women, Asian women, East Indian women . . . tall women, short women, voluptuous women, skinny women . . . old women, young women, and middle-aged women.

During my Lifestyle tenure, I've lost count of the number of stellar encounters I've had and can tally on one hand the number of not-so-great ones. I've been rejected infinitely more times than accepted, but have always forged ahead.

---

2 I know I incorrectly attributed this quote to Theodor Geisel. But I'd rather erroneously cite Dr. Seuss than properly credit financier, statesman, and political consultant Bernard Baruch. It just sounds better.

The truth is, I hope you'll find much of my advice unnecessary. I pray that personal hygiene is not a topic for which you need counsel. I hope you don't consider yourself God's gift to sex. And I wish with everything I've got that you treat everyone with respect, courtesy, and dignity. I really, truly do. But scores of pseudo-swingers (almost exclusively of the single and male variety) have made it so I can't assume anything. To do so would be a disservice to those more evolved, as it would fail to intervene on the Cro-Magnons lousing things up. So, to those of you who shower with regularity, who don't wield a *Hindenburg*-size ego, and who make it habit not to act with discourtesy toward your fellow man, I request you endure the mundane topics in order to gain insight from the more in-depth discussions.

I promise you, a cornucopia of copulation awaits. Porn ain't got shit on what's out there. However, there are no guarantees except unrelenting, soul-crushing, suicide-inducing rejection. Between the mysterious alchemy of personalities, the finicky pairing of sexual proclivities, or the elusive science of physical attraction, there are too many unpredictable and uncontrollable factors at play for surefire success. However, when the stars do align and the cosmic tumblers fall into place, nothing—and I mean nothing—is more satisfying.

There's one final group to address: those who feel I'm unqualified to speak to the Lifestyle. Who say a single male cannot, by definition, be a "swinger." Who believe my solo gender pollutes the sanctity of the swing community. With you, I respectfully disagree. I posit that I am *uniquely* qualified to comment on the Lifestyle, as I am painfully aware of what couples and women do *not* want. My nose has been repeatedly broken by the slam of the Lifestyle door. I've been rejected so many times that I was conditioned to expect it. My success and, more important, my failures qualify me more than just about anyone to comment. And so, for better or worse, I have.

Flirting

My Sort-of Sex Education

Long before I reached the peak of carnal mastery, I was five years old sitting on the big-boy toilet, as I had been doing successfully for some time, when for no discernible reason I began to grow. Horrified by the inflating and hardening that wasn't giving any sign of stopping, I shrieked at the top of my tiny, hyperventilating lungs, "IT'S GET-TING BIGGER! IT'S GETTING BIGGER!" Within seconds, my mother burst in to find me squirming rabidly on the toilet trying to escape my erection with the same futility with which a dog chases its tail. Suppressing hysterical laughter, I'm certain, she assured me that my genital mutation would return to normal if I relaxed. From God knows where, I summoned the will to stem the adrenaline and cease hyperventilating. As promised, I deflated.

In an attempt to dispel my penile-phobia, my mother read me *Where Did I Come From?* The illustrated children's book explained the basics of conception, pregnancy, and the birthing process. Problem was, my still-forming brain couldn't synthesize the material. As such, erections tormented me into middle school, at which time I took matters into my own hands (so to say) to wrap my brain around this thing called sex.

Because I was born into the pre-Internet age, banks of ready, available, and (somewhat) reliable information were scarce. It took years of scavenging for me to cobble the scant tutelage found in scrambled adult cable channels, a *Hustler* purchased at overnight camp, and a well-worn VHS tape of *Rosie: The Neighborhood Slut* into a working knowledge of sex.[1] Fully aware that my self-edification was rudimentary at best, I prayed it would be enough for my debut performance with Lindsay, my first serious girlfriend in college.

Tantamount to the miracle that I had found a woman to have sex with was the horror that she wasn't a virgin. She'd had two previous sexual partners of whom I was aware, which meant I was at a severe disadvantage. She'd had firsthand experience to which I could (and most likely would) be compared. But at the ripe age of twenty, I knew it was now or join the nearest monastery.

Due to the coronary-inducing stress of the experience, I recall little from that night. What I do remember amounts to the sexual equivalent of a Keystone Cops short. Two failed attempts donning a condom ended when Lindsay pointed out that I was putting it on backward. Then, despite possessing a decent theoretical understanding of the female anatomy, I proved exceedingly inept. After numerous attempts at entry, I relented and accepted Lindsay's guidance and frequent re-guidance throughout the forty-one-second marathon. I know it was forty-one seconds, as my deflowering culminated in Van Morrison crooning from Lindsay's stereo, "And it stoned me to my soul . . ." To this day, Van's voice curls me into a mental fetal position.

---

1 *Rosie* wouldn't prove the most creative or educational of adult viewing fare. However, neither was part of my buying criteria at the time. I'd had to circle the block for fifteen minutes to build up the courage to enter my first adult shop, and the anxiety of embarking on my first visit to an official adult store precluded me from progressing farther than the bargain bin beside the cash register. And so *Rosie* would have to suffice.

Sex with Lindsay over the ensuing year took on a haunting refrain, one in which I fumbled about, she exercised inhuman levels of patience and understanding, and all things physical resolved in a smattering of seconds.

That's not to say there wasn't the occasional triumph. One time, I lasted a full half hour.

"What happened?" Lindsay asked, dumbfounded and satisfied (for once), after the fact.

"I have no idea," I admitted, just as bewildered (and satisfied).

"Well, if you want to do that next time, it's cool with me."

It would have been cool with me, too, but I couldn't crack the code of that Olympic performance. And by spring semester junior year it was too late. I'd been accepted into my university's study-abroad program in London, and, a few weeks in, Lindsay admitted over the phone, choking on a deluge of tears, that she'd grown interested in someone else.

"It's just . . ." she gasped, ". . . our relationship . . ." Gasp. "Has become . . ." Gasp. "A friendship." Cough, snot, wheeze.

I didn't protest, because, well, she was right. The connection we'd had over those eighteen months had run its course. It was nobody's fault, just the trajectory of things.

Days after my transatlantic dumping, one of my housemates welcomed a visitor from the States. Melissa was on the thick side, with sandy blond hair and a pre–boob reduction Soleil Moon Frye chest.[2] Melissa's friend, my housemate, anchored the right wing of the political spectrum, so when Melissa voiced interest in exploring the red-light district, she was met with more than a hint of hesitation. But having just been released back into the dating pool, I was beyond game.

Dim lighting, neon displays, and every inch of shelf and rack space

---

2 For those unfamiliar with Soleil, shame on you! She was the title character from TV's *Punky Brewster*. Still don't know? Google her. I recommend season four, when she's at her most "breastally" developed.

crammed with devices engineered for maximum orgasm, the place was the mecca of adult emporiums—at least compared to the two shops I'd previously (and briefly) patronized. Behind the counter sat a man in a wrinkled tan Windbreaker and stained, unwashed khakis, both of which came off as oddly formal next to the store's extravagant wares. He looked like he hadn't showered, slept, or changed clothes in weeks, and the dubious dark circles weighing down his eyes typecast him as the pervert about whom every parent warned their child.

"This selection is uh-may-zing," Melissa fawned over the bondage wear, mesh blouses, and garments with areas cut away that most fashion designers considered essential.

As Melissa perused, I tried to discern why every article of clothing was priced in direct proportion to the amount of fabric it lacked, a seemingly illogical strategy.

"Need any help?" the clerk inquired in a Cockney brogue.

"Paddles," Melissa responded before our host could slur out the whole of his question.

We were directed to a wall offering what appeared to be every model ever made in the history of spankology. Melissa purred as her eyes zipped over the stock, instantly assessing each option's worth. Obviously, she wasn't lured by flashy packaging—flamboyant designs or corny sayings such as "Daddy's Little Helper" were immediately dismissed. Products receiving consideration followed a thematic trend of black with minimal flair. At first these designs struck me as boring, but soon I understood the intimidation in their understated appearance. It was the same way movie villains terrorized with deathly quiet and unshakable, even-keeled temperaments. Basically, if Hannibal Lecter were reincarnated as a sex toy, he'd have been the style of paddle Melissa contemplated.

"Li'l help?" Melissa requested as she armed me with a black leather paddle edged in maroon stitching that was quintessential Lecter. A lanyard hung from its handle, which, I presumed, was an effort at safety.

My mind briefly wandered to pre-lanyard paddles that had slipped from sweaty grips to shatter nearby vases or maim innocent spectators. How many of these senseless atrocities had transpired before a paddlesmith wisely added a leash?

"Ready." Melissa snapped me back to the matter at hand.

Her ass toward me and bent slightly at the waist, she awaited my assistance. I gripped the paddle and, heeding the adage "Safety first," slipped on the lanyard. Instinctually, I assumed a batter's stance and balanced my weight, the way my father had coached me to in Little League. I relaxed my shoulders, measured my distance, and administered what I presumed would be a decent smack but instead sounded muffled and weak against her denim. I swore I heard the clerk stifle a chuckle.

Melissa switched to a wider, firmer model studded with metal rivets and instructed me, "Don't hold back," before resuming the position.

It's all about the fundamentals, my father's coaching mantra echoed in my head. I lowered my center of gravity, kept my eye on Melissa's ass, and leaned into my swing.

"Oh, yes!" Melissa declared, then triumphantly snatched the Louisville Slugger (Deviant's Edition) from me. "Spreader bars?" she yelled to the now amused clerk, who pointed to another wall, where a collection hung like a shrine of industrial-size wrenches.

Melissa ran her fingers across the metal rods as though they were erotic wind chimes before removing one wrapped in a black leather skin with matching faux-fur ankle cuffs. She laid it on the floor and straddled it in a V stance, vertically mimicking the position when the bar was in use. She called out, "Do you take traveler's checks?"

That night we went to a pub and my housemates wasted no time interrogating me about my day trip. But since they weren't brave enough to tag along, I decided they weren't deserving of the details.

After many pints, Melissa and I began to flirt. Furtive glances escalated to stealthy petting and, before I knew it, we were the last two of our party. We trekked back to her bed-and-breakfast and had no sooner closed the door to her room than we began making out.

It should be noted that until this point in my limited sexual experience I'd yet to close a successful one-night stand. It wasn't for lack of trying. As a matter of fact, by this point I could boast many failed (and several aborted) attempts. 'Twas more than a few times I had cajoled lasses back to my dorm room.[3] But, other than a pity-fueled dry-hump session with the minister's daughter, casual sexual relations were not to fruit. I was (and still am) of the belief that one simply is or is not a closer. And though for years my libido had been open 24/7/365, I'd yet to have my first paying customer.

Within seconds, Melissa and I were naked on the bed and I was convinced I was about to experience my first actual, in-the-flesh, legitimate hookup. Luckily I'd had the presence of mind at the pub to buy a condom from the men's room vending machine and now retrieved it from my discarded jeans. But when I turned back to Melissa, she was in tears.

First Lindsay, now Melissa? I had inadvertently tapped into some innate talent to incite women to cry. And it was not a talent I particularly wanted, nor one that boded well for casual sex, I was certain.

"Did I do something?" I asked Melissa.

"I'm sorry," she sniffled. "It's just . . . he doesn't love me."

Though essentially brand new to hookup protocol, I knew crying wasn't a sign of impending intercourse. In fact, the last time a female's tears were lobbed my way, they immediately preceded a swift dumping.

---

3   "More than a few times" means exactly three:
    a. A rebellious Southern Baptist minister's daughter who couldn't quite pull the sexual trigger,
    b. A female friend who realized minutes into making out that we were destined to be just friends, and
    c. A girl I met at a campus party who had barely crossed my threshold before realizing she was still in love with her ex, serial cheater or not. (Since she physically entered my room, she qualifies.)

"Master tore up our contract," Melissa eked out before launching into a new fit of wailing.

Though fairly certain "Master" wasn't his given name, I didn't want to ask Melissa for details mid-bawl. What I wanted was to finally close the deal.

"The day before I left," she hiccupped. "He ripped it up and threw it in my face."

Trying to press through this minor detour, I asked as nonobliviously as I could fake, "What was the contract for?"

Melissa paused, breathed deeply, then howled, "Meeeeeeeeeeeeee!"

While modern-day enslavement was not a topic about which I knew much (or anything at all, actually), I could see my window of erotic opportunity slamming closed, so I threw up a Hail Mary.

"Would it help if I used these?" I asked as I lifted Melissa's earlier purchases from her suitcase.

Time froze. Melissa's tears slowed. Her erratic breathing calmed and her moist, swollen eyelids opened ever so slightly. My offer had parted the dark clouds of love lost and shone down warm, fertile rays of new hope, sparking life in the jagged remnants of her obliterated heart.

Melissa looked at me and, with the sincerity of someone whose soul has been genuinely touched, said, "Oh, honey, you can't handle me," then resumed crying.

She soon passed out, but I remained awake, smushed between the wall and her spasming body in the after-throes of emotional tumult. I listened to her breath strain through her throat parched raw from crying and endured the mocking of the paddle and spreader bar at the foot of the bed.

Oh, honey, you can't handle me. Their cackles gnawed at my shrinking sense of self-worth.

Though I was humiliated like I never knew possible, Melissa was right. I couldn't have handled her. If she'd taken me up on my offer, I would have embarrassed and possibly injured us both. I was barely experienced with one woman, whereas Melissa was a bona fide contracted carnal servant. The chasm of experience between us was intergalactic to say the least.

Lying there naked, crammed between the icy wall and Melissa's twitching corpse, I experienced a personal Big Bang. I vowed sexual mastery. I promised myself that I would be able to read my lovers' desires and reliably deliver. I was adamant that when next confronted with a spreader bar or paddle or any implement designed for optimal orgasm, I would be more than prepared. Someday—and by God, Allah, and Adonai, that day would come—I'd belong on this bed, instead of between the wall and mattress.

In retrospect, I see that cataclysmic experience was also an awakening. When I replay that night even today, I can still tune into the same internal stirring that woke in me that night. Some out-of-reach inner itch that, even then, I knew had to be scratched.

My Quest Begins

The next three years were a blur of insta-relationships, each resolving faster than the one before it. One lasted a single day. I kid you not. And while each relationship was unique and began and ended for its own reasons, the thematic trend through all of them was my sexual ineptitude.

Don't misunderstand; I wasn't beyond salvation. In fact, regular practice with girlfriends helped me to improve in certain areas. I'd been told repeatedly that I was an exceptional kisser and more than a few times my oral skills were highly praised. However, my central problem remained unchanged: I orgasmed on a hair-trigger.

Though beyond frustrated, I knew something deeper and more profound was at play. As if my void of stamina had meaning. Like it was letting me know I was doing something incredibly wrong. How one reliably messes up the process of tab A into slot B and repeat I couldn't fathom, but something told me that if I just pressed on, it would eventually reveal itself. At least I prayed it would.

While my girlfriends rarely, if ever, made mention of my "limitation," it bothered me to no end and I became gun-shy about sex. After I'd exhausted excuses of homework and time-consuming extracurriculars in order to avoid sex with girlfriends, I upped the ante to contagious illnesses and physical injuries. If I recall, a relative met his untimely demise more than once. On a positive note, though my sex life was on life support, I made the dean's list every semester.

A glimmer of hope appeared when I learned of Distraction Technique.[1] I'd seen some documentary on Ron Jeremy, who revealed that by focusing on non-arousing objects he distracted his attention from physical stimulation and thus was able to control his orgasm.[2] I experimented with Distraction on my own to some moderate success. But no matter how hard I tried not to, I couldn't *not* affect my results. Like playing checkers against yourself: you can't help but know your next move. To fully gauge its worth, I had to try it during actual sex. When I finally did roll out Distraction, I must have looked like Rain Main ODing on caffeine, my attention shifting by the nanosecond from the door to the lamp to the curtains, the carpet, everywhere but my girlfriend.

"Is everything okay?" she asked after I'd reset the world record for shortest consummation (yet again). "You seemed . . . distracted."

Though distraction was the goal, my partner taking note was not. As such, I filed away Distraction Technique before I made my girlfriend even more suspicious than I'd already made her.

Sexual rock bottom was my "slow dock" technique. Unable to exile myself from sex in a relationship, I resorted to doubling-up on condoms

---

1   ® Daniel Stern. All rights reserved for now and forever and all that legal jazz. That is, unless someone else beat me to the punch to this million-dollar idea.

2   I saw it as a riff on the Dead Puppies trick we adolescent boys used to battle unwanted and inconvenient erections. When such an embarrassing situation would arise (and arise with unbelievable frequency it most certainly did), we'd mentally repeat the chant "dead puppies" while simultaneously imagining horrific scenes of the same. The carnage of the innocent pups was supposed to counteract whatever stimulation plagued us. At best it had a 50% efficacy rate. But we were so desperate for any semblance of control over our hormonally raging selves that we tried anything.

to desensitize, genitally docking at a tortoise's pace, then requiring a lengthy period of silence and immobility from my partner so I could acclimate to my new environment. My hope was that this elaborate process—similar to entering a hot bath—would relax me enough to secure some stamina. Though it was exceedingly awkward to lie atop my girlfriend, both of us soundless and motionless, for several minutes before I attempted initial pelvic thrusting, I didn't know what else to do. And when "slow docking" proved useless after two humiliating attempts, I truly didn't.

Enter Missy, a tangential college acquaintance with whom I'd reconnected in New York City a few years after graduation through a mutual friend. It was in Missy that I'd found my first true *sort-of* sexual connection. "*Sort-of*" because we only non-sex hooked up. Non-sex because Missy had rediscovered religion and recommitted to celibacy until marriage. She wasn't a virgin, but she was resolute in her recommitment. And as I wasn't touting my sexual track record—in fact, I was trying to expunge most of it—I didn't protest, a response Missy mistook for respect for her spiritual rebirth. I didn't correct her because, well, it didn't seem to hurt anyone and, more specifically to my benefit, I was relieved not to have to circumvent sex to save myself further embarrassment.

To my surprise, non-sex hooking up with Missy was better than all the sex I'd had. The best was kissing. Our mouths fit perfectly and our lips knew precisely what to do. The entire act was . . . well . . . natural. As opposed to "slow docking."

My attraction to Missy wasn't physical, though she wasn't at all bad to look at; rather, it was of an intellectual nature. Missy was supremely intelligent, enviously quick witted, and brandished a sense of humor with samurai precision. She was different from prior girlfriends in that she kept me on my toes and challenged me, qualities I wasn't aware I desired in another until I experienced them with Missy.

Unfortunately, after a few months the non-sex bliss ended when Missy moved out of state for business school and I relocated to Los Angeles for better weather and an acceptable standard of living. We stayed in touch and a year later I visited her over New Year's. Only hours after my arrival, while we were resurrecting non-sex hooking up, Missy confessed, "I kinda want to have sex."

I was floored. "What about . . . ?"

"I know. I just . . . Wait. Do you want to?"

"Well, yeah. It's just that . . ."

"Just that what?" Her tone was laced with suspicion.

"I didn't bring any condoms."

My erection, Missy, and I drag-raced to the nearest drugstore, then back to her apartment, where we broke her recommitment. Then re-broke, bombed, and waged all-out nuclear war on it over the three-day weekend.

With each go I prayed that the intellectual attraction between us would transfer to the physical and elevate the experience to the one I'd been questing for. But alas, it did not. Instead, that internal stirring I'd felt after the Melissa debacle accelerated. I still couldn't pinpoint what it was saying, and my patience was growing shorter by the orgasm.

Missy moved to LA after business school and was hell-bent on making up for her sexual hiatus. We did plenty of nonsexual activities—ate out, saw movies, hung with friends—but everything was shadowed by the fact that I'd be called to duty at any moment.

As well as physically demanding, sex with Missy was mentally and emotionally taxing. Intercourse had become a game of twenty questions. *Does that feel good? Do you like that? What can I do for you? What position do you want? Are you ready to cum? How about now? How about now? Now?* A Fort Knox security clearance vetting couldn't have been more thorough. I knew Missy was trying to bring us closer as a couple, but her sexy-time interrogations kept me from being in the moment, which, in turn, precluded me from engaging with her on an emotional level.

That Thanksgiving Missy flew home to be with her family, and the day before her return, she called with an epiphany too important for her to wait to tell me in person.

"I think we should break up," she stated more than suggested.

Sure, we'd hit a rough patch—our Halloween screaming match on Wilshire Boulevard when I was dressed as Superman and she as Lois Lane wasn't a high point[3]—but were things so bad that she couldn't wait to talk in person?

"But I still need you to pick me up at the airport tomorrow," she added before I could respond to being dumped.

"Seriously?"

"Well, yeah. You have my keys. It doesn't make sense to have someone else pick me up only to take me to your place to get my car. Plus, you live closer to LAX."

"No, I mean about breaking up."

"Oh. Yeah. That, too."

We gave the emotional dust storm a month to settle before Missy and I met at a public park to end things civilly. She apologized for breaking up over the phone, admitted her airport pickup request wasn't well timed, and thanked me for dropping off her keys with her roommate rather than leaving her stranded. I apologized for making her feel she had to end things long distance. Then a bird shit on my shoulder.

On my drive home, I experienced an aftershock to my Big Bang: Relationships were obstructing my quest for sexual improvement. The

---

3 To this day I can't remember the exact substance of that argument. I'm certain it was something epically stupid and that I was to blame. However, I do recall that I couldn't stop thinking how ridiculous we must have looked to passersby. The two of us screaming at each other in matching costumes like comic book characters ejected from the pages for unruly behavior. I laugh now, but it truly did suck.

reality was, sex with a girlfriend would *never* just be sex. While a girl-friend was a regular sex partner, I realized the emotional entanglements packaged with monogamy were not something I wanted or needed at that time. And for the first time since that internal stirring woke from hibernation, I felt it begin to calm.

Swing and a Miss

I needed sexual batting practice. If I wanted to improve, I needed to swing for the fences and fail and fail and fail until I isolated the causes for my incompetence and devised methods to overcome them. But where and, more important, how?

My many failed one-night-stand attempts and my experience with Melissa in London proved beyond any shadow of doubt that I was not a natural closer. Long ago, I'd accepted that was my genetic luck of the draw. However, if I was serious about my quest (and I was), I had to formulate a system to get around that social Achilles' heel.

My problem with in-person interaction had always been its un-predictability. Too many variables led to countless outcomes, most of which didn't bode in my favor. As such, the bar and club scene was out; tack on alcohol to an already dicey setting and I was better off castrating myself. Hiring a "professional" also wasn't an option. Though a call girl eliminated the snag of emotional attachments and sped the process to sex, I couldn't clear the psychological hurdle of paying for sex.

Where I felt I had a fighting chance was with a non-"working" girl who was still all business. In the end, I had only one option. And it just so happened to be the most reliable and fertile source of anonymous sex in the history of ever: Craigslist.

After dozens of emails went unanswered or landed me on spam lists, I posted for a sex club recommendation. My rationale was, go straight to the sex. And within twenty-four hours I was referred to a website. After reading the club's rules and viewing pictures of its facilities, which included, among many amenities, a sex table/bench/hybrid thingy and an aboveground hot tub for twelve, I knew a club was too much too soon.

I Googled "alternative lifestyle" and was presented with hundreds of thousands of links. I clicked on the first and came face-to-face with a petite emo girl wearing black panties, lying facedown on an unmade bed with her arms tied behind her back in an intricate webwork of rope. My first thought was that there was no way I could hold my own with the Princess of Kink. But I had to start somewhere. And Google's number one result was as good a starting point as any. Plus, what could it hurt to open a free account?

Members were mostly low-rent versions of Princess Kink. Pasty skin, jet-black hair, bodies tortured into poses by ropes, chains, and other restraints reminiscent of those I'd encountered during my field trip with Melissa.[1] Everyone was "owned," "on loan," or "looking to be owned" and had screen names like Slave4XtremeUse, CploSubs, and DomDaddy. Less intimidating monikers like TinkerbellGirl and Luv-2Obey were exceedingly few and exceptionally far between.

After some consideration, I christened myself CuriousAndKind. It was perhaps more timid than most, and definitely not the most creative or arousing, but BrutalMaster was misleading and CluelessAndInept would no doubt draw little interest. I entered my physical stats and

---

1 I turned a deaf ear to the faint echoes of the cackling paddle and spreader bar in my mind.

sexual desires, and ticked off my levels of interest in knitting, museums, and Renaissance fairs (apparently, the site's fallback plan was a quirky dating site).

A few drafts of my self-description resulted in:

Easygoing, laid-back, and moderately experienced single male seeks good, adult fun. Looking to meet new people with whom to expand sexual horizons!

The only embellishment was my "moderately experienced" claim. But it wasn't too off the mark. The amount of sex I'd had qualified as "moderate" by any liberal and forgiving definition. Plus, I doubted anyone would take issue with my creative license when compared to DomDaddy's treatise on sexual enslavement and the mega-insertion fantasies of Slave4XtremeUse. I knew claiming to be someone I wasn't was a recipe for failure and, worse, could land me in a situation in which I had little to no chance of survival.

Finally, profile pics. At first, I was far less than enthused to upload pictures to a sex site. My initial plan was to opt out and let my words speak for themselves. But before I clicked submit, I spied the site's warning that picless profiles were viewed up to 90 percent less than ones with at least one pic. How they'd culled this data the site didn't specify, but the prospect of worsening my already slim chances of making a sexual connection right out of the gate gave me pause.

Before I heeded the site's advice, I decided to do a little research of my own. First I compared single female profiles with pics to ones without and discovered that both boasted an equally impressive number of certifications.[2] After that, I compared couples profiles and noticed a

---

2   *Certification* (also cert)—Online testimonial site members use to authenticate others and/or tender a performance review. Basically Lifestyle Yelp!, though exponentially more important. For most, certs carry more weight than profiles. In fact, some sites lend so much weight to them that they limit use

distinctly higher number of certs for profiles with pics. However, the picless profiles still had some certs, so I wasn't yet sold on the statistical claim. Unfortunately, I knew I couldn't rely on the evidence of couples' and women's profiles, as they both had something I lacked: a vagina.

After verifying that site members weren't informed the identities of those viewing their profiles, I perused the single males and instantly understood the value of the profile pic. Not one picless male profile was certified. It wasn't a numbers thing; there were plenty of single male profiles to be viewed. Nor could this imbalance be explained by quality of content; numerous certless profiles offered articulate self-descriptions. The only explanation could have been the existence of pictures.

I also found the single male profiles with pictures had differing levels of success that followed a surprising pattern. Guys who showed off defined six-packs, chiseled cheekbones, and carefully disheveled locks had certs. But the regular Joes, the everymen, the boys next door, these guys boasted a level of sexual achievement that would make Hugh Hefner perk up and ask for pointers.

Persuaded that profile pics were indeed in my best interest, I uploaded a few JPEGs that showed the real me. The next day my profile was approved, available for members to view, and ready to receive communiqués.

Officially open for business, I began my search.

Daddy2pleaseme was a twenty-something sub looking for a long-term Dom. She withheld a face pic, but her taut body wrapped in a black latex tube top warranted inquiry:

---

by noncertified members. Why so weighty? First off, the mere existence of a cert proves a member is real. Secondly, a cert is more objective than a profile's self-description. By way of analogy, in which would you place more trust about the quality of a movie: a studio's trailer or a critic's review? The critic's review, of course, because the reviewer doesn't have a vested interest in the film's financial success. At least, in theory. For purposes here, just know certs are worth more than gold.

Hi there,
I enjoyed your profile. I'm new to the site and am looking to meet some
fun people. Would love to chat.

I didn't get a response.

UseMeNow, a late-thirties, divorced mother of three, was a busi-ness executive by day who sought a take-charge man in bed by night. I sent a similar message. Again, no response.

I even conjured up some high school Spanish:

Hola ChicaCallosa,
Como esta? Tu es muy bonita. Las fotografías somos muy atractivas.
Gracis por las pagan. Interesada en muchacho solo?

I figured the fact that I wasn't a "certified" member was hindering my efforts. But I thought at least one of my dozens of emails would garner at least minimal interest. To make matters worse, I could see who had read my emails. It was one thing to blindly launch a message into the electronic ether, but it was quite another depressing state of affairs to know the recipient read your message, possibly viewed your profile, and still didn't consider you response-worthy.

All that ended one night with:

cute pic. ;-) wanna chat?
shayla (aka OpenMindedSF)

In her profile pic, Shayla was on all fours sporting a black butt plug that was held in place by someone else's latex-gloved hand. She displayed a large backside and thick thighs, both of which hinted at a larger-than-average body. Her self-description was tamer than most, stating that she was seeking to "explore sexually" and "experience physical pleasure," both of which calmed me immensely, as I wouldn't have to take a crash course in crops, forced orgasm, or knotcraft.

Over the next few weeks, Shayla and I commiserated over our respective frustrations locating compatible playmates. She claimed to attract all the crazies. My problem was I couldn't attract anyone. Shayla termed my dilemma "the curse of the single male." She also shared that she had been introduced to anal sex in Italy. "Over there, it's customary," she explained. I couldn't help but be awestruck by those Italian men who somehow made anal sex a cultural tradition.

Though physically not my ideal, Shayla came across as genuine and nice and her personality much better suited me than the one I suspected sub2bpunished possessed. Also, let's face it: Shayla was my only luck in six weeks, so who was I to be picky?

"Cum over?" she texted one night.

I stepped off the elevator and the thick, salty fryolator smell of fast food knocked me for a loop. Despite the off-putting aroma, the hallway itself was quite upscale. Thick, ornately woven carpet. Side tables with flower arrangements. Recessed lighting reflected by artfully faded mirrors created a warm, homey feel to justify what I assumed were grossly inflated rents.

The greasy fumes intensified as I progressed down the hall and knocked on the door to 211. I heard faint footsteps approach on the other side. The peephole went dark, then light. A few locks snapped and the door peeled back to reveal a tangled mop of blond curls framing a blushing, cherubic face inlaid with two baby blues that studied me curiously.

"You look like your picture," was her seemingly surprised verdict.

Confused as to whether this was a compliment or criticism, I responded, "Thanks?"

"That's a good thing. So many fakes. Wanna come in?"

I followed Shayla into her one-bedroom unit and found my assessment of her body spot-on. Half a foot shorter than me, she carried a noticeable amount of extra weight. She wasn't morbidly obese, but she was definitely flirting with cruiserweight status.

The air in her apartment was stifling and proved the source of the hallway tang. It was stagnant and hot, most likely due to way too much decor packed into the efficiently architected space. Trinkets crammed every flat surface, paintings tiled the walls, and framed photos clogged bookshelves. Oversize and overstuffed furniture mazed into tight corners and short, narrow walkways. Shayla wasn't a hoarder, just in need of an intervention for a shopping addiction.

Then it occurred to me that Shayla might actually be a genius. Intentional or not, so many large items occupying such a compact space diminished her size by comparison. I suddenly found myself in a life-size optical illusion that jostled my senses of perception.

Before I could acclimate, Shayla leapt into the air, crossed her legs, and landed on the U-shaped sectional in perfect posture. Her agility and flexibility were impressive, to say the least. The butcher block of an ottoman before her was littered with burger wrappers, a half-eaten box of fries, and a supersize soda.

"Sorry. Thought I'd have time to finish before you got here."

"Take your time." I meant it. I had to orient. The grease fumes, the stress of my impending first NSA[3] experience, and Shayla's M. C. Escher–esque interior design had me thoroughly discombobulated.

I sat opposite Shayla and was swallowed up by the cushions. I squirmed into a semi-upright position and shoved some throw pillows behind me to prop myself up.

"Any luck reversing the curse?" Shayla asked, then took a hit of soda.

---

3   *NSA (No Strings Attached)*—In short, casual sex. I realize many of you probably knew this one, but I felt it important to clarify for the clueless newbies that NSA doesn't stand for National Security Agency. As ludicrous a mixup as that may seem, I speak from experience.

"Honestly, you're my only lead. How goes it with you?"

"I met one other guy, but we didn't play."

"Why not?"

"Remember I said you looked like your picture?"

"That sucks."

"Some of these guys are Photoshop masters like you wouldn't believe."

"Speaking of pictures . . . Not to get too personal . . ."

"Whose hand is it?"

"Get that question a lot?"

Shayla laughed. "My camera's timer didn't give me enough time, so I enlisted a friend to help."

Her explanation had me questioning the strength of my friendships and I quickly concluded that butt plug assistance crossed more than a few personal boundaries.

"So, wanna play?" Shayla asked with the nonchalance of a server inquiring about my preference of soup or salad. But her question's subject matter instantly oriented me. My first lucid thought was this was really happening. I was actually and finally on the precipice of honest-to-God NSA sex. Hundreds of emails, countless dead ends, and a seemingly never-ending futile effort were finally bearing fruit! Perhaps not the most enticing fruit, but fruit nonetheless. What mattered was, NSA sex was about to commence. What mattered *more* was, I was petrified.

"You don't want to finish your dinner first?" I stalled in hopes of miraculously coming to terms with the reality of my situation.

"Nah. Lemme just brush my teeth. You can wait in the bedroom if you want."

Shayla trotted off and I knew I only had minutes to steel myself or lose this hard-fought-for opportunity.

Shayla's bedroom was barely bigger than a walk-in closet and almost entirely taken over by a queen bed with the excessive height of those slept in by princesses. The zenith of this monstrosity reached my rib cage and its girth left just enough room to squeeze in a dresser at its foot. Thermal dynamics might prove otherwise, but it felt as if the air currents in Shayla's apartment pushed every degree of heat and fume of odor into the four walls of the bedroom, where they festered, trapped.

Unsure of NSA protocol, I debated lying down versus standing, undressing versus staying clothed. I'd yet to resolve anything when—

"Toys?" Shayla asked, trailing in a minty scent that cut the greasy air.

"Up to you."

"I'm good."

Then, with the same Olympic grace exhibited on the sectional, she mounted the bed. My climb consisted of a leg heft, a full-body pull-up, and an awkward roll. With nothing left to say, I went for it.

Between the quicksand-like mattress, the snowdriftesque duvet, and our battling body types, sex with Shayla was a losing battle of positioning, balance, and leverage. Missionary wasn't to be, as the mattress forced me into a concave position that exceeded the limits of lumbar flexibility. Though doggy solved the bodily contortion issue, I couldn't secure adequate footing. We found fleeting success in cowgirl, but Shayla's silk sheets refused to absorb even one drop of our sweat and created a sort of Slip'N Slide. On the plus side, I was so distracted by the act's physical difficulty that I managed to sustain moderate control over my orgasm.[4] Even still, this atrocity had to end. And soon.

With Shayla on her back and me kneeling before her, I somehow secured some traction, pumped like I'd turn impotent tomorrow, and euthanized our effort at playtime. Sweaty, panting, and with lactic acid already eating into my overworked, out-of-shape muscles, I collapsed beside Shayla.

---

4 Though probably not exactly how Ron Jeremy recommends utilizing Distraction Technique, it served its purpose.

Once I regained semi-lucidity, it struck me that I'd finally done it. I'd had sex outside of a relationship. Sex for sex's sake. Granted, it wasn't an elegant performance, but it was a start. And it felt good. The accomplishment of my goal, that is. The act of sex itself was the most grueling physical ordeal I could recall ever surviving. And that includes the lifeguard certification course in high school I had barely completed as a pack-a-day smoker.[5] Despite the definitively subpar experience with Shayla, I'd set out to have no-strings sex and, lo, I had made it so.

I was still basking in the afterglow of my sexual triumph when Shayla proclaimed, "I'm officially no longer a virgin!"

I laughed at her joke and responded, "You're my first meet-up, too."

"Oh. Yeah. That, too."

That, too? Didn't she mean, *That's what I meant?*

I waited for Shayla to correct herself or retract her proclamation. At the very least, laugh at her joke. But she didn't.

My face must have contorted into a confused, terrified expression, because she finally broke her silence and asked, "I told you I was a virgin, right?"

Grappling to control my fight-or-flight response, I responded as calmly as possible, "You told me about anal sex in Italy."

"Silly," Shayla giggled. "Anal sex doesn't count."

Well, I thought, at least it couldn't get any worse.

5 Tread water holding a ten-pound brick above your head for two minutes while fighting a smoker's cough and you'll know from respiratory failure.

Lesson 1:

The Lifestyle and the Single Male

Despite your delusions to the contrary, swingers, by and large, are a civilized lot. We come in all ages, shapes, sizes, nationalities, and ethnicities. We have differing beliefs and opinions. We possess a wide range of IQs and varying senses of humor. We have families, friends, careers, hobbies, mortgages, and retirement plans. In short, we're just like everyone else. We don't strap on leather chaps and nipple clamps to go about our day. Wearing kinks on our sleeves like badges of honor isn't our style. Truth be told, we don't talk that much about our dalliances—at least not to Vanilla folk. We're not ashamed. We simply assume most of the world doesn't get our way of life. And more times than not, we're right.

Though we're like everyone else, our views on sex are admittedly not the norm. To us, sex is just another social activity, often involving refreshments and social etiquette. Also unique is the distinction we make between sex and love. For us, sex is physical and temporary, love emotional and eternal. For many couples, love is the bond that permits Lifestyle participation. And, for some, vice versa.

Now, for all its accepting nature, the Lifestyle considers single men

interlopers at best. Clubs and house parties prohibit single male attendance or, at best, tolerate it on specific nights. Couples and females
block men from emailing or even viewing their profiles. Solo males
are ignored, shrugged off, considered the incurable problem children
of the Lifestyle. Men, if you can't tolerate this reality, stick to whatever
online dating site in which you've already invested however many years
and spent however much in the way of subscription fees. Odds are, the
smattering of one-off coffee speed-dates you've obtained represent far
more success than you'll have in the Lifestyle. And before you think
otherwise, yes, the odds do absolutely apply to you.

Dissuaded yet, fellas? I'm trying my darnedest to do so. Not for my
benefit. I dissuade because I care. The Lifestyle isn't for the thin-skinned
or easily dismayed. Don't take my word for it. Google "swinging single
male" and read for yourself the cesspool of articles and blogs that attest to
the fact that you simply don't belong, aren't wanted, and should be shot
on sight should you be spotted anywhere in the vicinity in the Lifestyle.

Now, before you cry foul, this stereotype isn't wholly undeserved.
The number of stories I've heard about rude, pushy, selfish single males
is beyond reprehensible. Your abhorrent behavior has reached proportions so epic that I'm all too frequently embarrassed to wield a penis.
Not only have the vast majority of you sullied the single male reputation almost beyond salvation, but you've picked off playtime opportunities with the skill of a celibate assassin. Couples welcoming males into
their beds have shunned the lot of us after a single experience with one
of you. Your thoughtless behavior has convinced women craving sexual
exploration to weld on chastity belts. With impressively minimal effort
you have cast the single male population as the black plague of the Lifestyle. And these are just the stories I've heard. I cannot fathom the true
number of tragic tales that exist.

This isn't to say males are solely responsible for all bad times. Fact is,
the bulk of couple and female profiles are blocked to single males, and

the majority of swinger events are planned with their exclusion. Parties can even require an established guest "vouch for" or "sponsor" a male. And even then he's welcomed with heavy skepticism. Subject to this Lifestyle ban, single males can't be responsible for the majority of bad experiences. Mathematically, it's impossible.

However, any swinger can attest that the overwhelming majority of willing (and mostly able) swinging bodies belong to single men. Men create most of the profiles and publish most of the posts. If a woman desires immediate sexual attention, a male will rise to the occasion almost every time. Should a couple desire to "spice up" their relationship, their wish is far more easily granted by accepting the services of a single male than by searching for a compatible couple or solo female. But why, if males have the Lifestyle numbers, are they prohibited from most opportunities?

Consider a normal bar on a normal Saturday night. Droves of men buying women drinks hand over fist to demonstrate their chivalric natures. Their gestures are so transparent that their true motives to coax women to bed are easily quashed.

Now, consider another bar. Same Saturday night. Same people, same drinks. However, at this bar, sex needn't be coerced as it is the reason everyone gathered. That saying "A kid in a candy store"? We're talking Willy Wonka's sex dungeon.

It doesn't take a genius to understand that the mere possibility of sex fogs over a man's common sense and leaves him with a pushy, disrespectful disposition.

What's happened over the years is that these unattractive traits have become so omnipresent, so expected in single males, that the swinging community has been forced to cut them off. Couples, females, party hosts, and club owners limit interaction with single males to avoid even the remote possibility of another emotionally scarring episode. They've just been burned too many times.

However, what women and couples fail to realize is that by excluding males, rather than protecting themselves from horrors, they are instead poking the grizzly bear with a red hot iron. Repeated denials have nurtured a rabid beast in heat who reasons that if he just tries harder and pressures more, he'll be allowed to participate. This faulty reasoning has resulted in an eager, excited male whose well-meaning actions come off as aggressive and rude. Thus the origin of the single male stereotype and the fuel feeding the inferno of bad behavior.

Don't misunderstand. Women and couples shouldn't forgive and forget and welcome single males into their beds with open arms and legs. Though I might benefit from such a response, I wholeheartedly discourage it, as it rewards incivility and does nothing to remedy the growing problem. Instead, I propose single males admit their downfall is the result of *their* behavior and that *they* must take responsibility for *their* actions and change *themselves*.

The Lifestyle is about sex. There's no denying that. But sex is not all the Lifestyle is about—a fact many males ignore, push aside, or outright deny. Swingers seek fun, compatible people with whom they can enjoy good, adult times. Let me repeat that: Swingers seek fun, compatible *people* with whom they can enjoy *good, adult times*. Rude, pushy, insensitive single males remember the "good, adult fun" part but forget the "people" part. If the rude, pushy, insensitive male thought before he acted, he wouldn't be destined for failure. If he viewed the Lifestyle in terms of sexual matchmaking rather than as an orgiastic smorgasbord, he would not only achieve greater success but also better the odds for his comrades.

Despite their current, understandable ostracism, single men are needed. First off, not all heterosexual women want another female in the mix. Many want to be the sole center of attention. Not to mention, a second woman brings with her greater potential for romantic complications. Men are also necessary because, as crass as this may sound, parties aren't free. The inflated "donation" required by single men isn't pure profit. Hotels, refreshments, and condoms cost money. Prohibit single men from the guest list and women and couples are left picking up the tab, a none-too-enticing proposition, wouldn't you agree?

Just as I'm not suggesting women and couples unconditionally accept single males, I'm not proposing single guys band together in an act of civil disobedience until equal swinging rights are granted. As I've said, there's a place for solo males, but we have a lot of work to do. Deeply ingrained perceptions need to be changed. Trust and respect must be earned. Once a new, positive single male stereotype usurps the current, disparaging one, I am confident single men will be viewed as a benefit to the community. Well, at least that is my hope.

Lesson 2:

Pre-swing Considerations

If you were able to digest the current state of the Lifestyle, that's a good sign. For those who found the truth too harsh, don't fret. You're not alone. I said from the get-go, swinging isn't for everyone. Having said that, I encourage you to also read on, but as a voyeur into our little world. If the brutal reality of the Lifestyle struck you unkindly, then you're only in for more hurt.

Now, somewhere I heard, "You don't choose the Lifestyle. The Lifestyle chooses you." While I can't attest to the scientific truth of that statement, I agree that one is or is not born with the swinging gene. And while I also believe you'll never know until you try, there are certain Lifestyle benefits, drawbacks, risks, and repercussions to consider before venturing forth.

Lifestyle Benefits

Forgive the obvious: sex. The Lifestyle is a world of possibilities in which one can experiment and discover, push limits and expand horizons, dip one's toe in or belly flop from the high dive.

Another benefit is tolerance. While not everyone shares kinks, all swingers possess nontraditional sexual predilections. And this communal carnal palate fosters a more tolerant climate than is offered in the Vanilla world.

Then there's NSA. Some long-term couples met swinging, but they are by far the exceptions. Sex is sex in the Lifestyle. No one worries how long you have to snuggle before you can leave or how many days after a tryst to call not to insult. Swingers fuck. Simple as that.

The Lifestyle's taboo nature can also be attractive. It's a rare social gathering where one is encouraged to sleep with another man's wife or where a woman can enjoy multiple men at once. Additionally, being part of a subculture with its own parlance and customs can have a certain allure. I liken it to the life of a superhero. The Vanilla world knows you as one person, while the Lifestyle knows the "other" you. And if you're inclined toward fantasy and role-play, you can create new identities as often as you like.

Alas, nothing is all upside. Along with these benefits come . . .

Lifestyle Drawbacks

Joining a highly sexually promiscuous community increases your chances of contracting any number of STIs. In my experience, the overwhelming majority of swingers practices safe sex, submits to frequent testing, and is candid about health issues that could affect others. Posts and profiles openly admitting herpes, HIV, or AIDS are not uncommon. Some might find these confessions shocking, even distasteful, but would you rather be jolted at the outset by someone's candor or after you've unknowingly caught something? Having said that, an atmosphere of honesty helps, but don't rely on it. Be smart and responsible, and protect yourself.

Next, when meeting a stranger for the express purpose of sex, be cautious. Sexual assaults may occur more frequently with women than men, but I know males who have been the victim of theft and physical injury.

Something to ponder: Hunter is a friend who has a God-given talent for finding women seeking to explore sexually. He's arranged countless threesomes, gang bangs, blowbangs, you name it. After attending a few of his get-togethers, I asked Hunter if he was ever concerned about hosting strangers. In response, he reached beneath the couch cushion on which he was sitting and produced a steak knife. He then walked to a bookcase and removed a butterfly knife tucked between some votive candles. Finally, he pointed to a decorative box on the coffee table and told me to open it. Inside, a stun gun.

"Ever used any of these?" I asked.

"Once," he admitted. "That guy isn't invited back."

I'm not making this up.

Then there's society's view of the Lifestyle. Try working last weekend's gang bang into break-room conversation or recounting a mind-blowing threesome to your family over Thanksgiving dinner.[1] Admitting Lifestyle participation may lose you friends, diminish your dating pool, even jeopardize your job. I'm not suggesting swinging is shameful, but it's worth keeping in mind that there are people who don't approve of swinging and that you might want to consider their possible responses before revealing your participation.

Lastly—and this may be specific to me—swinging can temper normal sex. Orgies, gang bangs, and threesomes can dilute the prospect of a night in bed with one woman in missionary. Consider yourself warned.

• • •

---

1   Perhaps a tell-all memoir about your sexual escapades is the answer to familial disclosure. I'll let you know.

In addition to personal concerns, determine if swinging can help you realize your fantasies. The Lifestyle facilitates myriad experiences, but here are the most common:

Singles Scenarios

ONE-ON-ONES

For hetero unicorns, you can have one-on-ones whenever and wherever. However, as I've said, the Lifestyle is never in want of single men. As such, men, while one-on-ones are your Vanilla standard scenario, they are your most uncommon in the Lifestyle due to the insanely few active single females. Committed women with a hall pass are a possibility, but romantic complications easily arise. Word to the wise: Be sure a committed swinger has his or her spouse's permission to play. If not, be prepared for some serious drama.

In addition to being impossible to locate, single females receive an exorbitantly high volume of inquiries. Attention flatters, but too much overwhelms and intimidates. Women tell me all the time about men who harass with incessant emails. Guys, if that's you, chill. Ladies can't answer every one of the dozens of daily emails choking their in-boxes. They have lives outside of satisfying a stranger's sexual fantasies. If you want a woman's attention, men, patience and understanding will set you apart from the masses.

THREESOMES

Since most active swingers are couples, math dictates the greater likelihood of an experience with a party greater than two. Now, for the behavioral reasons discussed, a couple's first choice is almost always a single female. However, once couples discover the near impossibility of securing a female, and the maddening frustration of pairing with another couple, they warm to the possibility of a single male.

Most often a threesome will take place with a husband and wife, as opposed to a boyfriend and girlfriend, because a marriage has more time to grow stale, a common motivation for couples to "spice things up." So, unless the unmarried couple is experienced in swinging or supremely open-minded and confident, don't expect to find yourself in the middle of a budding relationship.

Since the threesome is the most prevalent scenario, it helps to know the difference between the MFM threesome and the MMF. The placement of the *M* implies bisexual play (MMF) or straight-only (MFM). Often couples new to swinging mistakenly search for MMF when really they want MFM. Don't be afraid to ask for clarification. Frequently, couples don't realize their mistake. And if they do know the terminology, asking will help everyone avoid a potentially awkward situation.[2]

By the same token, it's not given that a couple who says they're "straight" doesn't play bi. The male or female may not be comfortable admitting bisexuality or bi-curiosity. Or perhaps he or she doesn't think "bi" correctly defines them. Again, with such potential for confusion, ask.

Couples-Only Scenarios

HARD/FULL SWAP

The most common couples scenario is hard swapping. In essence a foursome, the hard swap is where couples engage in sex with other spouses. As a single male, I don't have firsthand experience here, but I'm not aware of the MFM/MMF rule applying. So, if it matters to you, you'll probably want to be certain whether any spouse is bi.

---

2   This rule applies to the FMF/MFF distinction as well.

SOFT SWAP

Less common than the hard swap is the soft swap, a scenario where spouses switch partners, but no oral or intercourse takes place. Physically, there's only kissing and petting. A soft swap is sometimes the precursor to a hard swap at a later meeting. Some couples need to warm to others before going the distance.

MISCELLANEOUS COUPLES SCENARIOS

Same Room Sex—Couples have sex with their own spouse in the same room with at least one additional couple present; no swapping.

Same Room Hard Swap—Hard swap with at least two couples playing in the same room.

Same Room Soft Swap—Couples swap spouses and kiss and pet only. However, they do so with their respective spouse present in the same room. Basically what happened in college if you had a roommate.

Different Room Hard Swap—Hard swap with each swapped couple playing in a separate room.

Different Room Soft Swap—Couples swap spouses and kiss and pet only. However, they do so in a room separate from their respective spouse.

Scenarios for All

GROUPS

Groups form as an efficient and reliable way to organize play and often focus on specific experiences such as BBC, BBW, MILFs,[3]

---

3   *BBC (Big Black Cock)*—Self-explanatory.
    BBW (Big Beautiful Woman)—What one considers a physically larger woman another may view as normal. Just know you're not getting skin and bones.

Dom/sub, threesomes, orgies, and gang bangs. Less common ones focus on specific fetishes. As a whole, groups are more intimate than clubs and, for some, less intimidating due to their smaller pool of participants and cozier venues. Another perk is "donations" tend to be less. Drawbacks include fewer playmates to choose from and, due to a group's smaller budget, lower-quality amenities (i.e., snacks and refreshments).

Single males, groups searching for you are virtually nonexistent because, let's face it, it's not a challenge to find a willing male. That being said, regularly active groups are great opportunities for the single male, as they tend to attract reliable swingers. They can also garner invitations to other parties or groups and, potentially, introductions to other swingers. So, if you can finagle an invite, do it.

Groups also form for geographical reasons. While a Lifestyle pen pal on another continent can be emotionally fulfilling, distance can preclude play. To avoid such logistical frustrations, most swingers search for playmates within a convenient distance. For those who live in spread-out or sparsely populated areas, groups can expedite the search for nearby swingers. Similarly, those who reside in morally conservative locales can benefit.

Application protocol includes submitting a recent picture along with your reasons for wanting to join. Be concise, truthful, and humble. Bragging about your sexual prowess or celebrity good looks can result in swift rejection, as no one likes arrogance. The most important qualities, in no particular order, are reliability, affable personality, and ability to perform. List those traits in your application and you've got a leg up on the field. Oh, and guys, unless the group specifically wants well-endowed men, refrain from touting size or girth. It's just tacky.

MILF (Mother I'd Like to Fuck)—A mature woman whom one finds sexually attractive. As with BBW, there is room for personal interpretation.

Avoid groups with too many members. I don't doubt their sincerity, just their ability to execute. It's difficult enough scheduling playtime for yourself, but when you're mobilizing hundreds? Sex is a great motivator, but it doesn't eliminate flakiness. Conversely, groups with too few members are just as inactive, as there's a greater chance of conflicting schedules and lack of leadership, both of which stall momentum.

Groups with too vague a mission also aren't ideal. What new or different experience does "Lovers of Swing" offer? Perhaps a chance to connect with those fond of redundancy? Or jazz?

Best are groups with specific missions, some membership criteria, and a core of active members. Not every group is for everyone, so join those for which you are right and that are right for you. Then be active in the group's success. If you can't find a group, form one. Then see who gravitates to you.

HOUSE PARTIES

House parties range from informal get-togethers to full-blown productions. Invitations are more exclusive because they are usually held at someone's residence. As opposed to clubs or hotel parties, both of which I discuss below, a house party doesn't always require a donation. However, since costs are involved, guests may be asked to help out financially or via potluck. The main benefit of a house party is the flake factor tends to be the lowest of all scenarios because guests are mostly friends or good acquaintances of the host and new attendees are commonly referrals.

A final benefit of the house party is that once you gain admission—and if you're deemed an asset—there's a good chance you'll be invited to future parties and, over time, will expand your circle of swinging friends.

HOTEL PARTIES

Whereas a house party may be a losing financial venture, the hotel party strives to break even or come out slightly ahead. Though a hotel party's expenses are higher than those of a house party, as the location is rented, single females are usually admitted free. Couples are asked to contribute a modest amount and single males pay the most. Since hotel parties must first cover their expenses, hosts aren't as stingy with the invites. This can bode well for single males, as odds of getting in are greater, but the likelihood of some bad apples slipping in under the radar also increases. The number of males invited usually correlates to the number of females, and a good host strives for a close-to-even ratio.

It's worth noting that hotel parties carry a certain amount of risk. You know that agreement you sign at check-in that you never read? Well, that microscopic print at the bottom grants the hotel permission to evict you for any reason. Generally, hotels don't welcome parties, much less ones with an overt sexual theme. A mob of adults getting busy in an enclosed space designed for four can quickly exceed acceptable noise levels. Ma and Pa Kettle on their cross-country road trip won't take too kindly to a carnal cacophony pumping through the wall at two in the morning.

I don't mean to scare you. I've attended dozens of successful and memorable hotel parties. It's just better to be smart than sorry.

LIFESTYLE CLUBS

The club is a hybrid house/hotel party. It's like a house party in that it's usually held at a private residence. But, as at a hotel party, guests are required to donate. Though clubs tend to be organized at private residences, they are run as for-profit businesses, with guest lists, posted rules, dress codes, hours of operation, websites, even security staff. Some have pools or hot tubs, sodas and snacks, even themed rooms. A club I attended had a *Star Wars*–themed playroom complete with wall murals and a *Millennium Falcon* hanging from the ceiling. The owner had a fetish I won't get into . . .

A major drawback to clubs is their cleanliness. This isn't a comment on guests' hygiene, but rather the result of a large number of people using facilities built for far fewer. Be sure to wear flip-flops.

Also, men, expect an explicit "no guarantees" disclaimer, which serves as the host's diplomatic way of warning you against bad behavior. Some clubs even mandate males take a guided tour of the premises (often given by the hulkiest of the security staff) as a discreet way of couching this warning. Despite their disclaimers, clubs are easiest to access for single men. The price of admission may be higher, but rarely does one have to scheme for an invite. Oddly enough, though clubs are most accessible to the single male, many newbies fail to play at them. A group setting for one's maiden Lifestyle voyage can intimidate even the most gung-ho first-timer.

MISCELLANEOUS SCENARIOS

Orgy—While this scenario can occur with multiple single males and females, orgies mostly occur with several couples at a house party, perhaps with a few singles mixed in.

Gang bang—For obvious reasons, GBs require multiple males, which means single males are virtually necessary to facilitate this experience. The GB experience normally occurs with either a couple arranging the experience for the wife or a group organizing one for a single female. For a single male, being part of a GB can be easier than other scenarios, as it can't occur without him.

• • •

Now, as house and hotel parties can be challenging to access and as clubs can be intimidating, impersonal, and unsanitary, I will be focusing primarily on obtaining personal playtime opportunities (i.e., one-on-ones, threesomes, couples scenarios). Not only do those options come with greater chances of success, but they can result in invitations to quality parties or active groups, and even club referrals.

Lesson 3:

The Swing Commandments

Understandably, the Lifestyle is a sensitive community. Owing to its very nature, you're broaching private topics and taking part in extremely personal activities. As such, discretion and trust are vital components to a safe and satisfying experience. The Lifestyle is meant to be fun, but with fun come real feelings and real people. Which means it is essential that etiquette be learned and followed.

COMMANDMENT #1
Thou Shalt Not Lie in the Lifestyle

Don't lay out every personal detail, but don't post a picture with a full head of hair when you're rocking the chrome dome. If your six-pack has ballooned into a keg, don't Photoshop otherwise. And, ladies, if motherhood has . . . accentuated . . . parts of your figure, please don't upload a pre-mommy pic. Everyone has unflattering personal features, but painting a false picture doesn't solve anything. After all, won't the truth be revealed when you meet in person?

In addition to physical appearance, refrain from dishonesty with:

- **Relationship Status:** Don't pose single if you're committed. Similarly, don't pretend to be part of a couple to solicit play when you're a lone wolf. No one appreciates being thrust into drama.

- **Age:** It's only a number, but it's not whatever number you want it to be. Yearn for your squandered youth, but don't lay that trip on someone else.[1]

- **Sexual Orientation:** Revel in your homosexuality, bisexuality, asexuality, any legal sexuality that floats your boat. Eat, drink, and fuck merrily, I say! But don't claim bi to play with the hot wife of a bi hubby, or feign hetero so you can cozy up to Hubby McDreamy and convince him to explore sexually.

- **STIs:** If you're sidelined, be up front. You'd want the same in return.

COMMANDMENT #2:
Thou Shalt Not Judge Others, Though Ye Shalt Always Be Judged

You may not be attracted to BBWs, but don't condemn one who is. A hairy chest might not be your cup of tea, but is denouncing another's preference going to help your cause? Tolerance is one of the best parts of the Lifestyle. Practice and perpetuate it. Everyone is sexy in his or her own way and to someone. Even you.

---

1   Ok, I'll grant some leeway on this one as it is a sensitive topic, but not a lot. Perhaps there isn't much difference between twenty-five and thirty, but there is between thirty-nine and fifty. Don't go crazy is all I'm saying.

COMMANDMENT #3:
Thou Shalt Embrace Rejection

Often you just aren't compatible. Perhaps you're a voyeur, but the couple wants play. Maybe you're 5'7" but wifey only considers men 5'10" or above. Women will back me on this; those few extra inches *do* matter. To some, they're the deciding factor.[2] No one doubts you're wholesome, educated, and display impeccable manners, but the unicorn wants a BBC bull and that ain't you. Many times you won't even know why you were rejected. Just because someone doesn't succumb to your advances doesn't mean you aren't worthwhile or that you aren't Lifestyle material. Rejection just means you aren't meant to play with that particular individual. But you are meant to play with someone else. And it's your responsibility to keep up the search without taking the rejection personally.

COMMANDMENT #4:
Thou Shalt Respond to Rejection with Politeness

The Lifestyle is a ridiculously small world in which one bad experience can domino into lifelong expulsion. When I'm rejected, which occurs multiple times daily, I always, *always* respond politely. Something to the effect of, "Thanks for your honesty. Best of luck in your search!" Most times I never hear back. But once in a while I do. Some of those responses become conversations, and in rare instances, those conversations result in playtime. Turns out my rejecters suffered a bad single male experience that soured them (sound familiar?), but my courtesy made them to reconsider. Guys, thank me later.

---

2 Don't believe me? Perhaps it helps to consider that this claim comes from a guy who, on a low gravity day and standing with impeccably straight posture, just reaches 5'7". Still have doubts? Well, you may just have to discover for yourself the unmerciful reality that is the heightist female.

Daniel Stern

COMMANDMENT #5:
Thou Shalt Persevere, *Not* Persist

Einstein defined insanity as doing the same thing over and over expecting a different result. A persistent swinger stubbornly adheres to the same, fruitless course of action. A perseverant one is resourceful, adaptable, and wise enough to know when to admit defeat. If your interest is not reciprocated, move on. On the flip side, if you garner even the smallest inkling of interest, do not under any circumstances pester, harass, bother, or annoy. No one likes a stalker.

Listen to Albert. Be perseverant, not persistent.

COMMANDMENT #6:
Thou Shalt Not Flake

The number of flaky swingers boggles the mind. God only knows why these idiots join websites, email, chat, and schedule meet 'n' greets only to flake. I know, I know; sometimes your car breaks down or you catch a wicked bout of food poisoning. Things happen. I get it. But have the decency to call. If the roles were reversed, wouldn't you want the same?

In summation: Be honest, don't judge, embrace rejection, always be polite, persevere, and DO NOT FLAKE. Not that hard. And with only six tenets, our community is far less stringent than most organized religions.

But though few in number, these behavioral commandments are the bedrock ensuring a safe and enjoyable environment where everyone can comfortably explore.

Before moving on, I need one more moment alone with the single men. Guys, since you're stigmatized with a bad reputation, here's some advice: If you're an asshole to a couple, there's a good chance they'll transpose your behavior onto the rest of the single male population. Meaning, your unsavory behavior not only reduces your chances of swing success, it fucks it up for every other single male, even those you've never met! You exacerbate the already Sisyphean struggle for Lifestyle acceptance to a virtual impossibility! Now, conversely, if you're respectful, patient, and responsive, odds are better the couple will consider playing with other solo males. See where I'm going with this? I'm sure most of you do, but I'm not taking any chances. So here it is, plain: Behave yourself! Do that, and no one can ask for more. Paying it forward will reap you infinite rewards, perhaps even brownie points with a certain writer active in the community. Just saying . . .

Foreplay

Ethiopian

The Deep End

"Hi. I'm Arianna, your hostess."

Framed in the doorway and haloed by the porch light, Arianna wore a powder-blue lace bra and matching panties. Her trim, petite frame was the well-exercised type one gets when one adheres to a work-out schedule for, like, years. Her unblemished skin and red hair glowed otherworldly in the moonlight the way ingenues' do in movies.

Just four hours prior I was at work when my cell rang from a private number.

"You answered the post?" The voice on the other end was gruff, curt, and male. It didn't specify the content of this supposed "post," but it could only have been referring to one from Craigslist.

I'd given up on CL months ago in order to focus my energies on the site on which I'd met Shayla. I figured a site dedicated to sex would garner better results as not only did it exist solely to facilitate sex,[1] but it also offered some measure of screening to minimize spam and fakes,

---

1   As once I'd failed to give away a couch on CL, it goes to reason that securing a sexual rendezvous would prove even more difficult for me, if at all in the realm of possibility.

a filter CL sorely lacked, evidenced by my email account choked with virus-laden spam. Plus, anyone who took the time to join a site, create a profile, and upload pics had to be somewhat serious, didn't they? But apparently one lingering CL response had meandered its way through the bowels of the Internet and landed in a legitimate in-box. So I did what any levelheaded, decently intelligent man who received a call from a nameless stranger contacted on the Internet recruiting males for anonymous sex would do.

"Yes," I answered him about responding to his post. "I did."

There were a few innocuous exchanges—probably a pleasantry or two—but as with the recall lapses suffered during my loss of virginity, the stress of interviewing for a second NSA experience has left holes in my memory. My recollection picks up, and you'll understand why, when the Voice asked, "So, you have experience with rough sex?"

The question set off a chain reaction in my mind's eye of CL posts rattling by at lightning speed. In less than a second, I saw it:

Assembling group of men to focus on lady. Theme: Rough sex. If you can't perform, don't respond. If you can, email pic and phone. NO PIC = DELETE. If interested, will voice verify. Fakes and flakes, move on!

I wasn't looking for rough sex. In fact, quite the opposite. I knew it was in my best interest—emotionally and physically—to ease into the world of anonymous sex. But after six months without a legit response, I was desperate. Half a year and all I had to show for my effort was a clumsy, unintentional deflowering. Frustrated, self-worth running on E, and one rejection shy from self-castration, I emailed any post that even remotely resembled the real deal. Odds were I wouldn't get a response anyway, so what was the harm?

I sifted through posts armed with only the basic skills of rational deduction and formed a three-point strategy to evaluate them as re-sponse-worthy:

1. Ignore Picless Posts. They were the hallmarks of spammers, Internet bottom-feeders who wanted nothing but to add my email address to their list so they could overload my in-box with offers for any number of bullshit products and scams. Dismissing these eliminated 90 percent of the fakes.

2. Ascertain Pic Authenticity. Many phony posters were aware of picless post avoidance and tried to bypass it by uploading any, and I mean *any* JPEG. So, with every post with pic I'd ask myself:

    a. Was the pic of someone recognizable? If so, I moved on. As much as I might prefer otherwise, Cindy Crawford wasn't searching for NSA. Other tip-offs to inauthentic pics were dated, scanned Polaroids or professional shots.

    b. Had the pic been used in multiple posts? If so, odds were I'd found a pic collector.[2] If I judged the pic reasonably authentic and nonserial, then I asked—

    c. Did the pic's subject need Internet sex? Not that I thought all web sex searchers were trolls, but women

---

2   For those unfamiliar with the unsavory species that is the "pic collector," allow me to paint a few unappealing pictures. One is the stereotypical obese, unshowered, agoraphobic crazy who lives in his mother's basement and who hasn't been exposed to a ray of sunlight since he discovered a dial-up connection and whose only contact with the outside world is made solely online. This breed does exist and doesn't appear to be going away anytime soon. For whatever reasons, he (sometimes she) fishes the interweb for pictures, often of the explicit variety, to assist in satiating whatever libidinous urges solitary life is still able to conjure up. Then there's the business-minded pic collector who accumulates stockpiles of images to populate websites. Again, these guys (and gals) are out there. Finally, there's the mischievous pic collector who amasses anthologies of pics in order to create profiles on other adult sites to do God knows what. Needless to say, the pic collector has very limited use, if any, to anyone other than himself (or herself). And I didn't want to be of use to him.

who could enter an amateur beauty pageant weren't trawling for web cock, I was quite certain.

3. Text Review. (*Applied ONLY after criteria #1 AND #2 were met.*) Curt messages like "want sex NOW" and "ready to suck cock," even coupled with a legit pic, I'd reject. Also, posts that "hid" phone numbers in the text—*five six two five 5 5 two 2 eight OHHHHHH*—were tossed out. I would only respond to messages that had some thought, coherence, and a basic spell-check performed.

Apparently my strategy had worked, as I found myself ear to ear with the Voice, who had presented me with a choice: Come clean about being a rough sex rookie or continue questing down the same desolate road.

"Yes," I lied about my rough sex experience. "I do."

Maybe I wasn't experienced in rough sex in the quote-unquote conventional way, and I was pretty confident I didn't possess the specific experience the Voice sought, but I'd had more than my fair share of *emotionally* rough sex. At that I was a grizzled veteran, which, I rationalized, qualified me more than most for the Voice.

"Still there?" I asked after a prolonged pause on the Voice's end.

"Yeah," he answered before another episode of radio silence. "Well, you don't seem too crazy . . ." he offered with a pondering tone. Unsure how to respond to his hesitant diagnosis of my mental state, I, too, understood the wisdom in opting for silence. And just when I'd assumed the Voice had hung up to call the next applicant, he instructed me, "Eight tonight. I'll text the address."

Four hours later I was gawking slack-jawed at Arianna in her bra and panties and defined abs. Mercifully, she snapped me out of my mental haze and asked if I'd like to come inside.

She led me down a candlelit hall that let out into a living room in mid-renovation empty of furniture, save for a refrigerator plopped in the middle of the space. To the right was an open-air kitchen with blueprints strewn over a skeleton of unfinished, topless counters and doorless cabinets. The air was thick with the smell of drywall and spackle. A sliding glass door revealed a tiny, walled-in backyard that contained an even tinier in-ground pool, around which were precariously stacked couches, tables, and other interior furniture.

My eyes had barely adjusted to the dimness when a shock of light ripped through the dark. I turned to find it emanating from the fridge, into which a muscular silhouette was loading a case of beer.

"That's Craig," Arianna said.

"Nice to meet you," I said to the silhouette.

"Beer?" it asked in response.

"Thanks."

Craig closed the fridge and, as he approached and handed me a cold one, my eyes readjusted and placed him in his mid-forties. Over layers of cultivated muscle, he wore jeans, loafers, and a tight-fitting V-neck sweater.

"How long you guys been renovating?" Craig asked Arianna.

"About a month."

"How much longer?"

Arianna sighed. "The contractor messed up the counters, so who knows."

"Preaching to the choir."

"Yeah?"

"Oh, yeah. But in the end everything turned out for the best."

"How so?"

"Well, for one, I switched from laminate to granite."

"Granite . . ." She exhaled, confounded, as if the granite countertop quandary was the most perplexing philosophical question of all time. "Yeah . . . We're torn."

"More expensive, but aesthetically superior," Craig lobbied. "Also retains value longer."

Knowing the sexual perversity about to transpire, I couldn't reconcile that I was suddenly in an episode of *Extreme Makeover: Home Edition*. Granted, I didn't know from normal pre–rough group sex discussion topics, but I was pretty sure home improvement wasn't on the list.

Before Craig could segue into the nuances of crown molding, there was a knock at the door. Arianna excused herself and left Craig and me alone in the awkwardness that can only be described as the one that results between two male strangers who are imminently going to have sex with the same woman at the same time, who, coincidentally, is just as much a stranger.

Desperate to escape the awkwardness, I tried to reintroduce the countertop topic. "So, granite's good, huh?"

But before Craig could answer, a door to a back room I hadn't noticed whipped open and from it bolted a man radiating energy, panting, and sporting an erection adorned with a studded leather cock ring. Candlelight reflected off the sheen of sweat coating his hairless body as he beelined for the fridge.

"Couple more minutes and she's all yours," he assured us in the same gruff voice that had only hours prior diagnosed me as not "too crazy."

The Voice opened the fridge, sat bare-assed on a shelf, grabbed a bottle of water from the door, and downed three loud gulps. He poured the last bit over his head and took a few deep breaths.

"Arianna taking care of you guys?" he asked.

"That she is," Craig assured him.

"She's hostess. Tell me if she isn't doing her job," he commanded us firmly.

"It's all good, Theo."

Theo steadied himself with a couple more deep breaths, instructed us to "hang tight while I finish prepping her," then disappeared back into the room from which he came.

A woman in lingerie? A man with a cock ring? Strangers who preferred granite to laminate? What insanity had I gotten myself into? This was not what I had envisioned for my quest. I wanted batting practice, not someone's virginity. And I knew I didn't want, and beyond a shadow of doubt wasn't ready for, whatever lurked behind that back door.

Feeling suddenly light-headed, I wanted to put an end to this retarded brainchild of a quest idea, drive home, and accept my hopeless state of affairs. Instead, that internal stirring whirred to life and had me blurt out, "Who's Theo . . . prepping?"

"Gina," answered Craig.

"Ah. Yes. Of course. Gina." I didn't have a clue. At this point, I could barely remember my name, much less venture particulars about Theo's "preparation" of this Gina. "Just curious. Who's Arianna?"

"Theo's sub."

"Ah. Yes. Of course. Theo's sub."

"Need another beer?" Craig told me more than asked me.

"Yes, please."

Craig went to grab me another beer and Arianna returned with six and a half feet of black, bald linebacker.

"Guys, this is Green Mile."

One would assume that someone nicknamed Green Mile would bear some resemblance to Michael Clarke Duncan. However, other than skin color, a shaved head, and a larger-than-life presence, Green Mile looked not a thing like Michael.[3] Regardless of his poorly attributed

---

3 I assume most of you have seen *The Green Mile*, but for those who haven't, Duncan plays a giant of a man whose physicality is dwarfed only by the size of his gentle nature. The film's plot has no relevance to my story other than Duncan's presence in it. But if you're in need of a movie recommendation, you could do much worse.

nickname, Arianna draped herself over his frame in a seemingly aphrodisiac trance, which triggered my deductive powers to surmise that "Green Mile" didn't refer to his overall physical appearance, but rather to a specific body part.

"She's all yours, guys," Theo announced as he reappeared from the back room and swept his arm to his side like a maître d' stepping aside for fine diners to proceed to their feast.

I trailed Craig and Green Mile into a bedroom barely large enough for the full-size bed that offered up the naked, blindfolded body of a woman whom I could only presume was Gina. Each of her limbs was tied to a different corner of mattress with thickly braided white rope, and over her petite, tanned torso were sprinkled condoms of seemingly every size and variety in the history of prophylactic manufacture. Gina appeared a sexual sundae of sorts.

"She likes it rough, guys." Theo slapped Gina's inner thigh, which elicited from her a moan and squirm. "So don't hold back."

Knowing I was well beyond my ken, I let Craig and Green Mile lead the way and did my best to keep up. Surprisingly, after a somewhat rocky and clumsy start, I relaxed and settled into a decent rhythm that wasn't too embarrassing.

Two late arrivals joined and, at some point, Theo cut Gina loose from her restraints and relieved her of her blindfold. Not long after, he worked Arianna into the mix, though it was understood that play with her must first be sanctioned by him.

Three hours later, I found myself the odd man out in the carnal configurations. Craig and the late arrival who hadn't departed were sharing Gina and, though I wasn't yet off-book with the Kama Sutra, I was pretty sure Theo and Green Mile were DPing Arianna. With all that had transpired, I had no qualms riding the bench to catch my breath and process everything. However, my reprieve was interrupted when Theo declared, "She needs another cock!"

Given the sexual logistics at the time of his declaration, Theo could only have been referring to Arianna's last available orifice: her mouth.

Craig and the late arrival shot me simultaneous bug-eyes that read, If you're not going, I am! I knew Craig's amped reaction meant that an opportunity with Arianna was not to be refused, so I leapt onto the bed, which proved identical to those adult-size obstacle courses in Japanese game shows where heavily padded contestants gallop through life-size *Mouse Trap*–esque challenges. Similar to those athletically challenged contestants with obvious death wishes, I wobbled around bodies and barely avoided limbs as I traversed the minefield of carnality. I was one step from Arianna when she opened her mouth to receive me. I secured a tenuous balance, took my final step toward Arianna . . . and clipped my head on the ceiling fan.

Myriad maxims apply to the lessons I learned that night. Do your best. Trust yourself. An active mattress does not provide stable footing. But one lesson more than all others, even a decade later, has proven integral to the person I am today: Bleeding puts a crimp in the sexy vibe.

A Threesome and Steven Seagal

Head-butting the ceiling fan brought about an impromptu play break that allowed me to bandage up and ice my forehead. It was also during this pause in the action that I overheard Craig mention a "Lifestyle" site on which he'd found success. From his description, "Lifestyle" members sounded more my speed, which explained the limited response to my emails on the emo girl site.

So the next day I checked out the site Craig spoke of and quickly learned the differences between "alternative lifestyle" and "swinging lifestyle," the major one being that the former customarily required specialized tools like the ones Melissa had purchased in London; the latter not so much. As swinging appeared more aligned with my quest (and definitely better suited to my still limited skill set), I joined the site, re-created my profile, and became the Tasmanian Devil of emailing.

Every day for what felt like eternity I checked for new profiles and contacted every woman and couple within a fifty-mile radius who even remotely entertained the idea of a single male. For weeks I received no response, flat no's, or, worst of all, stock rejections prewritten by the site

(*"Thank you for your email, but I don't think we're compatible. Good luck in your search!"*). Something about those canned replies really cut deep. On a positive note, a so-called straight man asked if I was interested in exploring my bisexuality. Though flattered, I politely declined.

Two fruitless months finally ended one Sunday whilst I brunched with friends.

"This is Annalisa," said a heavily accented voice coming over my cell from a private number. "We have been doing the email."

I had emailed so many couples that it took me a moment to recall that Annalisa and her husband, Marco, wanted an MFM.

"We desire for today meet, if that is to be possible to you." Italian, maybe?

I stepped outside for some privacy.

"Studio City is our preferred. Is the next hour to be possible?" Based on Theo's four-hour notice and now Annalisa's same-day request, apparently working fast was a Lifestyle motif I'd have to get used to.

To make it to the Valley in time I would have had to leave that minute. But the larger issue was, we had taken my friend's car. There wasn't enough time for me to cab it home, then make it to the Valley. I could take a taxi to meet Marco and Annalisa, then home afterward, but I'd have to delay retirement a few years to cover the fares.

"If today is not to be possible, I do not know the next disposable time."

It had taken two months of daily carpal tunnel–inducing searches, profile reads, compatibility calculations, and email sessions that garnered nothing but soul-rending, heart-breaking, ego-shattering rejection to get this one, single call. Who knew how many more months, years, decades would pass and what apocalyptic damage my ego would sustain from the emotional avalanche of denial—not to mention the battering my typing joints would suffer—before my phone would ring again, if ever it would. I knew I had to make this work.

"An hour is perfect," I assured Annalisa, then suggested the only bar I knew in Studio City.

I returned to the table and whispered to my friend, "I need to borrow your car. I can't tell you why and you can't ask me about it. Now or ever."

Without looking up from his eggs Benedict, he tossed me his keys, and minutes later I was chugging up Laurel Canyon in a baby-blue Ford Festiva. I crested Mulholland, descended into Studio City, and had just enough time to purchase some condoms before the agreed meet-up time.

As I entered the bar, it dawned on me that I didn't know what Marco or Annalisa looked like. Their profile didn't offer any pics, nor could I remember any physical descriptions.[1] Annalisa's call had caught me off guard, which precluded presence of mind to ask. And since their number was private, I couldn't call or text. They'd seen my picture, so all I could do was wait for them to find me.

Twenty minutes later, a middle-aged couple approached. Just over five feet, Annalisa was plump, with long, straight, dark brown hair. Her blue eyes were the size of saucers and she had a warm, timid smile. Marco was only a few inches taller than his wife, with a rugged look, salt-and-pepper stubble, and massive, manly hands disproportionate to his stocky stature.

"Marco does not speak the English," Annalisa informed me, then translated for Marco, who nodded in agreement.

The three of us sat at the bar. I spoke with Annalisa, who translated sporadically for Marco, who, in turn, paid us little attention. It was apparent this meeting was for Annalisa's sake, so I kept the conversation keyed on her. I inquired about their move from Italy, what they missed

---

1   On CL I wouldn't have dared consider emailing a picless post, as it was the key indicator of a fake. However, Lifestyle sites have filters that greatly reduce the fake and spam contingent, which meant it was safer to contact picless profiles on them, as long as the profile offered decently articulate text. Which, despite their obvious language difficulty, Marco and Annalisa's did.

about their homeland, favorite books, regular chitchat. When I asked if they had children, she flinched.

"Please, no. I don't like to . . ."

I couldn't blame her for not wanting to talk about her children with a man she'd just met and with whom she was considering having a threesome. I apologized for treading on too personal a topic, which she appreciated.

Marco was content sitting, drinking, and going outside for the occasional smoke. But Annalisa displayed increasingly frequent signs of doubt. Rather than pretend I didn't notice, I addressed the situation.

"Have you had a threesome before?"

"This is first. You?"

"For the most part, yes."

"What is that meaning?"

I recounted my experience at Theo and Arianna's, which involved more than three participants, but some configurations were threesomes, so I had a little experience. I also included my encounter with the ceiling fan, which made Annalisa laugh.

"So, why do you and Marco want a threesome?"

"Is idea of Marco."

I anticipated she'd respond, "It's always been a fantasy," or "We recently became curious." But now I felt like I was convincing Annalisa, which didn't sit well with me.

"And you're okay with that?"

"Sometimes yes. Sometimes not sure." Visibly uneasy, she sipped her champagne.

"Well, don't translate this for Marco, but we're not doing this unless *you* want to. We can just drink, talk, and go our separate ways. You can even tell Marco it was me who said no."

She smiled, relieved. "Thank you."

Annalisa and I chatted some more. Marco drank and smoked. Then he said something in Italian to Annalisa, who then asked me, "Do you know where is a hotel?"

"Are *you* asking me? Or is Marco?"

"Is me."

"If you're asking, then yes. I passed one on the way."

We caravanned to the hotel that resembled a winter lodge, complete with faux–log cabin facade. Towering plastic pine trees and fake snow were more than out of place in the suburban desert landscape of the San Fernando Valley, but I was on the verge of my first threesome and couldn't waste time locating a non-themed hotel.

I met Marco and Annalisa in the parking lot and, after standing around nervously a few minutes, I got the hint that I was responsible for renting the room. I decided a trio of adults without luggage renting a single room would draw suspicion, so I suggested Marco and Annalisa wait in the parking lot while I checked in.

The hotel's lobby strove to exude the warmth and comfort of a mountain lodge with electric fireplaces, thick red carpet, and artificially weathered leather couches. However, the taxidermied grizzly and assorted mounted animal heads were a tad excessive.

I steeled myself, approached the reception window, and proceeded to live out the scene in *The Graduate* where Dustin Hoffman stumbles through renting a room to have an affair with Mrs. Robinson. Granted, my situation wasn't exactly an affair, as it included *Mister* Robinson, but that distinction gave me little relief.

After a thoroughly clumsy check-in process that mostly involved me stuttering and trying not to sweat too profusely, I took the key in my sweat-slicked palm and bid the clerk good night (even offered a hearty yawn, à la Benjamin Braddock, to sell it).[2] On my way to the room, I sent Marco and Annalisa a text with the room number.

---

2   If you don't know Benjamin Braddock, then there really is no hope for you.

When they arrived, Annalisa excused herself to the bathroom. I lay on the bed and surrendered to the same awkwardness I'd experienced with Craig at Theo and Arianna's. Though this was only my third NSA experience—and second with multiple participants—I knew I'd never acclimate to being alone with a newly met man with whom I was about to share a woman. There were worse situations, I supposed.

To occupy himself, and perhaps to escape the discomfort, Marco turned on the TV. He flipped channels and stopped on Steven Seagal serving up an ass-kicking to some ruffians who, no doubt, deserved it.

"You like Steven?" Marco asked slowly, deliberately, in a resonant baritone.

These were the first words Marco had spoken to me. I didn't know if I should engage him in hopes of forging some bond prior to playtime, or if I should just answer and leave it at that. I couldn't help but think his seemingly innocuous question was really his attempt to connect with me on a deeper level. Perhaps it was his way of groping for some indication that the events about to transpire, the scenario he'd been encouraging his wife to embrace, would be as enjoyable and fulfilling as he'd always imagined. Whatever the motivation for his question, it struck a profound chord in me.

"Sure," I said as understandingly and reassuringly as I could. "He's fine."

Marco then sat in the antler-backed desk chair, silently faced the wall, and waited. Perhaps he really just wanted to know if I liked Steven.

Annalisa returned and approached Marco. They made out by the glow of the TV, serenaded by Steven breaking bones, ending lives, and clawing his way to justice one martial arts move at a time. Marco waved me over and I assumed make-out duties with Annalisa as he unbuttoned her top. I unzipped her pants and she massaged both of us through our jeans. We disrobed and moved to the bed, where I performed oral on Annalisa who did the same on Marco. Marco signaled me to switch with him and handed me a condom. I unwrapped it and was hit with a pungent strawberry aroma that had a strange calming effect on me.

Over the next half hour we experimented with multiple configurations of Marco and me pleasuring Annalisa, all while Steven saved the world. Before departing, Marco shook my hand and Annalisa gave me the gentlest kiss, which affected me more deeply than all the sex we'd just had. She pulled away, looked me in the eye, and said not a word. Perhaps this was how she always said goodbye, but I like to think it was something more.

I lay on the bed and replayed the night in my head. I noted aspects of my performance with which I was impressed—offering to be Annalisa's scapegoat and my limited but meaningful interaction with Marco (debatable, I suppose)—and aspects at which I could improve—the sex was still awkward; also, I could benefit from smoother hotel room renting. All in all, I was pleased with the direction in which I was heading.

When I finished my postmortem, it was late and I had work in the morning. I sat up to leave, then realized I was in a pickle. I had told the receptionist I was turning in for the night, even yawned as proof to my tired state. Checking out barely an hour later would raise his suspicion which would lead to him contacting the authorities who would interrogate me for days until the waterboarding grew too much to bear and I'd cough up Marco and Annalisa's identities who they'd locate and interrogate as well and conclude that their affinity for group sex was really a plan to overthrow America. Marco, Annalisa, and their children would be deported to Italy where Marco and Annalisa would soon come to terms with their new reality, but their children would foster a grudge against the American male who had fucked their lives in more ways than one. They'd spend their youths planning revenge scenarios to exact upon me once they turned of legal age, assumed fake identities, and returned to America. For the sake of my well-being as well as that of Marco and Annalisa and their family, not to mention the preservation of international peace, I had to uphold the cover story. I played out multiple plans of action and decided I had only one option: return my friend's car, wake up early the next morning, go back to the hotel in my car, check out, then go to work. Though a logistical pain in the ass, it was exactly what I did and, because of it, the morning clerk didn't suspect a thing, Marco and Annalisa continued to live the American dream, and the world remained at DEFCON 5. It felt good to be a humanitarian.

Tamer Waters

A one-night stand, an orgy, and a threesome. Not bad for less than a year of questing. What excited me more, though, was that my experience with Marco and Annalisa proved to me that what I sought could be found in the Lifestyle.

The alternative life wasn't my kink. True, it had led me to Shayla, but she was a fluke. And even if by some glitch in the Matrix she wasn't a stroke of luck, the odds of me finding another non-Goth female (preferably sexually experienced this time) seemed astronomically unlikely, evidenced by the fact that of the few hundred emails I'd sent, I'd received a total of two responses. One from Shayla; the other from a 24/7 Dom/sub couple whose profile pic displayed the wife in what Google educated me was the "teardrop" position[1] with Master stimulating her nether region with what Google also taught me was a cattle prod. And judging by the expression on the sub's purple-hued face, Master's im-

---

1   Imagine a person naked, hog-tied (arms and legs tied behind back), and suspended four feet off the ground from a master knot at which the ropes binding the four extremities meet. Medieval, to say the least.

plement was not a low-grade model. Even if you removed the prod, replaced Master's leather ensemble with something less diabolical, and freed the wife from her expertly fashioned rope prison, the photograph was professionally taken. It even had a freakin' watermark! Anyone sexually skilled enough to warrant professional pics was unequivocally beyond my abilities. It goes without saying that their response "Do you understand what you're getting into with us?" went unanswered by me. And when it came to CL, I'd long since reached my limit with blindly launching off email after email. It was a crapshoot and, as at casinos, the house always won.

So I stuck to the site on which I'd met Marco and Annalisa, resumed daily email regimens, and, before long, connected with more couples.

William and Vivian (aka FriskyFelines) were an early-thirties, blond, Caucasian couple from Calabasas. Though they blurred their faces in their pics, it was clear William was sturdily built and Vivian compact. Their Lenny and Squiggy pairing was jarring at first, but endearing once acclimated to. My favorite pic of Vivian showed her bowling in a Catholic schoolgirl outfit sans shirt. It was fun, sexy, and conveyed a great personality.

After a few emails, Vivian suggested we meet to assess compatibility, but said in no uncertain terms that they never played on a first meet.[2] Though I'd successfully closed a threesome with Marco and An-

---

2 Meeting members of a site devoted to sex and not playing may seem counterintuitive, even wasteful. But the truth is, no matter how hard you try, you can't truly know how you feel about another until you meet in person. How do you know if the person with whom you've been emailing, texting, and chatting is really who he or she or they claim to be? How can you be sure the online chemistry will transfer to the real world? And—this may just be me—but what if the other person smells bad? At the risk of permanently setting in print yet another humiliating admission (really, who am I kidding? I can't imagine another bucket of gasoline on the psychological fire is going to make any difference), I admit to possessing highly persnickety olfactory nerves. Perhaps my sense of smell is wired the same as everyone's, but the fact remains that I go to exceptionally great lengths to avoid even the slightest offensive aroma. Holding my breath to the point of light-headedness, electing to take convoluted detours to evade less-than-pleasurable odors, even spurning those with halitosis. Don't misunderstand. My smell issue is not isolated to others. Ever since puberty unleashed my body's

nalisa only an hour after meeting, I was relieved that my first meet with William and Vivian would be strictly platonic. I didn't have to worry about my performance, just conversation.

We convened at a Mexican restaurant deep in the Valley and talked about everything but the Lifestyle. Turned out William and Vivian grew up in Mormon families, but both came to the realization that it wasn't for them. Virtually everything Mormonism forbade were things about which they were curious. So they accepted familial shunning in favor of self-truth.

The night ended pleasantly; we went our separate ways and promised to stay in touch. We emailed for another month, and, while I was more than game to take the next step, their replies arrived farther and farther apart, making it evident the initial interest had waned.

Not long after William and Vivian, I connected with Frank and Lillian (HispCpl), who had joined the site a month before I had. Their profile mentioned a recently developed sexual curiosity they were eager to explore, but they weren't in any rush. Moreover, they disclaimed, they had two young children, which meant patience was a must for any-one wanting to progress beyond email. Lillian's head was cropped out of every pic for privacy reasons, but her body never failed to entice with its seductive poses and revealing outfits. We each had one MFM on our résumé, and, luckily, both were enjoyable enough for us to seek another. Frank and Lillian could get a babysitter Friday night, if I was interested in grabbing drinks. I accepted and Frank said we'd leave our options

---

ability to manufacture scent, I've toted around deodorant sticks and sprays to ensure that should I find myself in uncomfortably warm surroundings I can tend to matters. Beneath my sink, bars of soap are stacked five high and deep. My hand soaps have hand soaps. At any given time I have at my disposal an armada of air fresheners that never dips below four varieties. And don't even get me started on the miracles of Purell. My point is, sexual chemistry is a finicky science. Additionally, some use a "no-play" disclaimer to avoid having to reject another to his or her face. It's a lot easier to reject a person over email, a different experience entirely to do so in person. If a meeting is agreed to under the auspices of "no-play," then should one side dislike the other, it can claim "no-play" and be on its way. Others, for whatever reason, just don't play on the first date. I chalk it up to the Lifestyle version of the illogical "no kissing on the first date" rule some Vanilla folk adhere to. Whatever lets you sleep at night, I guess. Now, back to our regularly scheduled perversity . . .

open for the night. He asked point-blank if I'd flake. A babysitter wasn't cheap and they didn't want to waste a kidless night. I said I understood and promised to show.

Lillian was perched on a stool wearing a short skirt and high heels, which just so happened to be my favorite outfit from her pics. Though their profile listed them as in their mid-thirties, they looked much younger. Too young, in my opinion, to have two kids, a comment that made Lillian smile.

Half an hour of drinks and chitchat escalated when Frank informed me that Lillian loved to slow dance. On the dance floor, Lillian must have sensed the trouble I had hiding my erection while keeping what little rhythm I possessed and moved in to shield matters. Her proximity hid my predicament, but her body grinding against mine only exacerbated the situation.

"Let go," she whispered in my ear as her fingertips caressed the back of my neck, sending a chill waterfalling down my spine.

From somewhere in the long-forgotten muscle memory of my pubescent years sprang forth the ballroom dance classes forced upon me. I began twirling and spinning Lillian and the crowded dance floor opened up. Couples gave us space; many even stopped to watch. The song finished and I dipped Lillian deeply. We would have remained in that position forever if not for the bargoers' applause snapping us back to reality. Not until I righted Lillian did I again feel the pressure against my fly and did my best to conceal it with a deep bow, during which I struggled to adjust it.

"There's a motel nearby," Frank informed us when we returned to the table and saw he'd paid our tab.

We got a room and, while Lillian freshened up in the bathroom, Frank told me, "Lillian goes crazy with a good kisser and she loves to be the focus of two men. No need for a condom with oral, but it's required for sex. Also, she loves when guys talk about how sexy she is during sex. Nothing crude. She just likes to feel desired and wanted."

"No problem."

"With what happened on the dance floor, I didn't think it would be."

"Saw that, huh?"

"Everyone did." Frank and I couldn't help but laugh. "Any questions?"

"What doesn't she like?"

"She doesn't swallow. No cum on her face or hair. And I'm the only one allowed anal."

I assured Frank that I'd respect all limits.

"Thanks for asking," he said. "Not everybody does."

Frank was spot-on with his assessment of Lillian's affinity for being the center of attention, and supremely so with her love of being discussed. Every comment ratcheted her energy another notch. Soon we were in a carnal frenzy that resolved only after everyone was spent and satisfied.

In the parking lot, Frank asked, "Want to meet again sometime?"

"Yes!" I responded, perhaps too quickly and effusively, which caused Frank and Lillian to laugh.

"We'll be in touch," promised Frank.

On the drive home it struck me that Frank and Lillian were only my third meet from the site. Batting two for three right off the bench was nothing to scoff at. I was still a rookie, but if I could land fulfilling experiences this quickly, I couldn't imagine the number of stellar ones that awaited me. My quest was *definitely* on the right trajectory.

I struck up a correspondence with Al and Jennifer, an even-keeled Tahitian and a feisty Portuguese, respectively, that yin-yanged perfectly. Al was strictly voyeur, and Jennifer enjoyed being watched. Though San Diego was home, Al was traveling to LA on business and Jennifer decided to tag along with the hope of scheduling a few playdates. We hit things off over email, so we planned to meet at their hotel bar for a few cocktails. If the online chemistry translated to real life, we'd progress to their suite.

It took us less than fifteen minutes to conclude that the chemistry indeed translated. After a third cocktail, our lively conversation came to a natural lull.

"Shall we go up?" Al asked.

In the elevator, Al asked if he could take photographs. He assured me he'd avoid faces and, before I left, we'd delete any that made me uncomfortable. Though hesitant to put my sex life on record, I had a good feeling about them, so I agreed.

When Jennifer and I began to play, Al went to the balcony to smoke.

"Should we wait?" I asked.

"No. He likes to walk in on me."

Al returned just as Jennifer commenced oral on me. Out of the corner of my eye I saw him recline in the sofa chair and rest his feet on the ottoman. I nudged Jennifer's hip and she repositioned to 69.

"Honey," Jennifer called to Al after a few oral-gasms, "be a sweet and toss us a condom."

At first the camera flashes were jolting, but soon all I was aware of was Jennifer.

After play, while Jennifer and I cooled down and caught our breath, Al and I reviewed pics and deleted a few. He promised to email them to me once he returned home.

A few weeks later, I somehow wangled a meet with a single female. In her early forties, Alexis was on the heavy side but sported an impressive chest. She was the single mother of a teenage daughter and was "seeking a sexual renaissance." Specifically one in which she assumed a more submissive role.

Alexis arrived half an hour late to the country and western–themed bar and apologized, but I wasn't bent out of shape. At first she came off shy and demure, but a little alcohol relaxed her. We'd only talked ten minutes when she informed me that because she'd arrived late she needed to leave to pick up her daughter from dance class.

"But I could give you a blow job before I go," she offered.

We took my car a few blocks to a secluded spot and she made good on her offer. Before we parted, she asked if I could host Sunday night.

This time Alexis arrived punctually and proceeded directly to my bedroom, where we commenced play. She enjoyed herself, but I could tell she wanted more. Not since my failed night with Melissa had I attempted to assume a more dominant role. But with the success of my recent experiences I'd developed some confidence.

"On all fours," I ordered Alexis, who paused oral and looked up from between my legs with eyes radiating excitement. "Now," I commanded.

She obeyed. And she obeyed all my subsequent directives.

I told her to lie on her back and she hooked her legs over my shoulders. Her moaning intensified and, as she climaxed, she snapped off a rail from my headboard. Once her orgasm dissipated, she noticed the wooden rail clutched in her hand.

"What's this?" she asked, sincerely confused.

I pointed to the open space on my headboard.

"Well, well," she marveled. "Good job, you."

The following week, I received the pics from Al. While it was a turn-on to relive that night with Jennifer, it was unsettling and disappointing to see my stiff, rigid, hesitant self. Honestly, in some of the pics it looked as though a woman was having sex with a flesh-colored ice sculpture, that's how inflexible I appeared. I had eased into the Lifestyle, but I was still in the shallow end, perhaps still thawing out there. This quest might take longer than I had anticipated. Good thing was, I had no qualms about sticking it out.

Since joining the site, I'd been emailing with Gerard and Rose. But with one or another of us busy, out of town, or too exhausted with life, we could never mesh schedules. It seemed playtime was not in the stars for us. To be honest, the fact Rose was in her early fifties gave me pause. I hadn't been with a woman that old and I had many questions and major concerns. But, despite our age gap, Rose's profile pics were sexy and enticing, and radiated an alluring sense of humor. Moreover, her pics looked to have captured an authenticity, a quality to which I found myself becoming more and more attracted. Sure, there were multitudes of profiles of members with immaculate aesthetics. But, increasingly, they weren't drawing me in. Something inside me said that everything I needed to know about these people I could see in their pics. I'm not saying that I wasn't sexually aroused at first glance. But after that initial spark, nothing held my interest. With Rose, however, I wanted to know more. So I threw caution to the wind and, after three months of e-flirting, Gerard invited me to a GB he was organizing.

I arrived at the hotel lounge to find Gerard enjoying a cocktail. I'd be lying if I said I wasn't skeptical with Rose not present. But they had five certs, so I didn't bolt.

Gerard waved me over and, before I could slip in an allusion to Rose, he said, "Don't worry, Rose is getting dressed in the room."

We shared a laugh.

Gerard looked like his picture, with a full head of thick white hair and an even thicker 'stache that rivaled Tom Selleck's from his *Magnum P.I.* days. His voice was warm, resonant, and commanding, but not intimidating.

I retrieved a round of drinks for Gerard and myself and returned to find two more men at the table: Jeff, a young military type with too much energy who was pleasant enough, and Hal, dumpy and closer to Gerard's age. The four of us talked sports and other nonsense during which time three more men arrived, bringing our total to seven.

Then Rose appeared, in heels, a black miniskirt, and a sheer black blouse that revealed the silhouette of a bustier beneath. In unison, everyone offered Rose his chair.

"Such gentlemen," she said. "Done good, Gerry."

Rose was classy and sexy, like women of the silver screen in the '50s. She had a presence that demanded attention, laced with a cool, hypnotizing confidence. Rose was fully aware and completely in control of her effect, but she didn't abuse it. She was who she was and didn't pretend otherwise.

Everyone enjoyed a few more cocktails and small talk while stealing furtive glances at Rose's see-through blouse. The sexual tension had reached palpable proportions, almost to the point of discomfort, when Rose kissed Gerard and announced, "See you boys shortly." All eyes (ours as well as every other pair in the place) watched Rose take her leave.

Gerard gave us a few moments to gather our senses and pay our tabs before spelling out the rules: condoms, respectful behavior, no means no, the usual.

We crammed into the tiny elevator and rose to the eighth floor, where we spilled out and spaced ourselves to a more comfortable distance. Gerard opened the door to the suite to reveal Rose waiting on the edge of the bed in a black lace teddy and matching heels, casually smoking a Marlboro 100, which filled the room with a light, minty haze.

"We ready?" she asked Gerard.

"Only if you are."

Rose inhaled the last of her smoke and stubbed out the butt on the bedside ashtray. "Who's first?"

Rose's question was all the permission Jeff needed to push his way to the front. Tall, muscular, and more than adequately sized, Jeff had a limitless reservoir of energy. He wasn't selfish; just, like the model infantryman, perpetually ready. Jeff was the first to play as well as the first to climax. Slumped in the corner with a drunkish grin oozing down his face, he asked Gerard, "May we have seconds?"

Before Gerard could answer, Rose removed the cock in her mouth and replied, "I can take whatever you got, soldier."

"The lady hath spoken," replied Gerard.

And so went the night.

At one point, while I rehydrated and Jeff helped himself to fourths or fifths (I couldn't keep track), a tall, lanky guest with a shaved head appeared. He chatted with Gerard, and his voice had the affected tone of one who is hearing impaired, though he didn't wear any visible hearing aids.

My attention was drawn to Rose, whose vocal intensity indicated she was ramping up for yet another orgasm. Everyone watched as Jeff pushed her over the edge; seconds later, the only sound was that of Jeff and Rose panting. The deaf guest turned to Gerard and said loud enough for all to hear, "Even I heard that," which sent everyone into hysterics.

That night I wasn't the most endowed, talented, or experienced. At best, I fell into the middle of the pack. But I was patient and polite, and I performed. If awards had been handed out, I'd have received the sixth-man trophy. Even without a standout showing, Gerard asked that I stay behind afterward. Evidently he had asked Jeff to do the same, as we were the last remaining. While Rose cleaned up in the bathroom, Gerard requested our personal emails and cell numbers, as Rose had taken a particular shine to us. We obliged and Gerard promised to be in touch.

The next day I signed on to my profile to find my first certification:

What a great guy! He came to our GB last night and was just fantastic! He was a pleasure to be around, has a great personality, and really rocked me in bed! We are already making plans to spend time with this GENTLEMAN again. Ladies, you really don't want to miss out on this one! R (and G)

That night with Rose taught me that I didn't need porn star prowess. I could be myself as long as I complemented the overall experience. I didn't have to be something I wasn't. Nor did I want to. Not anymore.

Did I want to post this cert to my profile? the site asked unnecessarily.

Lesson 4:

Gearing Up

All hail the digital age! The technological revolution has made the Lifestyle more accessible than ever. Seedy personals at the back of adult periodicals have been replaced by an ever-growing list of websites. Online communities have made requisite in-person socials a thing of the past. And search queries have distilled compatibility to quasi-science.

But perhaps the greatest digital benefit is anonymity. Fear of exposure is arguably the main reason why those curious about the Lifestyle refrain from exploring it. But now, with identities shrouded behind email addresses, pictures easily blurred, and privacy settings allowing for the controlled dissemination of personal information with the click of a mouse, risking the loss of privacy is no longer an obstacle.

To take advantage of this iRevolution, you'll need some tools:

Email Address

Unless you link up with a well-connected swinger willing to usher you into the Lifestyle, you haven't a chance without email. I recommend a new address dedicated to your swing efforts. That way you can separate your two worlds. Want to risk family discovering your sexual exploration? What about colleagues? A dedicated email also affords a painless severing of ties. If you decide to quit the Lifestyle, you won't have to weed it out of your Vanilla life. Just cut bait.

Chat

Greater detail will come in "Courting," but for now, just know that chat is more conversational than email, which helps you better assess chemistry.

Phone

A Lifestyle cell phone may be excessive, but consider this: You're in a conference and you set your phone on the table. Halfway into the meeting, you get a text: *"I wanna suck ur cock!"* Did your colleague next to you see it? Even more awkward, did he ask to join? A dedicated cell is an added expense, but with the number of carriers and plans out there, you can find something in your price range. And, really, can you put a price on privacy?

If you refuse a dedicated cell, use your phone's security features. Create a passcode. Make sure texts don't display upon receipt. And hide caller ID for incoming and outgoing calls.

Pseudonym

A leaked email or compromising picture is all it takes for your private life to become very public. A pseudonym is an added layer of protection. Anything catchy, cheesy, pornish, or destined for a marquee is overkill. Everyone in the Lifestyle has a first name, never a last.

Websites

What is popular in Los Angeles is not in Dallas is sort-of used in New York and has never been heard of in Des Moines. Additionally, what works for Brad was a bust for Samantha but had lukewarm results for Steve and Evie and was hit-or-miss for Quentin. What I'm trying to say is, I can't recommend a site. But that's what free memberships are for. Create a free profile. Peruse the members. Rattle off a few emails, if the site allows. If the site doesn't pass muster, try another. You'll never be in want of a site to join.

When I started, I joined four sites. I found success with one, so I dumped the others. Find what works for you.

Profile Pictures

Before I talk optimal use of profile pics, let's prepare you to be photographed.

First, physical appearance: dentists, dermatologists, physical trainers, dieticians, laser hair removal specialists . . . Scores of medical professionals are ready to help you look your best. I'm not advocating *Extreme Makeover: Lifestyle Edition*, but you're seeking acceptance from a group who deem physical appearance an important (if not *the* most important) aspect of your person. Smoothing out the rough edges will make a difference to others and boost your confidence.

Second, wardrobe: Don't gut your closet and replace it with today's trendiest fashion. But don't expect to score playtime with your laundry-day outfit. Have a few decent outfits. That's all I'm saying.

Now, on to the pics.

Fair or not, the first impression others will have of you is your profile pictures. Thus, it is primarily the profile pic that determines your success, often within seconds. But now that you've become the best you, you're primed to take a few photographs. And once you have, here's how to unleash their full power:

1. Post at least one picture. I can't stress this enough. Many online members won't even view picless profiles, as they raise scores of red flags. "Is this couple fake?" "Could this guy be married but posing as single?" "What's she hiding?" If your privacy is so precious that you refuse to post a pic, blur your face. They say we eat first with our eyes. What do you think they say about sex?

2. Post recent pictures. You don't have to spotlight your less-than-ideal traits; just don't get crafty and hide them. The truth will come out at playtime, so you're better off getting rejected at the outset rather than after months of effort.

3. Post clear pictures. Don't appear like you have something to hide. Your pic must represent who you are and be easy to view.

4. Don't use professional pictures. Not only is the expense unnecessary, but the pictures can come off as compensating. In the end, if a pic is good enough for Facebook, it's good enough for your profile.

5. Express your personality. If you're introverted, don't post a pic of you cheering a *lucha libre* match. If you're gregar-

ious, don't share a shot of you engrossed in a paperback. Post the real you.

6. Don't include others in your pictures. Not everyone is comfortable with their image gracing a sex site, especially without their permission. If you want your friends to remain your friends, blur before posting.

7. Utilize private galleries. If you don't want your face broadcast to the membership at large, upload it to your private gallery, where you control access. Also, some swingers request candids (read: naked pics). If you're comfortable doing so, upload here.

Profile Self-Description

Self-Description #1:

I'm 25, 6' 3", 190 lbs. Daily workouts maintain my six-pack. I eat healthy, don't smoke or drink, and expect the same from you. Most important, I have an eleven-inch cock. Want proof? Ask to see my private pics. Don't waste my time if you're not ready to play.

Self-Description #2:

Just checking out the site to see if this thing is for me. I haven't posted any pictures, but I'm average height, average build, and average looks. Can't wait to hear from you!

Self-Description #3:

Looking for sex. Email me.

Which one of the above will garner the most interest? To no one's surprise, none are ideal. However, none is a total loss. Let's dissect.

Self-Description #1: Cockiness isn't attractive, but confidence is. Toned down, the profile has promise. Also, although your profile will most likely have areas dedicated to personal stats such as height, weight, and sexual orientation, reiterating them never hurts. Some women want specific cock sizes, so specifying that helps guide you to compatible playmates. Just don't gloat about your John Holmes status. Let it speak for itself.[1]

Self-Description #2: Be honest, not timid. No one wants to coddle a newbie. Exclude traits about which you aren't confident and focus instead on those about which you are. Are you humorous? Intelligent? Reliable? Put it in there. Easygoing and laid-back? Let it shine! With regard to the Lifestyle, have you always been curious about a threesome? Is there a sexual experience you wish to repeat? People want to know your desires and curiosities to see if they align with theirs.

Self-Description #3: Brevity is good as no one wants to read a biography. But if your profile can be tweeted, you lack detail. If you shirk on substance, members may question your sincerity and might even flag you as a fake or spammer.

Think of your profile as a movie trailer. Engaging, entertaining, informative, but not overly detailed. Spark members' interest and entice them to want to know more.

It's important to update your profile from time to time. We lose hair. We gain and lose weight. We age. Such is life. Just make sure big changes are captured on your profile. There's nothing more annoying than discovering the person with whom you've been emailing is ten

---

1   Point of clarity: I'm not saying your penis should possess vocal abilities. You get what I'm saying.

years older, fifty pounds heavier, and a full head of hair balder than his profile pics.

It's equally important to update your self-description. Don't cause frustration in others by discovering a penchant for dominance in the bedroom without listing such on your profile. If you do, then should someone claim they weren't aware of your dominant side, you aren't to blame.

Your profile will never be perfect, but it needs to represent the current you.

One last topic:

Your Home

One of the top reasons, if not *the* top reason playtime doesn't come to fruition, is location. Do you play at a hotel? Motel? If so, where? Who pays? It's complicated. But it doesn't have to be if you offer to host. It's private, cost-effective, and eliminates the number one obstacle to playtime: location.

Some swingers aren't comfortable playing at another's home because it feels like too much of a home-field advantage. There are safety concerns, the alien feel of a stranger's personal space, and other considerations. But for those who are fine getting down on a stranger's home turf, be prepared.

Repair, clean, and launder. Lay out clean towels, an extra roll of toilet paper, and a fresh bar of hand soap. Want to really impress? Have some nonalcoholic beverages, a music source, and a couch or love seat within view of the bed.[2]

---

2   Men, take heed. Voyeuristic hubbies greatly appreciate comfortable seating. Forcing a man to stand against the wall or sit on the floor while you enjoy his wife isn't the most gracious. Additionally, couches offer positions a bed doesn't. I speak from experience.

My last word on home prep is directed at the single men. Some of you find anything more than a mattress superfluous. Women and couples, however, view such "minimalist" design as you not giving a fuck. Doilies, duvets, and art collections are excessive, but basic home decor is not. If your home makeover skills leave something to be desired, enlist the help of a female friend. If your design touches earn her approval, they'll suffice for purposes of swinging.

Now that you've prepared yourself, your home, and your eTools, it's time to hunt!

Lesson 5:

The Hunt

Read profiles, view pictures, contact those who pique your interest. Simple as that. I recommend pacing with shorter daily searches as opposed to mega-sessions that will quickly burn you out. But even at a slow and steady clip, the hunt for playmates can overwhelm. To funnel your efforts as efficiently as possible, here are some tips.

Try Out Rejection

If a tsunami of rejection gives you pause, try this out: Email a dozen CL posts. This is just an exercise, so don't worry about ideal compatibility. Just stay within the realm of possibility.

How many responses did you get? The majority, if any, will be fakes or spam. More important, how do you feel? Did rejection emotionally destroy you? If not, it would appear you have a necessary component of the Lifestyle disposition. If you were affected more than makes you comfortable, reconsider your interest in swinging. I've said it before: The Lifestyle isn't for everyone.

Be Patient

Eagerness is natural, but take your time. Impulsive decisions can result in later regret. Don't make swinging one of those regrets. Survey the landscape. Read profiles without responding. You may be surprised to discover what interests you. Also, reading profiles may convince you to revise your own. Great! Revise away!

Use your first days on a site to window-shop. Perusing can settle nerves and help you acclimate. And who knows, maybe someone will contact you!

Read Certs

Profiles without certs don't necessarily denote members who haven't played or aren't sexually praiseworthy. Certless members may just deem certs too personal to share with the membership. On the flip side, profiles with multiple certs have evidence of playtime, but they aren't a guaranteed good time. This is because most sites bestow the power to post a cert to the profile owner. A member could have received a scathing review and declined to post it. So, while certs paint a more dynamic picture of a member, they aren't gospel. In the end, though, they are the primary barometer by which members are judged.

Email

Before I discuss successful email technique, I'm going to address:

METHODS THAT *DON'T* WORK

Mass Emailing

It's impersonal, shows a lack of effort, and is reminiscent of another form of despised electronic communication: SPAM. No matter the content, how friendly the tone, or articulate the language, the underlying message of every Lifestyle email is, "Wanna fuck?" How successful do you suppose a spammer is with that request?

One-Liners

I advise casting the widest net possible (within reason), but one-liners get deleted faster than spam. "How ya doing?," "What up?," and, worst of all, "Wanna fuck?" waste everyone's time and don't deserve the energy it takes to block your profile.

Winks/Flirts

While not email, per se, some sites offer "wink" or "flirt" functions. Though not as irritating as mass emails or one-liners, e-flirtations are generally perceived as lazy. If you want to be deemed playworthy, exert some effort.

Now that we're clear on the don'ts, let's focus on the dos.

METHODS THAT *DO* WORK

Before typing your email, be sure to . . .

Read the Entire Profile

Don't memorize or analyze for deeper meaning. Just read it. In its entirety. First off, doing so will ensure compatibility. How would you react to making it all the way to playtime with a couple only to discover the husband flirting with you? If you'd read the couple's *entire* profile, you would have caught the fleeting mention of hubby's bi-curiosity. What if you prefer control, but mid-play your playmate begins dominating? A few minutes of reading before initial contact will save future awkwardness as well as everyone's time.

More important, reading a person's profile will help you write your . . .

Initial Email

The first hurdle most wannabe swingers (as well as many experienced swingers) fail to clear—and because of this, foil any chance of success—is the initial email. Let's start by defining what the initial email is *not*:

1. The initial email is *not* an opportunity to impress.

2. The initial email is *not* your chance to brag about your sexual prowess, and,

3. The initial email is *not ever*, under any circumstances, an attempt to convince someone to commit to play.

What, then, is the initial email?

1. Your chance to make your presence known.

That's it. Nothing more.

What do you think would happen if you approached a woman at a bar and the first words out of your mouth were "Will you marry me?" Swingers fail to get past the initial email because they rush to the finish line before the starting pistol has been fired. Just because swingers have liberal views on sex doesn't mean they aren't human. And humans need time to get comfortable. Especially women.

Your initial email should be:

1. **Non-threatening.** No one likes a stalker. 'Nuff said.

2. **Non-pushy.** Interest is good; it makes one feel desired. However, forcing another to decide prematurely will, more times than not, end in rejection or a bad play experience.

3. **Proof you read their profile.** Include at least one reference to the profile in the initial email to show you've made an effort to understand what they want and that you're reasonably confident about compatibility. Also, referencing the profile potentially sparks conversation.

4. **Indicative of your personality.** Show, don't tell. If you're funny, be funny. If you're intellectual, be so. Stating qualities is boring, inactive, and potentially wrong in someone else's eyes. Engaging others to discover your character rather than filling in the blanks for them is what you want.

5. **Of requisite length.** Fortune cookies can be just as poignant as Dostoyevsky. Remember, the initial email is to make your presence known. Don't detail every bit of personal minutiae. No one wants an autobiography.

6. **Addressed to the proper recipient.** If you're contacting a single female or male, do so appropriately. If you're contacting a couple, *address the couple*. Swingers lose play opportunities because they don't acknowledge everyone involved. Ignoring hubby disrespects his marriage.

Disregarding the wife, ladies, makes the Mrs. suspicious of your motives. Also, men, acknowledging hubby is the first step to convincing him you are a respectful, non-threatening, and nice guy—single male stereotype be damned!

Here's a basic, winning email:

Hi there. I hope you both are doing well and enjoying the site! I truly enjoyed reading your profile. Thanks for taking the time to detail what you're looking for. I especially liked that you take the time to find compatible people. No need to rush into anything, right? Anyway, I'm sure you're drowning in emails, so let me know if my profile interests you.

A final piece of advice about the initial email: Leave the ball in the recipient's court. They should *want* to respond, not feel obligated. This will make them feel comfortable and ideally spark them to want to know more about you.

Before I end this chapter, here are a few hunting tricks I have developed:

The Passive Sign-On

Sites can search members by criteria, but they can't filter out inactive members, fakes, and spammers, all of whom exist (sometimes in bulk) on every site. So, while search has its benefits, many swingers favor online members over search results because online members prove their active nature. Essentially, by perusing online members you've filtered out the inactive, something search can't do.

Now, when I get burnt out with my proactive search, I'll sign on, then go about my life. Logging in casts my profile into the swinging pool and exposes it for all to see. I've had TV programs interrupted by Instant Message requests and also returned later to find emails waiting for me. Of course, there are times no one bites. But in those instants, I check my profile view tally and get a tiny boost of encouragement.

Theoretically you could remain online indefinitely, but I don't recommend it. Omnipresence makes you appear desperate or like a Lifestyle slut. Just use the passive sign-on to remind others you're active.

For hardcore searchers, there's—

The Night Owl

Night Owls are swingers who search late night to early morning. They tend to be very serious about playing, often looking for right then, right now. Most of the times I signed on during Night Owl hours, nothing resulted. But the times when I was contacted, it was for immediate play.

Now that you can effectively locate potentially compatible playmates, it's time to woo.

Lesson 6:

Courting

Generally speaking, playdates don't happen instantly, but rather after all parties involved decide that personalities click, sexual compatibility exists, and everyone is who they claim to be. The standard courting process unfolds as follows:

1. Email

2. Online chat

3. Phone call

4. Meet 'n' greet

5. Playtime

I've courted from a few weeks to a few months. One couple took over a year to meet. Personal and business schedules, family commitments, and life in general prohibit any reliable timeframe. All you can do is be patient and endure the process, which begins with . . .

Reconnaissance

You've read their profile, but not every single thing is in there. Start gathering intel. There are countless topics to discuss, and you won't be able to tackle them all, but here are some common ones to get the conversational ball rolling:

1. Dos and don'ts

2. Turn-ons and turn-offs

3. Specific areas of curiosity

4. Hard limits

5. Reasons for swinging

Additionally, the process of gathering information affords you the chance to double-check one's profile. Who knows when the content was last updated? The couple wrote they'd like an LTR with another couple. Is that still accurate, or are they now only open to a short-term arrangement? The female who contacted you specifically stated in her profile that she only plays with couples in which the husband is larger than nine inches and your profile admits to average size. Has she changed her preference or did she not read your self-description? Besides, asking about one's profile shows you're considerate, as you took the time to read it and get to know them.

Whether over email, chat, phone, or in person, casually pepper these inquiries into the natural course of conversation. Submitting a form email with a list of questions isn't the most seductive way to persuade another to play.

TABOO TOPICS

Revealing one's sexual fantasies is personal, but it's not the most intimate one can be. Feel free to discuss any aspect of sex—that's why you joined the site—but avoid personal subjects such as family, career, and children. They will ice conversation and jeopardize play chances. Your instinct is to get to know someone before sex, which is good, but anything that threatens one's privacy or anonymity is not appropriate.

EMAIL

There's no requisite number of emails in the courting process. Swingers have Vanilla lives, too, so instant responses aren't always possible. Patience is key.

Should significant time pass between emails, feel free to drop a friendly email like "Hope all is well" or "How's life?" Doing so keeps your presence alive in your potential playmate's mind without being annoying. And be sure to refrain from ultimatums such as, "So, do you want to fuck or not?" They are crass and a turn-off. And if you're a single male, in one email you've proven you're the pushy, selfish, rude, and insensitive stereotype.

CHAT

After you've developed email rapport, suggest an online chat. Chatting is more like a conversation than is email, so there's a sense of advancement to the courting process. But each side retains its anonymity and, more important, the power to cut ties should things not develop as desired. Chat can include conversing, trading pics, even webcam sessions. Just remember, don't do anything that makes you uncomfortable.

PHONE CALL

From chat to phone is a galactically larger step than that from email to chat, for a few reasons. First, a phone call is the first exchange of personal information: phone numbers. Some are fine swapping numbers, others not so much. Those in the latter group may ask for your number so they can call from a private number. If that works for you, go for it.

The second reason the phone call is a bigger step is there's more at stake. It tends to be considered the last stage before an in-person meet, so everyone wants to be sure all signs are go. Also, this is everyone's last chance to spot red flags before an in-person meet.

With phone calls, I try to ask questions rather than talk about myself. It shows my interest and sensitivity and, hopefully, puts them at ease. I also like to end a call before conversation gets boring. As with the initial email, a phone call is more successful when it ends with both parties wanting more.

Many calls end with a scheduled meet 'n' greet. But if yours doesn't, it doesn't mean you were rejected. Sometimes people need to collect their thoughts and assess their feelings. This is especially true with a couple, as they'll want to compare notes and reactions. More times than not, if you've made it to the phone call, a meet 'n' greet is around the corner. Just hold tight.

MINIMIZE COUPLES DRAMA

Once I sense courting is progressing at a nice clip, I make sure to connect with both husband *and* wife or boyfriend *and* girlfriend. My reason is that I want to make sure I'm not walking into a relationship war zone. I try to do this on the phone, rather than via email or chat, as it's more difficult to fake vocal communication. If I've only had contact with the wife, I'll say something to the effect of, "I've been so rude.

I haven't introduced myself to your husband. Is he around?" Usually she'll put him on and we'll chat. If she hesitates or has an excuse for why he can't talk, I'll say, "That's okay. Please give him my number so he can call whenever is convenient. Things are just going so well between us, I don't want him to think I'm disrespectful of your marriage." If I've only conversed with the husband, I'll ask to say hi to his wife. My request isn't unusual, as Lifestyle husbands want their wives desired. If hubby refuses to let me talk with his wife, I'll know something is amiss. If things progress to meet 'n' greet, we'll meet in person anyway, so asking to speak to everyone now isn't abnormal.

I like sex, but not at the expense of my safety. As such, I do my best to steer clear of troubled relationships. I'd rather not be woken up at four in the morning by an enraged husband who found my suggestive text on his wife's cell. Life's complicated enough.

By the end of the courting process, you should be 98 percent convinced you want to play with your potential playmate(s). Unfortunately, the last 2 percent can't be determined until you meet in person. And although 2 percent may seem negligible, it has the power to undo everything.

Intercourse

Synthesis

Certs opened doors, which opened even more.

There were Lawrence and Emily, a middle-aged couple madly in love, looking to spice things up. A GB group who invited me to a gathering for a petite, deaf Asian whose noises confused and alarmed me greatly. After the festivities, she spent ten minutes dissecting my diet to determine that it was the artificial sweetener I was using that made my cum taste smoky. I took her advice and changed my sweetener of choice.

Gary and Winona were a late-fifties couple, both on their second marriage, who invited me to their self-designed sex room that offered a selection of geometrically shaped pillows designed to optimize positions and a sex swing that hung from a makeshift scaffold operated by an electric winch.

There was Lila, a buxom brunette with a painful penchant for lip biting; Tanya, a twenty-something African American who brought with her a petite pink bag of "surprises"; and Cora, a twenty-one-year-old Latina pixie and self-professed old soul who liked sex very slow.

Miranda was a stout Cubana in her thirties who just liked to make out, and of course there were Ed and Savannah, who wanted to play until the sun came up.

Jezebel was adventurous with role-play, which came in handy when her five-year-old emerged from his room needing to take a midnight pee and she snapped from bad cop (with me) to compassionate mother (with him). Frankly, I would have preferred she began the night in the role of defendant under oath so I would've been aware of her kid.

Carrie's hubby was content curling up on the couch beside my bed to watch and then nap. If I'd known Carrie was a squirter, I would've taken some waterproofing precautions. Instead I had to do some subsequent mattress shopping.

Those hopelessly barren months treading water in the shallow end of the Lifestyle were no more. Some weeks I had two, even three play-dates on the books. I wasn't the Marquis de Sade, but I was a long way from where I'd started, which boded heavily in my favor when I received an email from D that his girlfriend, K, had agreed to be his sex slave the following week.

Online, D and K went by DsCpl. They had only one cert and a sparse profile that praised K, who had quite the toned body.

D told me that he and K were going through a phase of sexual exploration during which K expressed an interest in trying out subbing. D was more than happy to oblige. After a few emails, D stressed to me that safe sex would be mandatory and that K would like to see a recent STI test. As kismet would have it, I'd had a physical two weeks prior where I had one done and I had been cleared. Not that he didn't trust me, D said, but could I send him my results? I had my doctor fax them over. I blacked out my address and forwarded them to D. That night, D called and asked why some minor STIs weren't checked. I told him I instructed my doctor to run the gamut and that was the report she gave me. If something wasn't tested, I assured D, it wasn't me trying to hide anything. D said he believed me, but just wanted to make sure. Though new to the Lifestyle, D and K had had an MFM, which they thoroughly enjoyed and was why they wanted another. D wanted to meet up the next night, which was fine with me. He said to text him in the afternoon to confirm, which I did.

I left the office late, so I had to race home, shower, and dash over to D and K's. D answered the door. He was tall. Very tall. NBA tall. Sturdy and thick. He also had a bookish quality, with wire-rim glasses, a pasty complexion, and a deeply receding hairline.

"Welcome," he said in a hushed voice as he stepped aside for me to enter.

Jazz murmured from a stereo and candles lit the room. I'd made it to the couch when I realized no one else was there.

"K here?" I asked.

"I ordered her to the bedroom until summoned," D said, obviously taking the Dom/sub thing seriously. "Wine?" Before I answered, D was pouring.

I tried to make sure I hadn't missed anything about D's sexual orientation on their profile. I was pretty sure I hadn't, but I decided to drop a few reminders about my hetero status, just in case.

"K's pics were amazing," I said. "She work out?"

"Religiously."

"You can tell. Some of the sexiest pics I've seen on the site."

"Be sure to let her know. She loves compliments about her body."

D handed me a glass of wine and sat in the chair beside the couch.

Wine. Candles. Jazz. Less experienced guys would think D was seducing them. But I knew he was just screening me.

"So," D began. "How long you been doing this?"

"Almost a year."

"What's your experience?"

"Threesomes mostly. A couple orgies and gang bangs."

"And you're single?"

"I am."

"All that for a single guy?"

"I've been really lucky."

"Any one-on-ones?"

"A few. I'm not against them. Just impossible to arrange."

"Well, if you find a single female interested in a swap, K and I have been batting around that scenario."

"Will do. What about your experience?"

"So far only the one threesome."

"What made you want to try it out?"

"K suggested we try role-playing. Then we started talking other things."

"If you don't mind me asking, why me?"

"Your profile said you had experience. Like I said, we're somewhat new. We're more comfortable with someone who can guide us. Are you cool with that?"

"I'll do my best."

"Great. What are your thoughts on documenting tonight?" D picked up a camera from the floor beside his chair.

"So long as no faces."

"Discretion. Absolutely. Well, any questions for me?"

"Nothing comes to mind."

"Shall I summon K, then?"

"Ready if you are."

D entered the bedroom and shut the door behind him.

Then something occurred to me. What if D *was* K? What if he was in the bedroom right now transforming into K? I'd seen *The Silence of the Lambs*. I mentally compared D's physique to K's pics and though their bodies were nothing alike, it wasn't beyond the realm of possibility that D could have posted someone else's pics and fabricated the entire idea of K. After all, K's face was blurred in every pic, and I'd never spoken with her on the phone.

Just as I'd convinced myself that I'd unknowingly cast myself in E!'s *10 Most Shocking Sex Crimes*, the bedroom door opened and D led out K on a leash. She was Asian, wearing a pink silk half robe and a nervous smile. As they approached, I noticed the profile pics were genuine. K had an amazingly well-exercised body.

Without a word, D handed me the leash and sat back in his chair. I lowered K onto the couch next to me and opened her robe to reveal a pink bra with black lace trim and matching panties, both hugging her figure nicely. I released a breast and sucked on its nipple.

"Mmmmmm . . ." she moaned.

"Stand and lose the robe."

She did.

"Shift your panties so I can see your pussy."

Freshly trimmed with a landing strip.

"Come closer."

She did and I felt her.

"Very wet."

She giggled as I slid a finger inside, which triggered a long exhale from her.

"Lie down and masturbate."

K complied.

"Look at me."

K did as she continued. Out of the corner of my eye, I saw D had taken out his cock. And it was massive.

"Suck your master's cock."

K crawled to D and I handed him the leash. While K complied with my order, I knelt behind her and played with her. Then I laid on my back with my head between her legs. I pinched her nipples as I

licked her. She moaned. D then told K to be a good hostess and reciprocate my efforts. She obeyed and got me hard fast.

"Shall we go to the bedroom?" I suggested.

We did, and I insisted D and K begin. D asked me to photograph.
I grabbed the camera from the living room and returned to find them
going at it. K's legs were on the edge of the bed with her hands on the
floor. I snapped pics as they slid completely onto the carpet and continued doggy-style. I slipped my hips under K's face and she took me back
into her mouth.

K was a loud screamer. And I mean LOUD. D had warned me,
but I wondered if the neighbors were going to call the cops. It was that
intense. But I figured D and K knew if we were in danger of being cited
for noise nuisance, so I didn't interrupt the action.

D finished and K requested a quick break to catch her breath,
which we granted.

We returned to the den for a few drinks and chatted. Once K had
regained her composure, I told her to get me hard again, after which she
rode me. I led K back into the bedroom, bent her over the edge of the bed,
and had her spread her legs so I could take her from behind. She began
screaming again. I flipped her on her back and threw her ankles over her
head, which made her even louder, because the mattress wasn't muffling
her. I engaged her in conversation in an effort to quiet her.

"Do you like being a slut?"

"I LOVE BEING YOUR COCK SLUT! I LOVE BEING YOUR
COCK SLUT!"

I gave up trying to quiet her.

We doggied and I finished. K showered while D and I relaxed in
the living room. K came out wrapped in a towel, drying her hair, and
asked if I'd care for a shower before I left. I took a quick one, dressed,
and said goodbye.

My ears rang all the way home.

Vanilla Reprieve

I met Dee and Rick for lunch at a Mexican restaurant in Thousand Oaks. Dee was forties, petite, white, blond, buxom. Rick, a guy's guy, thick with muscle more for utility than aesthetics, close-cropped hair, trimmed mustache. They were play buddies and, judging by the thin swath of untanned skin circling Rick's ring finger, I surmised their spouses were none too accommodating of their atypical sexual appetites.

We swapped stories. They told me about rude males and incompatible couples and their constant struggle to find playmates. However, their search was harder than most because they could only play during the weekday, possible further evidence to my "married to others" hypothesis.

Dee recounted their first play experience. They were in Vegas when, after a few drinks, Dee admitted she'd always been curious about MFM. Without hesitation, Rick dared her to pick up a guy in the casino to help her realize this longtime fantasy. Dee called Rick's bluff and fifteen minutes later returned to the room with a BBC.

"I haven't had a cock that size since," Dee confessed.

Dee's story reminded me of Green Mile, which I shared. Rick suggested I arrange a GB for Dee and invite Green Mile. Dee responded ecstatically at the prospect and, most likely as a way to sweeten the offer, told me about their friend Joanna, whom they'd bring. I pretended to be tempted, but I'd grown my Rolodex beyond what I could ever have imagined, so I wasn't hard up.

All this BBC talk had Dee horned up, so we settled the tab and proceeded to the motel, where Dee and Rick already had a room. As Dee changed in the bathroom, I asked Rick for her dos and don'ts.

"Condoms."

"What about spanking? Hair pulling? Oral?"

As if my inquiry was as personal as asking what toppings he liked on his pizza, Rick responded, "Sure, why not?"

Dee returned in a pair of leather knee-high fuck-me boots with a black thong and matching nightie. She approached me, pulled out my cock, and started sucking. Slow. Very slow. She held it in her mouth and rolled her tongue over it while locking onto my eyes. Dee had the horniest fuck-me eyes I'd ever seen. So as not to cum, I laid Dee on the bed and reciprocated.

"I like him," she told Rick, who'd been observing from a reclined position on the other half of the bed. "He's fun."

I asked Rick if he'd like to take the reins. He accepted with a gentlemanly nod and didn't waste any time. He fucked Dee while I resumed occupying her mouth. Dee moaned, enjoying herself tremendously. Rick flipped her on her stomach and continued to have his way with her while I stood at the foot of the bed to continue with her mouth. Rick instructed me to pull her hair while I did so. I obliged. After Dee came a few times, she requested a break, which we granted. But Rick only gave her a few minutes to catch her breath before he grabbed her by the hair and pulled her mouth to his cock. I grabbed a condom and lifted her hips to doggy. Rick told me to do so harder and harder. I heard and felt Dee loving it, so I sped up and pounded harder. Dee responded equally and, with one exceptionally timed and incredibly vicious buck, launched me off the bed. I landed on the floor, hard. But with adrenaline still pumping, I leapt back to my feet and finished the job.

Based on the shock waves of pure, raw agony that tidal-waved through my body the following morning, "finishing the job" had been a mistake. My nervous system had crossed into the danger zone and was on the precipice of collapse. Convinced the skeleton hand of death had reached inside my pelvis and was shredding my nerves like Jimi Hendrix on a full-blown acid trip, I was forced to have my general practitioner's answering service page her.

"How'd you do this?" my GP inquired when she returned my call what felt like hours later, but was really only minutes.

Even in my pain-addled state, I knew anything I said was protected by doctor-patient confidentiality. However, I was a little more than slightly embarrassed that I'd injured myself—seemingly quite seriously—whilst having sex. Not to mention, I hadn't yet shared this extracurricular part of my life with anyone and didn't particularly wish to start with my internist. "Not a clue," I told her.

In that case, she told me, I needed to see an orthopedist. But her referral wouldn't be in the office until Monday, so, in the interim, she could call in some morphine to nearby urgent care. I declined and said I'd just call the orthopedist Monday, which I did, but he didn't have an opening until the following Monday, so I endured a week of Quasimodo posture and repeated failings to position pillows to alleviate the intensifying and unceasing pain.

"Any idea how you did this?" the orthopedist asked when I finally got in to see him.

If I wasn't comfortable telling my GP, I certainly wasn't going to confide in a referral I'd known only minutes. He commenced a battery of stretches on my leg and concluded that I was the unlucky genetic recipient of a malformed ball-and-socket joint.

"Medical advances have radically improved," he explained in an effort to soothe my nerves. "Rather than dislocating the hip joint to shave the bone, surgeons now use a minimally invasive procedure that keeps the joint intact and even allows the patient to remain conscious." His chipper tone was the same used in commercials by spokespeople touting products to the masses. And, as with the nonsense spouted by those spokespeople, I wasn't buying it. In fact, I felt light-headed at the prospect of bone shaving—minimally invasive or not—and considered coming clean. "Well, Doc," I could've admitted, "my injury may have been sustained during the fuck-slam I gave a woman I'd known for all of twenty minutes who bucked me off the bed and sent me careening to the floor. But you're the medical professional here, so I defer to your judgment." Of course, his only logical response would've been, "If you don't want to tell me, fine, but there's no need to get pornographic."

I opted to keep mum.

The doc took a few X-rays to confirm his diagnosis and, after an inconclusive set of images, instructed me to get an arthrogram before he prescribed corrective surgery. And based on his tone slipping from chipper to foreboding, I knew I shouldn't be optimistic about the forthcoming procedure.

For those unfamiliar with the oh-so-pleasant medical procedure known as the arthrogram, it's a variation on the MRI.[1] In fact, an arthrogram *is* an MRI, except that since the hip is a collapsed joint, the patient must first have his hip inflated with fluid so a useful image may be captured. It goes without saying that if you can avoid this procedure by, say, oh, I don't know, confessing the likely cause of injury to

---

1 *MRI (Medical Resonance Imagery)*—A medical imaging technique used in radiology to visualize internal structures of the body in detail. Though not a Lifestyle term, it conveniently fits in with BDSM play.

your medical professional, you'd be wise to do so. However, as you're no doubt well aware by now, I tend not to favor the wisest courses of action.

Doc told me I wouldn't be capable of driving after the procedure, so I should have someone take me. As I was quite certain asking a fellow Lifestyler to do me a solid and chauffeur me to and from the imaging center wasn't protocol, I was forced to ask my brother.

"What did you do to yourself?"

"Don't ask."

After consciously enduring a twelve-inch knitting needle navigated into the unseen recesses of my pelvis and almost passing out at the sensation of my hip inflating with fluid and somehow clinging to my sanity through the hour-long, migraine-inducing blare of the imaging contraption, which resembled a compact wind tunnel, possessed the amplification capability of a Marshall stack, and pushed my patience beyond the limits of superhuman endurance, I was informed by my orthopedist that the image of my still-smoldering hip had revealed, and I quote, "just a little inflammation." In the world of orthopedic medicine, "a little inflammation" apparently qualifies as sound diagnosis. Still, I had a few questions; in particular about treatment options.

"Maybe your internist has some ideas," was the evasive response the good doctor laid on me despite the calligraphied sheepskin hanging over his mahogany desk that was blanketed in an array of gold-plated objects, all of which served as further proof of his consummate medical expertise.

Having plummeted to a new low of desperation, I reconsulted my GP, who said in a tone that implied I was a moron for asking, "If I had any ideas, I wouldn't have referred you elsewhere."

So, after two-plus weeks of suffering what felt like a red-hot fire iron lodged in my hip, without a single night of decent sleep, and a checking account five hundred dollars poorer thanks to my health plan's

Daniel Stern

deductible, I was back where I started. I figured if a set of X-rays, an arthrogram, and the combined knowledge of two degreed and licensed medical professionals couldn't yield a prescribed fix for my injury, admitting my sexual tryst wouldn't shed any light on matters.

I had resigned myself to a life of pain, discomfort, and hunched-over posture when my brother suggested I visit his chiropractor. I had nothing to lose—unless the chiro knew of a procedure more torturous than the arthrogram, but I doubted it—so I did. Miraculously, after the first session of basic stretches, hot compresses, and electro muscle stimulation, I saw a glimmer of hope. Six weeks of therapy was what my new chiro and bestest friend in the whole wide world predicted would get me back to the old me.

Being out of commission those six weeks gave me time to reflect. Without any playdates due to my injury, and with a self-imposed moratorium on online activity, as sitting at my laptop aggravated my hip—I also wanted to steer clear of any temptation to get back into the game before I'd fully healed—I had a significant amount of free time on my hands. Not to mention twice weekly chiro sessions that involved lying in a dimly lit room atop a cushy examination table under multiple hot compresses with therapeutic currents of electricity pulsing through my slowly healing muscles, there wasn't much else to do but ruminate. To say my time in the Lifestyle had been quite the ride would have been the grandest of understatements. I'd secured a foothold in an extremely private, highly guarded community that not more than two years prior I was convinced was only a fantasy. My growing number of certs testified to the fact that not only had I gained admittance to this community, but I had thrived and been deemed worthy of membership. Those cringeworthy years of sexual avoidance, though long past, were still a vibrant memory, but when compared to how far I'd progressed, seemed someone else's past.

And I'd conquered my seemingly incurable knack for premature ejaculation. The panacea, it turned out, was not some magical, ingestible elixir or a piece of ancient wisdom inscribed onto a stone tablet. Rather it was the journey itself: a regimen of exposure therapy, so to say. By subjecting myself to sexual experience after sexual experience, I was demystifying the act of sex, desensitizing my reaction to it, and chipping away at the fear it held over me and beneath which I was pinned. Now, years later, I'd escaped that tonnage of performance-hindering anxiety and understood sex for what it was: fun.

Though laid up with an injury sustained during this "fun," I could confidently claim that I had far surpassed the level of sexual ability I had originally sought. I now had stamina, control, adaptability, and a sense of carnal confidence I never could have dreamed possible when I began my quest. So, yeah, I was satisfied with myself.

But while it had been a wildly adventurous and wholly satisfying adventure, it had also been, for the most part, temporary. I remained in contact with a handful of swingers, but the vast majority had been one-off encounters. This observation hadn't occurred to me before, or at least I hadn't acknowledged it had, which got me thinking. I had begun my quest to slay my personal dragon of subpar sexual performance so it would no longer inhibit me from fully engaging in a relationship. Well, I had slain my dragon, butchered its corpse, roasted it over a bonfire, and had been feasting off its flesh for some time. I felt the tug of the Vanilla world and decided it was time for a homecoming.

Utilizing the Internet prowess I'd developed from swinging, I perused the Women Seeking Men section on CL and found a post that challenged readers to name seven Oasis songs. Apart from my affinity for brainteasers and all things trivia, I was encouraged to have stumbled upon a woman (at least, I assumed she was a woman) who actually liked Oasis; not one of my exes had. I responded and received a surprisingly fast reply.

Cayley was an Irish transplant who came off smart and articulate over email. I kept things platonic the first few days, as I needed to recalibrate to Vanilla flirting. Once you've been conditioned to sex as a given on the first date, it's tough to shift your thinking. A week was enough for me to feel sufficiently re-rooted, and I asked her out. She accepted. Then it occurred to me that I had to plan this date. It had been some time since planning a date didn't mean any equidistant, public location a short drive from a moderately priced, reasonably clean hotel/motel.

I settled on a Japanese restaurant in Santa Monica, where we had dinner. Cayley told me about missing Ireland while feeling LA was her home. She had been working at a high-end soap store, but her real passion was designing greeting cards. She loved all manner of paper and pens, and we stumbled upon a stationery store after our meal, where she taught me the pros and cons of different products. I listened, asked questions, paid attention best I could, and tried like hell to be interested, but I just couldn't be. I felt like I'd been driving NASCAR all my life only to find myself pulling a rickshaw. I was bored. *Very* bored. Having been ensconced in the Lifestyle for so long, I found my threshold for stimulation had been raised, arguably too high.

That internal stirring returned. I hadn't felt it in so long, not since I'd sworn off relationships, that at first I didn't know what it was. But quickly my thoughts were thrown back to that night with Melissa when I first felt it and then after the breakup with Missy when I set out on my quest. Pretending to listen to Cayley debate ballpoint versus fountain versus pencil, I finally understood what that inner disturbance was trying to tell me, had been trying to tell me all these years: that I was not Vanilla.

Standing there with Cayley, I was betraying myself. I had dressed up in my old self, but it no longer fit. In fact, it was confining and suffocating. Making matters worse, a week after our date, I received a birthday gift from Cayley: a bar of soap carved into a golden retriever (the breed of one of my childhood dogs) and a handmade card. I thanked her via email for her thoughtful gift and complimented her on her card talents, then never contacted her again. Maybe she deserved an explanation, but I wasn't sure she'd understand. After all, I was still processing everything. My quest was supposed to be an exercise in sexual improvement, not a journey of self-realization. Plus, I didn't feel that telling Cayley that sometimes I just needed a little kinkiness was second-date subject matter. So I decided it was best left unsaid.

The night I returned home after my date with Cayley, I resumed the online hunt and within days received an invitation to a GB hubby was organizing for his wife. Heather's face was blurred in her profile pic, but her twenty-four-year-old body with twenty-four-year-old breasts crouched on an unmade bed and clothed in a plaid schoolgirl skirt and self-tailored white midriff tee was enough for me to request an invite. Heather's hubby asked everyone to meet at a strip club before heading to the hotel, which gave me pause. Not because the plan sounded fishy, though it most certainly did (what couple chooses to meet a group of already horned-up guys at a strip club?), but because I'd never been able to function at a strip club. Something about the mix of commerce and faux sex messes with my sense of reality. I know what you're thinking: this from a man with a penchant for the perverse? I get it, but the fact is, strip clubs freak me the fuck out. However, the Cayley date still had me mentally and emotionally lost, so I sacked up.

We were to meet at the club at nine, after which we'd caravan to the hotel. I arrived at nine-fifteen in order to minimize my time there. After the doorman frisked me and made me promise every which way but an official pinkie swear only to look, not touch, the performers, the hostess snatched my twenty-dollar cover, which entitled me to two drinks, and I entered the dimly lit room to see a long-legged stripper exhibiting her big top-worthy acrobatic skills on a pole so tarnished it looked to be decomposing in real time. A dozen or so patrons were enjoying the performance that was taking place on a stage the length and width of two pool tables. I proceeded cautiously in order to let my eyes adjust to the lack of light and, when they did, I spotted the only couple in attendance. They were at the foot of the stage and, even from behind, I recognized Heather's long brown hair. I got a few steps toward her when another hostess, a non-stripper visibly less than enthused about her job, blocked my path.

"Drink?" she grumbled over the thumping bass.

My nerves relaxed at the prospect of liquor. "I'd love a Bud Light."

"No" was all she said.

"Okay. How about Heineken?"

"No," she spat again at me. Just no. No explanation or elaboration. No drink menu. Nothing. Just, no. And a blank, vacant, disinterested gaze.

Before I could venture a third attempt to order, a stripper in a silver-sequined G-string and clear platform heels inserted herself between me and Ms. Congeniality, clamped my hand on her ass cheek, grabbed my cock with her other hand, and, two inches from my face, informed me through fumes of cinnamon breath that assaulted my olfactory senses, "I'm Roxy. You're hot. I like you."

Total laryngeal lockdown took effect and I stared in paralyzed bewilderment.

"Order your drink so we can talk," Roxy advised.

"I—I've been trying," I stuttered out.

"We're fully nude, sweetie. We can't serve alcohol."

"Oh." I sighed, relieved that I hadn't lost my grip on reality. I turned to the hostess. "Diet Sprite?"

Before the hostess could serve me a hat trick of denial, Roxy interjected. "He'll have regular Sprite."

"Change?" Ms. Friendly Hostess told me more than asked. My twenty-dollar cover included two drinks, so her question confused me and I didn't know how to respond. "Do you want change?" she drawled out patronizingly slow, like I was the weak link on the McJobs program.

Then it dawned on me. She wanted to know if I needed change to tip the performers. Perhaps my strip club IQ really was in the lowest percentile.

I opened my wallet to find I only had a hundred-dollar bill, the very one I'd received in the mail the day prior from my father for my birthday. As I was pretty sure strippers' G-strings weren't where my father envisioned his present going, I was about to ask if they had an ATM on premises when the hostess snatched the bill and dashed off. Roxy then yanked me by my still-ass-clamped hand to an unoccupied corner of the space, threw me on a couch upholstered in some pseudo-velour lacquered with what felt like weeks-old maple syrup, and cranked the stripper flirting to eleven.

"Do you want me to dance for you?" she asked, filling my nose with cinnamon fire. "I really want to dance for you. Can I? Please? Ooooo, I really need to."

Woozy from the onslaught to my senses, I politely responded, "That's very nice, but I just—"

"You just what?" she exclaimed in a faux-shocked, obviously rehearsed manner she must have employed whenever her mark put up the slightest protest. "You don't like my tits, do you?" Before I could defend myself, Roxy relocated my hand to one of her enhanced breasts.

"Wow. Okay. Um—"

"What? You don't like tits?"

"They're very nice. And very . . . lotioned."

"But you don't like them, do you?" she asked with a fake pout to elicit guilt, which kinda sorta worked.

"I do. I like them very much. It's just I'm here to meet some friends."

"Well, if you like my tits, then you must not like *me*," she squealed like a petulant child. "I like you, but you don't like *me*!"

"I didn't say that."

"You didn't have to. I know because you didn't ask to feel my ass. If you asked to feel my ass, I'd know you liked me."

"The doorman made me promise not to touch."

"I say who touches. Not Jesse."

"Well, Jesse didn't tell me that."

"Does that mean you want to feel my ass?"

Not wanting to make any more of a scene than we already were making, I bit. "Roxy, may I please feel your ass?"

She grabbed my hand not vised onto her breast, sat on it, and began grinding. "Will you let me dance for you now?"

Thankfully, Ms. Personality chose that moment to return with my mini Dixie cup of Sprite. However, since both my hands were occupied, I couldn't accept it.

"Roxy," I said as nicely as possible so as not to incite her to another practiced, bitter response, "I really like your ass, but I need my hands for a moment."

"Okay," she chirped.

I accepted my drink, after which the superbly mannered hostess thrust a three-inch thick brick of singles at me.

"You didn't have anything larger?" I asked, already knowing her response.

"No."

"Didn't think so."

I accepted the boulder of bills, peeled off two for Little Miss Sunshine, who snatched them and left, and crammed the rest of the cinder block into my jeans pocket.

"So, are you ready for me to dance for you?"

"After I meet my friends, okay?"

Roxy thrust out her bottom lip. "You're going to forget about me."

"I don't think that's possible."

Having wasted enough time on me, Roxy bounced off to find another victim. I took a moment to compose myself, downed my warm Sprite, and headed toward Heather. I stopped behind the unoccupied seat next to her and leaned into her field of vision. She was stunning. Light brown skin, angular features, model-grade looks. Luck was most definitely a lady tonight.

"HEATHER?" I shouted.

She leaned closer, cupping her ear. My introduction had been drowned out by the music and the DJ's announcement, "Please welcome Roxy to the stage," which was followed by Roxy bouncing onto the platform to the ominous musical lead-in to Phil Collins's "In the Air Tonight."

I accepted that the music's decibel level might render communication to nonverbal means, so I extended my hand to Heather, who accepted, then screamed, "NICE TO MEET YOU! THIS IS RICH!"

Rich's handsomeness was the male equivalent of Heather's beauty. He was late thirties, well-muscled, and toned. Together, they were a striking couple.

I waved hello to Rich, then pointed to the empty seat beside Heather, who motioned for me to sit. Not long after, she noted my pained state.

"You don't look so good," she screamed.

"Sorry. Strip clubs don't agree with me. But, don't worry; I'm totally cool at a gang bang or orgy."

Heather and Rich laughed. Even I had to, at my absurd strip club phobia.

Roxy crawled to the section of stage in front of me, slung her legs over my shoulders, and began grinding her now G-stringless crotch inches from my face. I endured best I could, as I didn't want to disturb her performance and risk a repeat of her wrath.

Heather must have seen my horror, as she yelled into my ear, "Tip her and she'll go away."

I yanked a fistful of singles from the meteor in my pocket and extended the money to Roxy, who instructed me, "Cascade them down my body."

"Come again?"

"Cascade them down my body, sweetie," she repeated, then mimed so I'd get it.

I dropped the money onto her abdomen like a lead brick. It couldn't have landed in a more perfect stack if I'd set it there and balanced it with a level. Roxy picked up the bills and proceeded to rub them over her skin like some magical, orgasmic lotion. I assumed the action had twofold purpose: to show her appreciation for my generosity while also enticing others to do the same in exchange for a similarly climactic response. Mercifully, she unhooked her legs from my shoulders and crawled to her next victim.

I regained some of my composure and looked to Heather and Rich, who were rolling with laughter.

"She likes you," Heather astutely observed.

"I kinda got that."

"Starting to calm down?"

"A little."

"See. Strip clubs can be fun."

"I'll take your word for it. Hey, where's everyone else?"

"It's still way early."

We watched Roxy do her thing and I actually started to calm down. True, I'd placed myself in an uncomfortable position, but even that couldn't trump the fact that I was back in the swing of things, and that had me feeling good. I mean, how could I not? Rich and Heather had planned a GB, but if no one else showed, there was a good chance it'd be MFM, which meant I'd only be sharing Heather with one other guy. And if Rich was more voyeur than participant . . . But I was getting too worked up and forced myself to relax.

High on my decision to return to the Lifestyle, I leaned over to Heather and admitted, "I have to say, I doubted whether you'd show."

"Huh?"

"Meeting a couple at a strip club. At first I thought I was being set up."

"Oh, you're here to meet a couple?"

I instantly knew the subtext of Heather's question, but my ego refused to accept it. All sound died away except for Phil Collins crying, "OH, LO-ORD! OH, LO-ORD!" Then the only sound echoing through my head was Heather's voice.

"You're here to meet a couple?"

"You're here to meet a couple?"

"OH, LO-ORD!" screamed Phil.

"OH, LO-ORD!" screamed my shriveling ego.

From somewhere in the depths of my pulverized humility, I mustered the courage to ask, "Did you just ask if I was here to meet a couple?" hoping with every ounce of faith I possessed that I had misheard Heather, even though I knew I hadn't.

"Isn't that what you said?" she asked. "That you're meeting a couple?"

You know that sensation when you've stumbled but haven't yet fallen but it's definitely coming and it's only a matter of how hard you hit the floor and how badly you injure yourself? And how that millisecond between your pain-free life and paradigm-shifting hurt feels like years as you teeter in limbo waiting for your tenuous balance to tilt in gravity's favor? And all your internal organs drop through a trapdoor into your lower intestines and leave you feeling empty and a shell of a human? Well, it was that feeling of inescapable and imminent pain and humiliation that shot through me like an ultra-strength laxative to my soul, when I realized I had introduced myself to, befriended, and, worst of all, painted a graphic picture of my sexual perversity for two complete strangers.

"So, you're not Heather?" I sputtered out in embarrassment, poorly pretending to be casual.

"What? No. My name's Nadia. Oh, is that what you asked when you came over? If I was Heather? Sorry. I couldn't hear you over the music."

"No problem." I tried to play it off. But before going home to flagellate myself, I had to be certain. "Just so I'm clear, you two aren't swingers?"

"No," Rich chimed in. "We're Buddhists."

What Buddhism had to do with not being swingers I hadn't the foggiest, but for whatever reason, Rich felt the need to prove his Buddhist status and handed me a business card for a spiritual retreat.

"Well, all I can say is, I'm sorry," I said to both of them.

"No worries, man. It's totally cool."

"Really, it's not. But thanks." I stood to save what shred of dignity I had left. "I have to ask, what did you think when a stranger asked to sit next to you at a strip club?"

"We thought you were friendly," answered Heather.

"And when I shared my sexual . . . tastes?"

"Yeah," Rich said. "That was a little weird."

"That it was, Rich. That it most certainly was." I could hear the Buddha laughing heartily, wherever he was. "Well, Rich, Nadia, sorry again for the interruption. Enjoy the rest of your night."

I turned to run away, but came face-to-face with Roxy, her lower lip curled into the pout of all pouts. "Were you leaving without letting me dance for you?"

Three minutes later I was in the V.I.P. room sprawled out on a chaise sofa even gummier than the prior couch, being smothered by Roxy's naked, lotioned, and now glittered grinding body.

"Oooo, your dick feels so hard," she commented in her patented rehearsed tone.

"That's the singles," I corrected her.

"What?"

"Never mind."

Perhaps this wasn't exactly what I had in mind for my first time back from injury, but in a humiliating way, it felt good to be back.

Same Book. Dusty Cover.

"Watch," Louise instructed, then walked across the room to demonstrate a painless, limp-free gait courtesy of a recent hip replacement. Louise's exhibition was in response to my sharing the story of my hip injury, from which I'd almost fully, I'd argue miraculously, recovered. Unfortunately, Louise wasn't making me feel any better, because, somewhere in her sixties by my estimation, she anchored the low end of tonight's age range.

"Better than ever and barely a scar!" she boasted as she pivoted and made her way back toward us, as if making a return trip on the catwalk.

From beneath the strap of her black lace teddy peeked a decades-old tattoo, the ink greened, faded, and blurred. Her skin having long ago lost its war with gravity, what may have once been a lion or tiger had aged into a shar-pei-esque blob melting down her shoulder blade.

"Oh! And there's this new osteoporosis medication I found!" Louise chirped as she squeezed back into the love seat, squashing me between her and a female octogenarian whose hearing aid had already deafened my left ear with its high-pitched squeal.

When I'd RSVPed for tonight, I hadn't expected to be the youngest by three-plus decades. To be honest, I hadn't expected anything. I didn't have the mental capacity. The excitement over my first house party overwhelmed me and kept my thoughts abuzz for three weeks.

Jim and Valerie suggested Harry and Jackie invite me. Understandably, Harry and Jackie were skeptical about bringing a single male into their close-knit group, but Valerie vouched for me, which persuaded Jackie. I leapt at the invitation—any single male would have—but now, learning about the most recent medications to assist smooth menopausal transition, I was seriously rethinking my decision.

I excused myself to the buffet, where I found Jim, a late-forties regal type with a weighty, elegant air.

"The ladies are fighting over who gets to break you in." He laughed devilishly.

I glanced around, desperate for anyone remotely close to my age bracket onto whom I could glom and seek shelter, but I was only met with eager glares from elderly women with percolating libidos. Now I knew what Eric Carmen meant by "Hungry Eyes" and I very badly wished I could still claim ignorance.

"See that one?" Jim asked as he nodded toward a bottle blonde in leopard-print lingerie with a face-lift that had remolded her eyes into asymmetrical ovalish orbs. "That's Mona. She'll fuck you silly. How old would you say she is?"

While Mona's multiple cosmetic surgeries might have persuaded some to generously shave off a few years, the galaxies of liver spots the diameter of saucers that oozed from beneath her nightie led me to conservatively place her in her late seventies. But I didn't want to make a misstep in the minefield of women's ages, so I pled the fifth.

"Sixty-five!" Jim exclaimed in genuine astonishment. "She looks at least ten years younger, doesn't she?"

Fighting the horrific mental images of intercourse with a woman who could run in my grandmother's social circles, I responded in faux disbelief, "Yeah. At least."

"Make sure you carb up before playing with her. I learned the hard way."

Don't get me wrong, I support adults of all ages enjoying all permutations of sex. As long as it's legal, consensual, and everyone enjoys themselves, shtup away! What I don't subscribe to is the requirement that I participate in, bear witness to, or even have the smallest inkling regarding certain carnal combinations taking place. Some things are just better left unknown. And as I surveyed the landscape of—to put it delicately—veteran swingers, I added tonight to my list of items about which I should remain blissfully ignorant.

What if one of the guests got injured? Pump a little too hard and someone slips a disk. Experiment with the wrong position and a bone snaps. God forbid the throes of passion are too much and we have to break out the defibrillator or, worse, summon the paramedics.

I know full well that I've always been prone to overreacting and catastrophizing, but my concerns were nothing if not well founded, rational, and imminently and incredibly possible. Biologically speaking, the human body deteriorates after a certain age. That's not prejudice, just pure, unadulterated science. And when one is pushing the envelope for life expectancy as it is, that inevitable physical decline becomes one's primary focus. Granted, I couldn't rule out the possibility that tonight's revelers were the keepers of the fountain of youth, but even more than an over-reactor, I'm a realist. And my realist instincts were giving me fair warning that if anything close to my imagined, doomsday scenarios was realized, I would never, *ever* psychologically recover.

"When playtime starts, don't be bashful," Jim instructed me. "Grab anyone who strikes your fancy and go to town."

The room tilted and I felt light-headed. In an effort to balance myself, and to appease Jim's carbing-up recommendation, I ladled out some mashed potatoes and returned to my seat. I focused on eating and tried to keep an open mind while Louise listed her favorite fiber supplements.

I'd just swallowed the last of my meal when Jackie leapt onto my lap and launched her tongue down my throat. Her kissing technique, while passionate, was reminiscent of a weed whacker. Her tongue lashed about my mouth like a rabid wildebeest, flaying my cheeks, and beating my gums to a pulp. I was supremely thankful Jackie didn't possess a tongue stud as, if she did, the force with which she orally assaulted me would have resulted in an emergency dental visit.

In tandem with her abusive kissing, Jackie dry-humped my thighs at jackhammer speed, the friction from which was akin to one trying to start a campfire with two sticks. A fleeting image of my denim set ablaze by Jackie's crotch was interrupted when she broke from me and commanded, "Let's go have some fun." I emitted a terrified squeak, but quickly converted it to a shy giggle, which Jackie interpreted as consent for her to continue her ravaging.

Jackie physically dragged me (emotionally kicking and screaming) into the living room and began ripping at my clothes. I didn't want to be rude by requesting a female closer to my age or several levels less aggressive, especially since Jackie was hostess, so I had no choice but to suck it up. I thought about the suffering my past girlfriends had endured with my sexual shortcomings and how they grinned, bore it, and pressed on to save my feelings. Couldn't I walk (or fuck) a mile in their shoes? Surely I'd benefit in some way from viewing matters from a different vantage, wouldn't I?

If Jackie's voracious make-out session had left any doubt, she quickly confirmed that, despite her age, she had a limitless reservoir of energy. So when she summoned two additional males, I was more than happy—bordering on blessedly thankful—to share. The three of us did our best to keep up with Jackie, but at some point she pushed the two other males away and ordered me in a low growl to "fuck me NOW!"

I had two options: obey and hope to survive, or refuse Jackie's direct orders and endure whatever punishment she deemed appropriate. In general, I pride myself on shrewd decision making. So, when faced with a possessed woman demanding immediate sexual gratification that might very well be hazardous to my physical being, my supreme analytical skills kicked in and told me to shut up and slap on a condom.

I hadn't finished unrolling the rubber when Jackie jerked me to my knees, slung her legs over my shoulders, slid me inside, and began grinding like one of those electric sanders. I've only gone horseback riding three times, but I couldn't imagine a cowboy with the strength or expertise to break the wild stallion that was Jackie. Lactic acid coursed through my quads and lower back. Muscles I didn't know I possessed cramped and locked. But I pressed on and managed to barely keep up with Jackie's violent thrashing.

When Jackie snapped her fingers like a malevolent dictator, the two males she'd thrust aside earlier resumed their positions, one on each flank, so she could recommence oral activities. Even with a team of three capable, in-shape men working at peak performance, Jackie wasn't getting near what she needed. She again thrust aside her oral slaves and took matters into her own hands. She tackled and mounted me, vised her legs around my pelvis, and clamped her talon-like nails onto my pectorals. I stared up at Jackie's red, ravenous face waterfalling sweat and suddenly and miraculously was overcome by a Zen-like peace. Perhaps it was an unprecedented endorphin rush taking hold, but despite the excruciating, all-encompassing pain being inflicted upon me, I somehow relaxed and submitted to the experience. My surroundings fell away and all I was conscious of was my sense of self.

Jackie rode and rode and achieved several impressive and vicious orgasms that echoed through the house and received encouraging responses of "Get 'em, Jacks!" from disembodied voices. Even under the pelvic-snapping force of Jackie's relentless pounding, I was conscious of the fact that never had I performed with such stamina. Every ounce of blood drained from my head to keep every other muscle operable. Though my nervous system was on the verge of overload, I was still in control of my faculties. I could have gone on indefinitely; there wasn't a doubt in my mind.

Then Jackie froze. Her body seized up and she locked a vaginal death grip on me. Every fiber of her being shook. Every muscle bulged to the point I thought her skin would snap like an overinflated balloon. Her maroon complexion deepened to purple and she stopped breathing. This was the orgasm of all orgasms. The Mt. Vesuvius of climaxes. A sexual supernova of intergalactic proportions that would shatter all preconceived notions of physical pleasure and forever redefine the limits of the human nervous system. I didn't care that she'd rearranged my internal organs with her legs' hydraulic compression. The fact was, I could claim partial credit for helping Jackie reach this pinnacle of ecstasy.

Lying there watching her eyes blanch white as they rolled into her skull, I beamed with pride. Her head lolled to her chest and she collapsed like a heap of russet potatoes on top of me. I waited for Jackie's sweaty, overheated body to move, but it didn't. I nudged her with my shoulder, but again, nothing. Just a motionless . . . (gulp) . . . corpse.

Preoccupied with my own sense of pride in a job more than well done, I hadn't considered Jackie's age. And now . . . Oh, Jesus.

I craned my head to look at one of the flanking males, who was baffled, which was actually a confusing visual, as his eyeline passed through his still erect penis, so one could easily have mistaken his reaction as bewilderment at the sight of his hard-on.

"Dude, what did you do?" he asked.

"Me? I didn't do anything."

"That sure as fuck wasn't nothing, man," said the other male, who looked like he was going to make a run for it.

My nightmare had materialized. I had fucked Jackie to death, her still-tightening vaginal grip proof rigor mortis was setting in. Any moment now, paramedics and firefighters would burst in and set about using the Jaws of Life to free me. The media would dub me the Cock Killer. My actions would single-handedly revise the legal definition of a lethal weapon. My court-appointed counsel would tell me my odds were grim and that a plea deal was in my best interest. But I'd trust that the witnesses would testify that I was merely a tool for the deceased's/victim's enjoyment. I'd request a jury trial, certain that I'd be exonerated. But on the trial's first day reality would set in and I'd know there was no way a jury would sympathize with me. Even before the verdict was handed down, multiple movies of the week would turn society against me and I would forever be guilty in the public eye. My quest was officially vanquished.

But then I felt a tiny, rapid thumping against my stomach. Could it be? Was it? Oh, please God, let it—

Jackie shot up, gasping an enormous breath like a drowning person surfacing. Her head bobbled, eventually sustaining an upright position. Her eyes reemerged from her head and she found her sense of balance. Her breathing calmed, she looked at me, and, still woozy, declared as if nothing were amiss, "I need a break," then dismounted and stumbled off.

Seconds after realizing they wouldn't be named as accomplices to the Cock Killer, the two men scattered as well. Fucking cowards.

I just lay there. Alone, baffled, but eternally grateful. And once I accepted that life as I'd known it would resume, I sat up. I spied on the couch opposite me Louise.

"In the twenty-seven years I've known her," she said, "not once has Jackie needed a break."

Still incapable of summoning the ability to speak, I smiled shyly.

"How about making *me* need a break?" Louise asked as she crawled toward me.

I played with Louise. And Gladys. Even Dehlia and Hattie at the same time. And I was glad to have done so. I even tried my luck with Mona. Jim was right about the carbs.

Lesson 7:

Know Your Couple

I've said it before and I'll scream it till the end of time: The Lifestyle isn't for everyone. But it is for the right people with the right reasons with the right attitude.

Who are these "right people," you ask? In general, adults open to alternative sexual scenarios. Who aren't as judgmental as the layperson. Who are tolerant and accepting. Who are at peace living—at least part of the time—outside the conventional definition of "normal."

"Right reasons" are harder to define, as they have many shades of gray.[1] Broad reasons to sexually experiment or explore are just as valid as specific ones to experience a certain position or scenario. At their core, right reasons have a selfish motivation that doesn't minimize another's. Say you want a threesome and a married couple invites you into their bed. As much as you may think otherwise, you haven't stumbled across a pair of prostitutes with altruistic, kinky hearts or sex therapists working pro bono. This couple has a personal stake in the threesome as

---

1   No E L James allusion intended.

well. If you're aware of this fact and sensitive to it so you don't make the experience all about you, then you're swinging for the right reasons. To quote one of modern civilization's finest thinkers, Bill S. Preston, Esq., "Be excellent to each other."

A quick example of a *wrong* reason to swing: I met a couple who behaved snippily toward each other at our bar meet. Perhaps ignoring the obvious because of my horned-up state, I chalked up their crabbiness to their personal—albeit odd—version of foreplay. I don't judge, remember? I'm one of the "right people." We moved things to the hotel, began playtime soon after arrival, and, while the wife performed oral on hubby, he began to snore. I heard it and prayed she didn't, but when I looked up from between her legs to see her grip tightening around his cock, I knew she had. Before the door to their marital cage match locked me inside, I made a speedy exit. It goes without saying they were swinging for the wrong reasons.[2]

Unfortunately, I can't articulate the "right attitude." All I know is, it's the result of being one of the right people with the right reasons. The right attitude has friendliness, patience, and understanding. A sensitivity and responsiveness to others. Adaptability, honesty, and, above all, mindfulness to everyone.

While these qualities are present in all true swingers, Lifestylers come in many colors. Meaning, not everyone is compatible, especially couples. When there are two personalities that must also act as one, the recipe for compatibility complicates exponentially. Unquestionably, when deciding whether to engage in a swing experience, cou-

---

2 Though you may have surmised these, here's a sampling of wrong reasons, to bring this point home:
- Having sex with as many people as possible without concern for their feelings
- Swinging to satisfy a deficient emotional need
- Injecting "spice" into an already troubled relationship
Get it? Good. Moving on.

ples must consider their individual personalities *and* their marriage. This means each spouse contemplates a possible swing situation from *three* vantages (his, hers, and theirs). Talk about frustration! Sure, one spouse could "take one for the team" or throw caution to the wind, but that's not a marriage anyone wants to be part of.

To alleviate some of the aggravation in the couples hunt, you'll want to glean as much as you can from interactions and conversations to ascertain what type of sexual sandwich you're considering slipping into. However, even before you expend all that effort, it helps to know the basic couple types with whom you are and are *not* compatible. Being able to dismiss a couple type before investing your time and effort getting to know them is a relief.

Now, while I can't pigeonhole every single couple, there are some archetypes to consider:

The Experienced Couple

Your gold-standard swingers. Your bread-and-butter playmates. Of all types, Experienced Couples are the most common, easily located, and, thankfully, least likely to cause drama. They eliminate so many variables from the equation that dealing with them *only* means matching personalities, attraction, and logistics. Not to say those aspects aren't challenging, but when you don't have to worry about flakiness, doubts, etiquette, and naiveté, it's a fucking godsend.

Most often, Experienced Couples are in long-term marriages built on strong, loving foundations. They understand the essence of swing and engage in good, adult fun. Swinging is just a part of their shared life—not its central focus—which makes play a stable and virtually worry-free experience. If only all couples were like this . . .

The Lifer Couple

Lifers are Experienced Couples turned up to eleven. Swinging plays a much more prominent role for them. Often it's one of their highest priorities, evidenced by social calendars frequently dictated by Lifestyle cruises, resort takeovers, and swinging events in general. Lifers have extensive Rolodexes of regular playmates—I've known some who keep date books—and expect their regulars to play with reasonable consistency or face replacement. Lifers have little tolerance for bullshit and abhor those who waste their time and efforts.

Should you try a Lifer, be prepared for the unusual and extreme. I don't mean sexually, but rather with regard to effort. For example, some Lifers own RVs for the purpose of touring the country to play. That's some serious dedication to the Lifestyle *and* the pocketbook. Another example was described to me by a female friend who attended a gathering at a Lifer Couple's summer home. According to her, the compound had a custom medieval turret that offered a period role-play experience and a "moon room" carpeted in water-bed mattresses, with glow-in-the-dark constellations painted on the walls and ceiling. I doubt anyone would disagree that that's some hardcore swinging shit.

Generally, Lifers aren't for newbies. Get some experience under your belt before sampling them. Lifers have been there, done that, and want to go and do more. Keep up with them or get the hell out of their way.

The Newbie Couple

At the opposite end of the Lifestyle spectrum is the Newbie Couple. The most important thing to remember about Newbies is they are a total crapshoot. Inexperience is a *highly* unpredictable variable, and

Newbies are chock-full of it. They are pervasively hesitant, have never-ending questions, and are all but guaranteed to flake. While Newbies can create a torturously horrendous time, they can also turn to you to be their Lifestyle Jedi, a dynamic that has the potential to provide a beyond stellar experience. A Newbie Couple either has swinging in their DNA or curiosity has led them seriously astray. Consider yourself warned.

The Dabbler Couple

Dabblers are more experienced than Newbies but less so than Experienced Couples. Dabblers have swung, but don't do so regularly. They come and go from the Lifestyle and tend to maintain contact with a handful of active swingers with whom they play almost exclusively. That's not to say they don't entertain expanding their circle. It's just that since they come and go with such frequency, they tend not to have the temperament to dedicate time searching for new playmates. They get in, get satisfied, and get out.

The Half 'n' Half Couple

Strange as it may sound, there are couples with one spouse who plays and one who doesn't. I'm not talking voyeur/swinger couples—throw a condom and you'll hit one of those—I'm talking couples composed of one Lifestyler and one Vanilla. I'm not denying the existence of healthy, alternative marriages—if you haven't noticed, I've been promoting sex outside of committed relationships for quite a few pages now—but the Half 'n' Half arrangement isn't the norm in our admittedly abnormal community.

The Half 'n' Half experience can be quite awkward. For example,

I attend a regular house party that includes on its guest list a certain couple. Without fail, the wife of said couple spends the duration of every party enjoying a rotating harem of men while hubby sits on the couch. He doesn't watch and doesn't really acknowledge what's going on just feet in front of him. To date, I've yet to hear him utter a word and the most I've seen him do was read the newspaper. His inattentiveness means he isn't a voyeur and, as he doesn't seem to take particular umbrage regarding his wife's activity, he's not a cuckold. Yet, party after party, there he is. Just . . . sitting. While everyone else has a grand ol' time, this stone-faced gentleman keeps on every stitch of clothing and rides the bench. Not the sexiest of vibes.

The ProAm Couple

The ProAm (Professional-Amateur) is similar to the Half 'n' Half in that each half of the couple possesses a different level of experience, but it differs in that both play. More times than not, the Pro half had been part of a swinging couple and is now introducing his or her new half to the Lifestyle. Playing with a ProAm couple can be awkward, as you're jockeying between differing levels of ability, but it's a far cry from the discomfort of the Half 'n' Half experience. ProAms are most compatible with patient and adaptable couples.

The Non-Couple Couple

Non-Couples are Half 'n' Half/ProAm hybrids. Both Non-Couple spouses play (like the ProAm), just not together (like the Half 'n' Half). Though they're outside the Lifestyle couple norm, the fact that both Non-Couple spouses swing is comforting. That being said, it can take time to acclimate to playing with half of a couple in the absence of his or her spouse.

Personal experience: I met a couple at a party. The wife and I hit it off, so we swapped numbers (with hubby's consent) and planned to play at a not-too-distant date. The day of our rendezvous, hubby answered the door in his robe, wearing reading glasses and gripping the day's crossword. He offered a friendly handshake, informed me, "She's upstairs expecting you. If you need anything, give a holler," and went about his puzzle. So, yeah, that was a new one for me.

The Puppy Love Couple

Puppy Lovers (PLs) are drowning in gooey love and reminiscent of the Lov-ahs, the Will Ferrell/Rachel Dratch characters on *Saturday Night Live*. PLs are in constant, and I mean *constant* contact, both physically and verbally. For me, it's the verbal stuff that's most off-putting. It takes some serious concentration to pleasure the wife while hubby pets her hair, stares deeply into her eyes, and utters in the most loving tone, "How's his cock? Is it hard? Is he fucking you good, sweetie? I bet he is. He looks like he's fucking you *really* good and *really* hard. I love you so much, honey." (True story.)

While a loving couple is ideal because they keep drama minimal, finding yourself in the nougaty center of a Puppy Love relationship can feel icky.

The Connoisseur Couple

Think of them as Puppy Lovers with toys. This couple *loves* sex in all its incarnations and goes to phenomenally great lengths to explore as much of it as possible. Some have rooms outfitted for fun. Others offer an array of sexual "enhancements" that includes swings, tables, chairs (I've played on a custom sex seat hubby hand-smelted for his wife that boasted reinforced steel legs, durable padding, and waterproofing [she was a squirter of diluvian proportions]), Sybians, exercise balls, restraints, nylon ropes, you name it. It can be fun (and educational) to play with Connoisseurs. Just keep an open mind. And stretch out beforehand.

The Dom Couple

I don't mean Dom in the BDSM sense. I mean it simply in a controlling manner. Some couples want a very specific experience and are very vocal about it. I once received a last-minute invite to a visiting couple's hotel room. I was given explicit instructions to arrive in the lobby at a specific time and to call the husband's cell when I got there, at which point I'd be supplied the room number. Then I was to come to the room and knock "delicately" so as not to startle his wife. Once let in, I was to quietly take a shower, then redress, after which I'd be escorted by hubby to wife, who would be blindfolded in a chair. I was to refrain from speaking and allow her to undress me while she remained blindfolded. Once naked, I would engage physically with the wife, but should still refrain from speaking. During intercourse I'd be provided condoms, and penetration should be done slowly and carefully, as the wife possessed a "sensitive vagina." I was to pull out before ejaculation but to cum in the condom, then proceed to the bathroom, dispose of said condom, shower, redress, wave (not speak) goodbye, then depart. Their follow-up email complimented me on my ability to follow directions.

If you're okay following orders, perhaps the Doms are your cup of tea (or bottle of lube; har, har).

The Undeciders

Almost exclusively Newbies. Undeciders' inexperience is so paralyzing it short-circuits any cognitive ability to decide, well, anything. Where to meet, where/if to play, how to play, in what acts to engage . . . A few Undeciders I've encountered had me questioning whether they had the ability to decide to enjoy themselves. If you require (or even just prefer) a symbiotic playtime experience with give and take, avoid Undeciders like herpes. But if you have no qualms taking the reins, charting the course, and making every decision at every turn, what the hell, give them a shot.

• • •

What qualities do you want in a couple? More important, what qualities *don't* you want? Would you prefer a couple whose level of experience is on par with your own, or one from whom you can learn? Are you okay following orders, or do you want a say in playtime? Settle on couple types *before* you begin your hunt and you'll save time and effort and, hopefully, set off on the right path to the experience you seek.

Lesson 8:

Meet 'n' Greet

Some swingers agree to play before they meet in person. Others make it clear that the first meet will only be platonic. In my experience, most leave open the possibility for play and let the meet 'n' greet decide. As such, prepare for a meet 'n' greet as if play were guaranteed. That way, you're ready should luck come your way. It's awkward when, after weeks of emailing and chatting, you meet, personalities click, everyone's libido is primed and ready, but you've come straight from spin class, haven't trimmed your pubes, and didn't bring protection.

Although you should prepare for play on the first meet, don't expect it. If you do, you'll exude eagerness and desperation and won't be focused on getting acquainted, the real goal of a meet 'n' greet. I've said it before and I'll preach it until the day I die: Swinging is not only about sex; it's about finding compatible adults with whom to enjoy sex. Failed swingers try to get laid. Successful ones seek compatible playmates.

Here's how to prepare for your meet 'n' greet.

Grooming

Shower, deodorize, brush your teeth. Do that and you'll be in the top 10 percent of swingers. It's true some take a shine to the natural look down below, and if so much was expressed, then by all means let it grow. Just know that unspoken etiquette calls for a trim or full shave. Balls, too, gents.

An extra tip: Keep a nail clipper in your car, just in case; Edward Scissorhands (or feet) is not a welcome bedfellow.

Location

Meet 'n' greets generally take place in public: at coffeehouses, bars, restaurants, lounges . . . I don't have to tell you there are lots of crazies on the Web. A public location provides everyone a safe environment at which each other's sanity can be verified.

Men, the locale should be convenient for the woman or couple. Remember, you're the one with the bad rep. Be accommodating. Plus, chivalry will earn you brownie points. The one caveat regards anyone who wants to meet far from his or her or their neighborhood in order to ensure privacy. In that case, make your preference known. Also, make sure the location is conducive to conversation. A noisy club isn't ideal for getting to know one another.

If, prior to the meet, both parties expressed interest in play, choose a location near where you're going to play. Whether you're hosting, they're hosting, or a room is rented, meet close to your final destination. The farther you are from bed, the more likely someone will get cold feet.

As for paying, there's no protocol. Because I'm financially able to, I normally offer to pick up the tab, as long as no one ordered

Cristal or Maine lobster. As for the hotel, guys, be ready to foot the bill. If that's an issue for you, discuss it with the couple or female prior to meeting. Money is a sensitive subject for some, so it's better to resolve it prior to meeting face-to-face so an awkward situation is avoided.

BYOC

Protection is everyone's responsibility. If you have a preference, bring it. It saves time having to hunt down a store carrying your contraception of choice.

Don't lug a dispensary with you. Have one type of a basic condom with lube and one without. Though you may be a connoisseur in this department, I wouldn't stray from name brands. Trust is important and unknown brands may cause concern. Also, unless requested prior, avoid anything flamboyant like ticklers or crazy flavors. Not everyone's into that stuff. I also recommend staying away from spermicide. I respect that it's another layer of protection against pregnancy, but I'm told it tastes bad.[1] Finally, some people—mostly women, in my experience—are allergic to latex. So if you haven't broached that topic prior to meeting, bring along a non-latex option, just in case. A bottle of lube is also advisable, as condoms can dry out a woman. Be sure to use water-based, as oil-based ones eat latex.

You should know that some swingers prefer, even require, the use of condoms they provide. The thought behind this is they aren't taking chances with a person who, for all intents and purposes, they just met. You may not be comfortable using protection supplied by someone else, so if you aren't, there's no shame in politely declining playtime.

---

1   You're welcome, ladies.

"The Break"

This is a nugget from my personal tool box. At a meet 'n' greet, once everyone has had sufficient time to form an opinion of one another (fifteen to twenty minutes on average), I excuse myself to the restroom, whether nature is calling or not. This is "The Break" and it serves a few purposes.

If you're meeting a couple, The Break allows them to huddle-up, share notes, and decide whether they want to proceed to playtime with you. I know couples who use hand signals and trigger words, but private conversation is best for everyone. If you're meeting a single female, especially a newbie, The Break gives her time to gather her thoughts and feelings. The situation may be stressful, confusing, even overwhelming. Give her some breathing room. Also, for safety reasons, many women inform a friend where they are going and plan to check in via text or a quick phone call at a designated time. Allow her privacy to do so. It'll settle her nerves, which will, in turn, make it more likely for her to agree to play.

Couples, it may feel awkward to excuse yourselves to the bathroom at the same time, but if you're meeting another couple, they'll appreciate the break as well.

In addition to the emotional pause it affords, The Break displays a sense of confidence. The mere act of walking away from the situation illustrates that you are, in fact, willing to walk away. It may also grant a sense of control to some. In your absence, they are reminded that it's their decision as to whether things progress. This power fosters a feeling of comfort and plays to your advantage.

Lastly, The Break lets you gather your thoughts. Sitting face-to-face with a potential playmate with whom you've been discussing sexual fantasies can cloud anyone's thoughts. Cool off and decide with sound mind if you truly clicked. There's no shame in declining play if you don't feel a connection. However, if you've emailed, chatted, spoken on the phone, and met in person without racing for the emergency exit, odds are everyone is game.

Keep The Break to less than three minutes. That should be more than sufficient for everyone to decide. Besides, the longer you're absent, the more time they have to think up reasons not to play. When I return, I usually say something joking, to the effect of, "Well, you had your chance to leave. I guess you're stuck with me now." The joke tends to lighten the mood and hint at my interest in playing. It also seamlessly segues to the topic of play. After my joke, the woman or couple will either consent to play or we'll agree to part ways. Either way, no more time is wasted, which benefits everyone.

No Expectations

The Lifestyle attracts scores of flakes. There's no way around it. But one way to deal with it is to avoid holding expectations. By doing this, you'll create a mind-set that allows you to accept whatever outcome presents itself.

Make your goal of the meet 'n' greet to meet someone new. Nothing more. If the person shows as promised, you'll have achieved your goal. Then you can let the meet 'n' greet run its course. If he flakes, then you aren't disappointed, because you had no expectations. Letting go of expectations opens you up to whatever experience befalls you.

Lesson 9:

The Club Scene . . . Grudgingly

I'm not a fan of the club scene. Sex "for profit" is not my idea of the Lifestyle. While I understand clubs incur unavoidable expenses, it doesn't make it feel any more right. To me they'll forever smack of meat markets where people "play the odds" to ferret out sex. There's an old joke about a guy who asks every woman he meets, point-blank, if she'll fuck him and, not surprisingly, gets turned down every time. His buddy asks, "Why do you keep asking so bluntly?" To which he replies, "Because eventually one of them will say yes." In a nutshell, that's my take on the swing club mentality.

But I promised help. So here's what I know about clubs.

Where Are They?

Some clubs operate in the open, laws be damned! Others are speakeasy-like, requiring passwords and member vouching. An official club yellow pages doesn't exist, at least not that I'm aware of, so some searching is required. However, swing sites and Internet groups almost always offer a club section, so it's not too hard. But, like everything else on the Web, consider club listings with a healthy dose of caution. Even if a club is listed on a bona fide swing site, do your due diligence. Make sure it's legit, that you meet the requirements, and that the crowd it draws is the type you seek.

If site listings don't pan out, try word of mouth. Personal referrals are more reliable anyway as, in my book, a firsthand account from a trusted source always trumps anonymous Internet reviews or ad buys. Also, referrals can give you an advantage. Perhaps your "source" can get you on the list more easily than you could on your own. However, the downside to a referral is you're "outing" your interest. So, for the more private individual, this option isn't ideal.

As a last resort, there's Google.

Protocol

Don't just show up; you'll be turned away. Call and get on the guest list. Some clubs require applications, so if that makes you uncomfortable, politely decline. While I can't vouch for all clubs, most pride themselves on privacy and discretion, which goes to reason because, if they didn't, they wouldn't last.

For single males, it's a virtual certainty you're going to pay a sizable "donation." Don't haggle. If you don't want to pay, dozens of other guys are raring to take your spot.

Everyone should expect a "no guarantees" disclaimer of some sort. Remember, it's a "donation," which means you're not promised anything in return. To bring this point home, many clubs post rules in conspicuous places that disclaim any expectations. Some of the most common rules are no means no, respect everyone, sex only in designated play areas, and clean up after yourself. A club doesn't want to build a reputation as a flophouse for sexual deviants (read: adult theaters and bookstores). A club wants to be seen as a welcome place for mature, like-minded adults. Perpetuate that reputation.

One last thing: While some clubs permit BYOB, never drink to excess. Even more than being unpleasant and rude, drunken swingers are a liability. The volatility of an intoxicated, horny adult in an overtly promiscuous setting is a recipe for disaster. Should you have a few too many, you'll be escorted off-premises and there's a good chance you'll be blacklisted.

Packing List

Treat your club visit like a day at the beach. Pack enough supplies to sustain you and keep you comfortable. The short list includes condoms, lube, a towel, and a robe. Condoms and lube are self-explanatory, but the towel and robe may not be. Allow me to explain.

Some clubs boast hot tubs and/or pools, and while many supply towels (some even a robe amenity), who knows the last time they were laundered. Secondly, even if the club doesn't have a pool, still bring a towel, as most clubs have a "dress code" that forbids normal clothing. This rule guards against voyeurs who attend just to sit around in jeans and T-shirts and gawk creepily at all the naked folk. You won't be forced to have sex, but you are expected to dress like the natives. I also recommend a swimsuit, because while many clubs with pools are clothing optional, some aren't.

Optional items include bottled water, soda, and alcohol (if allowed). Some clubs offer nonalcoholic drinks, but if you enjoy a specific beverage, bring it yourself. Don't lug cases. They're overkill and, frankly, weird. A six-pack is plenty.

Lastly, I *highly* advise flip-flops. Clubs tend to exist in structures not purposed for heavy foot traffic. Architecturally speaking, a single-family home is not designed to accommodate a party of fifty. Not to mention, fifty engaging in activities that produce an impressive volume of fluid by-product. Moreover, I promise clubs don't offer the requisite "facilities" for the number of guests they host. They are getting by in this regard. Commercial establishments are required by law to supply a certain number of restrooms based on maximum occupancy, but it's safe to assume code enforcement hasn't paid a visit to a swing club, like, ever. You've been warned.

Oh, and if the hot tub looks like a ginormous shabu-shabu pot, it's okay to take a pass.

Items you should *not* bring:

1. Valuables. Some clubs supply lockers, but many don't. And while in my limited club experience I've found the honor code to prevail, I've heard stories of theft. Leave your valuables at home or, at the very least, in your car.

2. Cash. Pay your "donation." That's it. There's no cash bar or souvenir shop of which to partake.

3. Camera and cell phones. In today's age of technology, everyone's tethered to their smartphones. However, be sure to keep all recording devices far from club doors. Clubs religiously guard discretion and privacy, and any potential threat can lead to the denial of admission.

Club Etiquette

Don't expect a brothel setting with women lined up to be selected. Nor should you anticipate being yanked into a sex pile. Like any social gathering, a club requires interaction and conversation prior to fun. To maximize your chances of play, here are behaviors to avoid:

1. DON'T be creepy. Refrain from spying a woman from afar, stalking her for hours, then appearing in front of her with a hard-on primed for action. It's tasteless, tactless, and scary as hell. Not to mention it will probably result in your speedy ejection from the premises. And, women, avoid instant clinginess. Not attractive, especially with one you've just met.

2. DON'T play dark and mysterious. In a club setting, it comes off as cocky and unavailable. Project friendliness and accessibility if you want to play.

3. DON'T pressure. It'll garner you the same fate as being creepy, usually much faster.

Now some advisable behavior:

1. BE accessible. Hiding in the corner waiting to be selected isn't productive. You don't need to be the life of the party, but be on everyone's radar.

2. BE patient. Striking out is the chance you take (no guarantees, remember?), but you can mitigate disappointment. If you attend a club with the goal of meeting people—not fucking—then you'll preempt disappointment and won't reek of desperation. If play doesn't happen this time, try again. Just, whatever you do, don't rush, pressure, or force. It'll backfire dramatically.

To be clear, I'm not condemning clubs. They serve a specific purpose and provide an experience that house and hotel parties can't. Rather, I'm being honest that they simply aren't my thing. However, if they pique your interest, give them a go.

Orgasm

Poker Night

After three weeks of viewing the same profiles on my regular sites, I perused Craigslist in an attempt to scare up some variety. A curious couple looking for a male for a long-time fantasy. A theme party tolerating select single males. A retired porn starlet organizing a get together for which I requested more info with no intention of attending (the detailed invites are beyond entertaining). Underwhelmed, I was about to call it quits when a post caught my eye:

POKER NIGHT—(SFV)

24/7 committed dom/sub couple seeks 8 guys for a poker night where winner takes all . . . including me! If interested, and if you can play Texas Hold 'Em, email with pic. No Pic = Delete. Guys must be DDF and respectful of Master and His rules.

Normally I'd never consider a picless post, but faced with no other viable option I figured what the hell and rattled off my standard intro

Daniel Stern

email. I took a jog to work off my frustration with the dearth of play opportunities and, upon return, found a response:

> FROM: slavenatalia@XXXXX.com
>
> SUBJECT: Poker Night!
>
> Thank you so much for your interest! As you can no doubt imagine, Master and i have received hundreds of emails and, i'm sad to say, we only have room for eight at the table. As i will be occupying one of the seats, that leaves seven.

At least the rejection was courteous. I was about to hit delete when I read:

> Master and i have culled the pool to 35 . . . and you made the cut!

Perhaps there was hope . . .

> After W/we figure out the final seven, W/we will set a day and time convenient to all. But keep your eyes peeled, as it won't be too far off! i just can't wait that long! If you have any questions, don't hesitate to ask. Lastly, W/we have a difficult decision on our hands getting to the final table, so if you'd like to supplement your original email, please do so now.

The fact that this party wasn't a moneymaking venture, coupled with natalia's adherence to Master/sub capitalization rules, lent credence to the post's legitimacy. Though I'd taken to never holding expectations, I felt a tinge of hope having survived the first cut. I decided

| 180 |

against submitting additional info as I didn't want to come off desperate or compensating. Instead, I replied that I was flattered to still be in contention and wished natalia and Master best of luck culling down to the lucky seven.

Two weeks later:

> Master and i finalized the list . . . and you're one of the lucky seven! The game will take place at Master's home in Sherman Oaks at 7:00 this Saturday, so I'll need an RSVP from you ASAP. Also, Master desires to speak with you prior to the game, so include your phone number.

Attached was a pic. On all fours facing the camera, raven-haired natalia wore only a metal choker secured with a heart-shaped lock. She was in her early twenties with ample, natural breasts perfect for her frame. Most striking were her eyes. Dark and intense. I eagerly RSVPed, included my cell, and played some online poker to brush up on my skills.

The following afternoon at the grocery store my cell rang from a private number. It was Blake, natalia's master. His voice was surprisingly gentle and warm.

"Can you talk?" he asked.

These calls had become so routine, there was no need to interrupt my shopping.

"Sure," I said, switched to my earpiece, and picked up a carton of eggs to check its expiration date. "How are preparations?"

"Surprisingly good."

"And the flake factor?"

"Not bad. But there's still time."

We shared a knowing chuckle. I placed two dozen eggs into my cart and pushed on.

"Natalia's pic had to mitigate a lot of it."

"You like?"

"You're kidding, right?"

"I'll be sure to pass on your compliment."

"Please do."

"So, I take it you read the emails?"

"I did. Very thorough. Always nice to know what to expect."

"Equally nice to talk with someone who actually *reads* emails."

"Least I can do after the amount of work you and natalia must have put in. I hope you haven't gone too crazy trying to line up everything."

Blake laughed. "Close, but not quite. So, will we see you tonight?"

"Can't wait."

"I'll text you the address."

"Can I bring anything? Food? Drink?"

"Just whatever you'd like to drink. See you in a few."

I grabbed a four-pack of Boddingtons on my way to check out.

At home, I had just enough time for the usual cleanup, grabbed some protection, and set out over the hill. Blake, or someone I presumed was Blake, answered the door. He looked more surfer than Dom, which probably meant he was a damn good one. (Dom, that is. I had no clue as to his surfing acumen.) He showed me in and I immediately spotted natalia at the poker table. Naked. Her now-curled hair was pinned high on her head, which drew my eyes to the choker around her neck. She casually counted out poker chips under the stares of two guests trying to play as though a naked dealer was a regular Saturday night thing for them.

"Pet, we have another guest." Blake's tone was soft and subtle, but precise. Another sign of what I was certain was a talented Dom.

"Yes, Daddy." Natalia approached and embraced me. Her body was warm and soft, even through my clothes. "Thanks so much for coming!" she tittered with excitement.

"Thanks for including me."

"You were in her top three, buddy," Blake informed me under his breath.

"Wow. I'm flattered."

Natalia relieved me of my beer. "Would you care for one now, sir?"

"I would, yes."

She disappeared into the kitchen and I glanced around the one-bedroom apartment, which was nothing out of the ordinary. Couch, TV, CDs, a few pieces of wall art.

"Come meet Mick and Sam," Blake suggested as he led me to the poker table.

Sam didn't say a word as I shook his hand. He was schlumpy, doughy, a wallflower at best. The type of guy who'd wear a T-shirt, boxers, and socks during a gang bang. And exactly the type of guy who I needed to keep an eye on. Guys like this are always the dark horses. In the Lifestyle, they almost always attract quality women. Whether because they carry a mysterious quality or because the silent type is a favorite in the community, I haven't a clue. All I knew was, I'd be wise to keep Sam on my radar.

"Sexy as hell, isn't she?" interrupted Mick before I'd released Sam's hand. "I wouldn't kick her out of bed for eating crackers."

Mick was whatever the opposite of a dark horse is. His lame attempt at humor was a poor cover for the abject horror he was suffering internally. It was obvious he didn't possess swinger DNA; his downfall was he didn't know it. Whereas I was wary of Sam, I was gunning for Mick. I just couldn't stomach the prospect of natalia having sex with him. True, they had invited him, but I'd wager he was much different, much more sedate over email and phone. It was only when tonight became reality that his true, irritating personality revealed itself. Should Mick win the tournament, all of natalia and Blake's efforts would be for naught. The least I could do was try to make it pleasant for them.

"Yeah," I said to Mick as I ratcheted up the intensity of my grip as a not-so-subtle message. "She is."

Natalia handed me a frosted mug just as there was a knock at the door. She answered it to find some guy of barely legal age, frozen at the sight of her nudity.

"Darren?" asked natalia, who received no response from the traumatized soul.

Sensing his terror, natalia didn't dare hug him, but rather extended a cordial hand. Limply, Darren took it, which gave natalia the opportunity to gently guide him inside.

Like Mick, Darren didn't belong here. But unlike Mick, he was fully aware of it. Tonight was to be more of a personal journey for him than a sexual one. I could have laid out in excruciating detail every reason he should have packed it in and called it a night, but doing so wouldn't have done him one bit of good. Everyone has to come to the realization themselves. Should I have convinced him to about-face, the second he got home he'd have questioned his decision to leave. He'd have concluded he'd made a terrible mistake, jumped back online, and searched for another invite to another party until he secured one. He'd have attended and ended up in the exact spot: standing in front of a naked woman he'd just met asking himself how he came to stand in front of a naked woman he'd just met. Had I convinced Darren to head home I'd only have succeeded in delaying his epiphany. Instead, a sort of paternal instinct kicked in for me and I decided to keep an eye out for him.

"Want a beer?" I asked Darren louder than normal to snap him out of his trance.

"What?"

"Beer? Want one?"

My offer to Darren triggered a memory of my first group experience, at Theo and Arianna's. The memory wasn't of Gina blindfolded and restrained to the bed, nor Theo's leather, studded cock ring. Not even the perfect fit of Arianna's powder blue lingerie. It was of the unac-knowledged coolness that Craig extended to me that night, the way he looked out for me without letting me know he was looking out for me. Just as I'd done with Darren, Craig had calmly, nonchalantly offered me a beer, knowing how in need of it I was. He didn't even so much as hint that he sensed the Thunderdome of emotions that all but paralyzed me. But looking back on it, I knew there was absolutely no way he couldn't have. Key to my experience that night was that Craig hadn't called me out on my newbie status, or even insinuated that he knew. And, thank god, he hadn't. For if he had, I would surely have bailed. Craig couldn't have possibly known how far I'd travel down this path, but he did know enough to remain silent because he knew I had to determine on my own whether this life was for me. I made a mental note that if I ever crossed paths again with Craig, I'd thank him.

"Yes, please." Darren gratefully accepted my offer of a beer and I watched a visible sense of relief wash over him.

"He can have one of mine," I told natalia.

She disappeared into the kitchen as Blake's phone chimed. He read its screen, announced, "That's Ralph. He's parking," then re-pocketed his cell. "Gary called earlier to say he was waiting on a jump for his car. We can start without him."

"Who's number seven?" asked Darren.

"A flake."

"Better odds for us," chuckled Mick, again to no response.

Saving him from the grotesque silence, the door opened and in tottered a mid-sixties, rotund, bald grandfather of a man who glanced around the room of men, confused.

"Is this . . . ?" he stuttered. "Am I . . . ?"

Natalia emerged from the kitchen with Darren's beer and, upon seeing Grandpa, exclaimed, "Ralph!" She rushed to him and threw her arms around his girth (as much as she could), which clued me in to the fact that Ralph was her top pick. Gary must have been number two, as there was no way Darren, Mick, or Sam had placed higher than me.

"Shall we shuffle up and deal?" asked Blake.

We took our seats. Natalia sat on Blake's lap as she distributed the starting chips.

"Everyone read the email, so I'll keep this short," Blake addressed everyone. "The winner of each hand gets natalia. Enjoy her. But no oral or intercourse. That's for the winner." Blake turned to natalia. "Did I forget anything?" She whispered in his ear. "Right. Natalia is wearing her contraceptive ring. So heads up."

Darren's blank stare read that he didn't know from birth control besides the Pill. My paternal instinct didn't cover basic contraceptive devices, so Darren was on his own for that one.

Natalia dealt and before she finished Darren reached for his cards and spilled his beer, my beer, all over the felt. The entire fucking beer sudsed into the fibers, warped the cards, and gummed up the chips. My paternal instincts evaporated, as he was already fucking shit up. I feel confident that Craig would have rescinded his unspoken guardianship of me that night should I have spilled lube all over the bed, ruining the vibe. Though not a swing commandment, fucking up the shit of another swinger should be automatic grounds for dismissal. At least chiseled onto my stone tablets, it should be.

"Sorry! Sorry!" squealed Darren.

"It's okay." Natalia sprang into action with paper towels.

After the cleanup, repeated apologies from Darren, and a fresh deck, the hand was re-dealt. And wouldn't you know it, fucking Darren took it down. But he was too busy stacking chips to accept natalia, so she had to wait to sit on his lap until all his chips were in perfect color-coded order. Jesus, kid, OCD or not, get your priorities straight. Making matters worse, for the entire next hand, Darren didn't once touch or even look at natalia. He showed less interest in her than a shopping mall Santa does in the kid on his knee toting a steaming load in his overalls. So I was eternally grateful when Ralph raised Mick out of the pot and accepted natalia, though his mediocre tit massage was only slightly more entertaining than Darren's indifference.

Luckily, the next hand I found myself heads-up with Mick and raised him into a fold. I welcomed natalia to my knee and wasted no time making out with her as I pinched her nipples, which caused her to squirm and moan. I shot a glance at Blake and saw his amused approval.

Fully occupied, I folded the next hand without even looking at my cards and relinquished natalia to Sam, whose tepid enjoyment of her rated somewhere between Ralph's and Darren's. Not for lack of trying, mind you. He attempted to make out with her as I did, but it was sloppy and uncoordinated and he knew it, so he ended it in a matter of seconds.

It quickly became obvious that I was the most experienced poker player at the table and undoubtedly the most brazen when it came to enjoying natalia. As long as I didn't get stupid or cocky or unlucky with the cards, I couldn't lose.

Half an hour into the game, Gary arrived. Forties, hard body, good-looking—"G'day, all"—and Australian. "Sorry I'm late." He spied natalia and stopped in his tracks. "Well, well, well . . ." Gary looked to Blake. "May I?"

"Be my guest." Then to natalia, "Pet."

Natalia approached Gary, who assessed her tits. Satisfied, he turned her around, bent her over the only empty chair at the table, and put his face between her ass cheeks. Natalia's face spasmed with pleasure. Gary was the real deal. He laid a firm smack on natalia's ass, then rose to his feet, smacked his lips, and addressed the rest of us.

"Apologies, gents. Didn't mean to interrupt."

I was encouraged that Gary would take full advantage of natalia as I'd been doing, but the way he gingerly picked up his cards and blankly stared at them told me he hadn't a clue about poker. I grew concerned that his talents wouldn't get to be exercised on natalia.

We made it a full revolution of the table, with Darren, Sam, and Mick picking up every hand and completely dropping the ball when it came to natalia, so I intervened. I raised without even looking at my cards. Everyone folded and natalia was back with me. I stood and commanded her to lean over my chair. She obeyed and I proceeded to fingerbang her. Everyone else could barely concentrate on their cards with this distraction, so I had to assume dealer responsibilities as well.

"Ralph?"

Natalia moaned.

"Huh? What?"

"You're up. Ten to call."

"Fold."

"Gary?"

"What's it to call?"

"Still ten, Gary."

Natalia sighed long and low.

"Which one's ten?"

"Red."

"How much is blue?"

"Blue's five."

A thin, high-pitched squeal eeked out of natalia.

"Are you enjoying yourself, pet?"

"Yes, Daddy," she stuttered out.

Gary tossed in a blue chip.

"Blue is five, Gary. It's ten to call."

Gary tossed in a red chip.

"A raise has to be at least twice the big blind."

"The big what?"

"Either take back the blue chip to call or raise to twenty."

Gary tossed in another red chip. "Can I do that?"

"Gary raises to twenty-five," I decided for him.

"May I cum, Daddy?"

"Yes, pet. You may."

As natalia came, impressively I might add, I peeked at my cards: 3-7 off-suit. Worst hand in No Limit. I could have raised Gary out of the pot—he'd no doubt fold as he hadn't a clue what was going on—and kept natalia, but I knew she'd be more than appreciated in his custody.

I folded.

"Did you enjoy that, pet?"

"Yes, Daddy. Thank you."

"Don't thank me."

Still bent over the chair, natalia craned her neck to me. "Thank you, sir."

"You're welcome. Off to Gary, now."

Wobbly, natalia ambled to Gary. Satisfied I'd raised the bar to an acceptable height, I took my seat.

The game progressed uneventfully, except when Gary or I won the hand. Darren got knocked out by Mick and on the next hand Ralph met the same fate. Blake thanked Ralph and Darren for coming and escorted them out.

"How's everyone feel about a break?" asked Blake to those of us still in the game.

I got some air while Blake and Gary partook of a smoke.

"Ralph was an amazing find, huh?" Blake commented.

"First on natalia's list?" I asked.

Blake nodded. "Sucks he got knocked out."

"Yeah. Super-nice guy."

"As you and Gary are the only ones taking full advantage of natalia, what do you think about staying after, regardless of who wins?" Gary and I exchanged an excited glance before eagerly accepting. "Good. Natalia will like that."

Blake stubbed out his smoke and gathered everyone to resume the game. First hand back, Gary made a terrible call and got knocked out. A couple hands later, I won and instructed natalia to straddle me.

"I want you to win," she whispered into my ear as I massaged her clit with the tip of my finger.

The gods must have heard natalia's wish, as I was dealt an ace-king off-suit. I raised the pot, inducing Mick to fold, and continued my enjoyment of natalia, which elicited from her a long moan.

"I call," declared Sam, who I couldn't remember having said a single word that entire night.

Flop came king-two-ten. As further proof the gods were listening to natalia's wish that I be crowned victor, I now had top pair, top kicker. I could feel worry radiating from Sam and it ignited in me a sense of mounting excitement, as I knew with Sam knocked out it would only be a matter of hands before I'd take down Mick and win natalia. I hadn't a doubt I could milk some serious chips out of Sam, but I didn't want to be stupid, so I went all in to end the hand. Sam checked his cards before responding to my monster over-bet with, "I call."

Shit. Before he flipped over his cards, I said, "King ten?" Sam looked at me as if I was an honest to God psychic, then turned over what I'd predicted. Behind in the hand, my only hope was an ace. It didn't materialize and I was out.

Natalia looked at me with disappointment. "Really?" she asked.

"That's poker," I said. I relinquished natalia to Sam and joined Gary on the couch. He told me about a new slave he'd met online. I'd never been into the whole BDSM scene, so I didn't have many stories with which to reciprocate. But we got along nicely enough.

Pretty soon Mick and Sam were all in and Sam won. Like I said, the dark horse.

"She's yours, good sir," Blake pronounced to Sam, who followed natalia to the bedroom.

No sooner did the door close than Blake escorted Mick out, then turned to me and Gary. "In the interim . . ." He pulled a photo album from beneath the coffee table and sat between us on the couch. "Care to see natalia's Valentine's Day gift to me?"

We didn't have to respond; Blake knew our answer. He opened the bound album of professional photographs of natalia. She was naked in some, sporting bondage gear in others.

"Fuckin' hell, mate," exclaimed Gary, ocularly climaxing over the glossies.

"You two enjoy while I check in."

As Blake slipped into the bedroom, the rhythmic squeaking of a bed and natalia's moaning escaped.

Perusing natalia's portfolio, Gary and I knew we'd struck gold. The odds of finding a woman online of natalia's caliber were astronomical. In Blake's absence, we wisely opted to bask silently in our unbelievably good fortune.

"Well, he's definitely enjoying himself," Blake updated us on Sam upon his return.

After another twenty-five minutes, natalia joined us in the living room. Sweaty, a little out of breath, and seemingly embarrassed, she massaged her jaw.

"How was it?" asked Gary.

"He couldn't stay hard," she sighed.

"Bullshit!" exclaimed Gary in sudden rage at the suggestion that any man could be anything but fully erect in natalia's presence.

Natalia shrugged, not knowing what to say.

Gary held aloft Blake's Valentine's Day gift. "These here, these got me rock hard. Both of us, they did." He indicated me. "And we was looking at them with each other. Now I don't know about him, but I'm only into the ladies. No offense."

"None taken," I assured Gary.

"So, what does that tell you that two new mates flipping through a book of photos of you react like that?"

He was far from eloquent, even grammatically correct, but we understood his point.

"So, you liked them?" Natalia cracked a hopeful smile.

Gary grabbed natalia's hand and placed it on the pulsating bulge in his jeans. "What do you think?"

"Awww." She blushed. "That's so sweet."

Sam emerged from the back and Blake shoved his remaining beers into his arms and showed him out. Blake locked the door the second Sam crossed the threshold, then turned and addressed the three of us.

"You're not done yet, pet."

"I'm not?"

Blake looked to me. "Care to supervise natalia's cleaning?"

"It would be my honor, good sir."

I followed natalia to the shower. She got as far as a quick, soapy lather before I joined. I instructed her to suck my cock, but in under a minute she was massaging her jaw again.

"Sorry," she said. "TMJ."[1]

I had her stop as I didn't want her too sore to tend to Gary and Blake. We rinsed, dried off, and rejoined Blake and Gary.

"Gentlemen. The bedroom?" suggested Blake.

The room was minimally furnished, with only a dresser and a full-

---

[1] *Temporomandibular joint disorder*—Umbrella term covering acute or chronic pain, especially in the muscles of mastication and/or inflammation of the temporomandibular joint, which connects the mandible to the skull. Sorry to disappoint; it has nothing to do with sex.

size bed. As I'd had the honor of showering with natalia, I had no problem taking a backseat to Gary, but before long everyone was enjoying themselves. Unfortunately, playtime ended before we'd have liked, as we ran out of condoms. We said our goodbyes and promised to stay in touch.

A Day in the Lives

For five years I had lived, breathed, and consumed nothing but the Lifestyle. My morning-and-night ritual of email barrages and member searches had garnered me steady participation in the community. My roster of reliable play partners had grown impressively and was regularly spiced up with new playmates. I was more than content with the level of sexual ability I had achieved, and the days when I was convinced avoiding sex was the only way to protect my self-esteem had become a distant, laughable memory.

Most impressive to me was how I had unconsciously and seamlessly woven this "other life" into my normal one. This isn't to say I informed every friend and family member of my sexual revolution and flaunted my experiences to all who'd listen. Far from it. But I had become skilled at balancing the two. This merging of worlds was epitomized by the day after my threesome with Wayne and Gwen, an event that itself went until three in the morning.

My day began (or rather continued from the prior night) with me hitting snooze a few too many times. Not until eight forty-five did I finally accept my sleep-deprived state and surrender to daylight.

I grabbed my phone and checked my Vanilla email. Just a handful of spam that had snuck in under the radar, scattered among the smattering of newsletters to which I'd grown disinterested but was too lazy to unsubscribe from.

Then my Lifestyle account. I'd accrued four thousand–plus legit messages (not including my online accounts) and hoarded these emails for the lean times. The times when I didn't have four or five playdates on the books. When my regular play partners were occupied with Vanilla engagements or had decided to take a break from things. When these times came, and come they did, my electronic Rolodex was always there in reserve.

On a good day, I'd get five legitimate messages. That morning: three. The first was from Raymond, the leader of a GB group of which I was a member and occasional participant.

SUBJECT: Get Lucky with Saint Abby

With Saint Abigail's Day fast approaching, what better way to get lucky than with a sexy lass! Well, thank your four leaf clover because our favorite slut, Saint Abby, patron saint of orgasm, wants to celebrate with you. She has promised to kiss the blarney stone of all who attend. For those unacquainted with the unparalleled talents of Saint Abby, attached is a lovely pic.

Redheaded Abby was captured mid-BJ, her face obscured by a discretionary camera angle. But her more-than-ample cleavage was front and center.

Raymond's group had always been plagued with flakes. The last two events were rescheduled due to under-attendance. If we didn't rally at least seven for Abby, we'd have to postpone yet another one. I did my part and confirmed.

The next email was from CplLuv4More, a newbie couple with two young kids who sought a respectful SM to play with the wife while hubby watched. MFM was possible but would be a game-time decision. Family issues had forced them to cancel our prior scheduled meets, which I understood. And it was this understanding that kept me in play contention. They asked about next weekend. I responded that I'd love to meet up. We'd see what happened.

The last was from SnglFem, a strawberry blond, golden, rainbow unicorn with whom I'd been enjoying heated chat. Her email said simply, "Enjoy!" which I assumed referred to the three attached JPEGs.

I opened the first. Perky-breasted SnglFem stood against a nondescript wall in a pair of camouflage panties and black high heels. Her playful look of seduction was not a bad way to start my morning.

Pic #2 was set in a hotel room (I'd seen enough to know). She wore a naughty police uniform of Daisy Dukes, midriff shirt, cop cap, and black thigh-highs. She faced away from the camera but looked over her shoulder into the lens with the same look of carnality from the first pic.

The last one was located in a partially renovated room with exposed wall studs, plastic sheeting, and half-finished wiring. SnglFem repeated the cop pose but had reverted to the camo panties and added a tool belt. Perhaps women contractors were a fetish, just not one of mine. But I wasn't complaining.

I pulled up the first pic again, rubbed out a quick one, and started my day.

While the shower heated up, I trimmed my pubes in prep for Friday's meeting with LatinaSF. Neither one of us enjoyed the natural look, so I did my part. I grabbed the shaving cream, a fresh razor for my balls, and stepped into the shower.

Thirty minutes later I was at the office weeding through P&Ls and balance sheets when Lisa texted: The wait is killing me . . .

Lisa and Nick were vacationing in Vegas in two months and had extended an invitation. Petite, mid-fifties, tan, bleach-blond suburban Jerseyite Lisa had admitted she was desperate for DP. Nick supposedly just watched, but Lisa claimed she could coax him into playing. Especially since she delighted in the attention of two men at once. I was considering joining for a day or two, as life had grown exceptionally boring, but I hadn't yet committed.

> I texted: Tom Petty was right . . . The waiting is the hardest part . . .
>
> She texted: OMG yes!!!
>
> I texted: ;-)

Needing further distraction from my financial slogfest, I signed on to Yahoo! Instant Messenger. I'd long ago oriented my desk so I could see anyone approach my office and have time to sign out before a dirty chat session was discovered. Even if someone slipped past, my monitor faced away from the door. When I left my desk, I always, *always* locked my computer.

One time, I left for lunch when my colleague called needing a file saved on my hard drive. He needed the document right then, so I had no choice but to give him my password. I couldn't remember if I'd signed off chat, but I clearly recalled the last message I received: *promise 2 fuck my ass 2nite.* If my colleague saw that, I wouldn't bother returning to the office; I'd just fax in my letter of resignation.

After what seemed like forever, he said, "Got it! Thanks," and hung up. When I got back to the office I changed my password.

SINGLFEM is online.

REGGUY4FUN: hey u

SNGLFEM: hiya ;-) how's ur morning?

REGGUY4FUN: very relaxing thx 2 u

SNGLFEM: really?

REGGUY4FUN: mm hm

SNGLFEM: glad I could help ;-)

REGGUY4FUN: me 2. u r quite photogenic . . .

SNGLFEM: moi?

REGGUY4FUN: vous

SNGLFEM: por que?

REGGUY4FUN: construc and law enf not usual turn-ons, but u made it so

SNGLFEM: i respect many professions ;-) u should 2

REGGUY4FUN: open to xposure . . . ;-)

SNGLFEM: lol . . . i'll see what I can do

REGGUY4FUN: how's ur day?

SNGLFEM: not as relaxing as urs

REGGUY4FUN: sorry

Daniel Stern

SNGLFEM: no pix this AM :(was hoping . . .

REGGUY4FUN: long day yesterday. will make up for it. promise . . .

SNGLFEM: hope so.

SNGLFEM: morning dragging

REGGUY4FUN: want help?

SNGLFEM: intriguing . . .

REGGUY4FUN: alone?

SNGLFEM: sorta

REGGUY4FUN: alone enough?

SNGLFEM: can b discreet

REGGUY4FUN: take off panties

SNGLFEM: don't waste time, do u?

REGGUY4FUN: stalling?

SNGLFEM: hells no!

SNGLFEM: brb

REGGUY4FUN: nope

SNGLFEM: ?

REGGUY4FUN: at ur desk

SNGLFEM: cubicle??

REGGUY4FUN: yup

Ten seconds.

> REGGUY4FUN: stalling?
>
> SNGLFEM: hold

Twenty seconds.

> SNGLFEM: takes longer with coworkers nearby
>
> SNGLFEM: now what?

Colleague entered my office. So much for my strategically positioned desk.

> COLLEAGUE: "I hear there are vacancy issues at the downtown properties."
>
> ME: "I wouldn't say 'issues.'"
>
> COLLEAGUE: "What would you say?"
>
> REGGUY4FUN: put 2 fingers in your pussy
>
> ME: "I'd say six point seven."
>
> SNGLFEM: yes sir
>
> REGGUY4FUN: good slut
>
> COLLEAGUE: "Why the increase?"
>
> ME: "Management says the school district laid off six hundred teachers."
>
> SNGLFEM: now what?

REGGUY4FUN: taste

COLLEAGUE: "Do they think we will have to increase concessions?"

ME: "I'm due a rental survey. But I would assume so."

My phone chimed with a schedule reminder: Raquelle GB Burbank noon.

I'd forgotten Kevin[1] had arranged a lunchtime GB with a supposed 5' 10", recently dumped, ex–track runner. "Supposed" because Raquelle was a newbie and, like all newbies, cautious about sending a pic. Kevin had organized this one on faith, which was almost always the kiss of death. Normally, I avoided newbie parties like gonorrhea. But I was overworked and insanely bored, and although my chat with SnglFem was entertaining, something in the flesh was preferable.

ME: "Lunch with the insurance brokers."

COLLEAGUE: "Everything okay?"

ME: "Prepping for renewal."

COLLEAGUE: "No worries. I've got things here."

ME: "Much appreciated."

Exit colleague.

---

1   Kevin more than deserves a shout-out. Everyone knows single males comprise the biggest segment of flakes in the Lifestyle, despite it going against all logic. However, even in the face of this ludicrous reality, Kevin has successfully and impressively run a steadily active group for years. He has maintained a rotating roster of members, posted his group's availability for women seeking the services only a group of men can provide, and located an inordinate number of females who have taken him up on his offer. What Kevin has pulled off over the years truly is an amazing feat. May all you men be so lucky as to find your very own Kevin.

SNGLFEM: tangy :)

REGGUY4FUN: mmmmm

SNGLFEM: next?

REGGUY4FUN: lunch meeting in valley

SNGLFEM: :(such a tease

REGGUY4FUN: i'll check in after

SNGLFEM: promise?

REGGUY4FUN: :)

SNGLFEM: :)

I grabbed my keys and a pad of paper (had to make this "meeting" look legit), made sure I signed out of chat and locked my computer, and headed out.

The 405 was a parking lot, so I detoured to Benedict Canyon to Mulholland to Laurel, grabbed a three-pack of Trojans at a gas station, then weaved surface streets to the motel with fifteen minutes to spare.

A scrap of paper in the rear window of Kevin's Civic had "245" written on it. I parked, found a random envelope in the glove box for my $20 donation, grabbed my newly purchased protection, and headed to room 245 to find Kevin and three guys standing around awkwardly with that hallmark, uncomfortable feeling of rabid horniness in a room of just men. Not the most refined host, Kevin had provided as refreshments a pair of two-liter bottles of generic soda and a bag of mini Snickers. I dropped my envelope on the dresser next to the refreshments and turned to Kevin.

"Any word?"

"No news is good news, right?"

"Have you seen her?"

"Spoke on the phone. Seems legit."

Coming from anyone else, I'd have given this party five minutes. But Kevin's fake/flake radar was second to none. So I forced myself to be uncharacteristically optimistic.

A few more guests increased our attendance to six. We continued to wait, keeping our horny gazes averted.

Conversation at these things is always the same. Some guy has a fresh lead on a couple open to a single male. Another paid an insanely high donation to attend a party where he thinks he'll get play if he goes back. Most, though, stand idly, waiting, hoping, tolerating the discomfort the best they can.

Kevin got a text, the chime of which made everyone perk up.

"Says she's two miles out."

A text declaring imminent arrival tends to be the precursor to a last-second flake. The hesitant guest of honor has no real intention of showing but wants to delay the inevitable as long as possible in order to save face. Newbies, please know that we'd much rather get a straightforward "Too scared to go through with it" than wait in vain. It's not like any of our worlds are going to end because a lunchtime GB went bust. But it's hugely irksome waiting, especially with the tiniest glimmer of hope.

"Give her another ten?" suggested Kevin to the group.

Nods all around.

Unbelievably, seven minutes later, there was a knock on the door. We held our collective breath as Kevin peeled back the door to reveal a tall, lean, sexy black woman with shoulder-length curls. Mid-twenties, she wore heels, so she easily topped six feet and dwarfed just about everyone.

"Raquelle?" asked Kevin. As if the odds were so great that another woman matching Raquelle's exact description would happen to knock on the door to our motel room at the exact time we were expecting a Raquelle.

She smiled in response, revealing a mouthful of braces.

"Come on in."

Raquelle entered and began unpacking her gym bag, setting its contents on the nightstand. Three bottles of lube, a couple boxes of condoms, a stack of folded hand towels . . . This may have been her first time, but the lady had done her homework.

"Do they know the rules?" she asked Kevin.

"Gentlemen," Kevin formally addressed the room, "we have gathered here this afternoon to help Raquelle realize a longtime fantasy she has described to me as 'porno-style sex.'"

. . . vibrator, dildo, silver bullet . . . The woman had taste.

"She requests as many hands on her at once as possible. Bareback oral. Condoms for penetration. And she'd very much like to try DP. Am I right so far, Raquelle?"

Raquelle nodded as she unloaded a toothbrush and toothpaste . . .

"Feel free to cum on her stomach or tits. Just not her face."

. . . still camera . . . video camera. Seriously?

"Pics are okay. But no faces. Did I cover everything?" Raquelle held up a hand to Kevin, wiggling her fingers. "Oh, right. Everyone needs to wash their hands before we start. Any questions?"

Not wanting to delay the main event a second longer, everyone crammed into the bathroom to wash up. Guys muttered to one another. "Can you believe it?" "Fucking gorgeous!" "Holy shit, did Kevin score with this one or what!"

Having developed patience over the years, I had no problem hanging back and sanitizing last. I returned as Kevin was untying Raquelle's wrap from her neck to reveal a pair of tiny breasts with abnormally large nipples. Then her shorts. Then her panties. She was freshly waxed.

I'd been so focused on Raquelle, I hadn't noticed most of the guys were naked and primed for play. Raquelle wasted no time. As I observed the action, the full effect of last night's epic threesome hit me. I'd gotten a front-row seat to a beautiful, athletic woman being enjoyed by a fleet of more-than-capable men, and I was a dead fish down below. I'd been relegated to voyeur status until the visuals hopefully kick-started me.

Men were on Raquelle. In her. Around her. Whatever she wanted or needed was within arm's reach.

"Raquelle," Kevin interrupted the action. "Would you like to try DP?"

Raquelle paused to inspect everyone's size and girth and selected a slimmer, longer cock for her ass and a larger one for her pussy. Slimmer Cock laid on the bed and Raquelle mounted him reverse cowgirl. Once she balanced herself, Larger Cock entered her from the front. As a cherry to the Raquelle sundae, Kevin stood on the bed and slipped into Raquelle's mouth.

"Would you like this on video, Raquelle?" asked Kevin.

Mouth full, Raquelle nodded.

One of the sidelined guys grabbed Raquelle's video camera and struggled to figure it out. Another equally ineffective nonparticipant stepped in to help. I laughed to myself, watching two naked men with condomed hard-ons fail to operate a video camera. Dumbly pushing buttons and flipping switches, they looked like a pair of chimpanzees that had discovered a shiny can of corn. Intrigued, but clueless.

"Stop! I can do it," Tweedledum barked at Tweedledee, who then chastised Tweedledum with an "Obviously you can't. Give it here." Before a fight broke out between the primates, Raquelle snapped her fingers and motioned for the camera. Still airtight and with only one hand, she clicked a switch, pushed a button, and handed the camera back to one of the Tweedles, who proceeded to track around the action, zooming at opportune moments, careful not to intrude on or affect Raquelle's experience.

I thought to myself, This must be how nature photographers capture wildlife in their natural habitat. I imagined a David Attenborough narration playing over the scene, "Observe closely the newbie female in her natural habitat. While clearly outnumbered by the pack of men, the female remains in control and conducts the carnal orchestra to her bidding."

Luckily, all the action had caused me to react. I disrobed, grabbed a condom, and replaced Larger Cock, who appeared to be losing steam. A few minutes in, I started to deflate. I was certain there would not be another chance for me today, so I quickly finished and dismounted.

I did a quick cleanup and returned to voyeur status. After fifteen minutes, I figured I was just deadweight, so I said some quick goodbyes and slipped out.

I reversed course and made it back to the office by three o'clock.

> COLLEAGUE: "How'd it go?"
>
> ME: "A little disappointing, but I'll get over it. Anything exciting here?"
>
> COLLEAGUE: "As expected."

I signed back on to YIM and a few messages from SnglFem popped up.

> SNGLFEM: where r u?
>
> SNGLFEM: sooooooo bored . . .
>
> SNGLFEM: want u 2 entertain me :)

As much as I wanted to chat, I was exhausted from my lack of sleep and my midday release. Not to mention, I figured I should probably get a little work done. So I signed off, managed a couple hours of actual work, and left for the day.

I grabbed a sandwich on the way home and ate it while I checked the sites for any women or couples open to single males. There were just a few, one of which I was certain was a spammer. But I emailed her anyway, as I could just flag her should she solicit me for an outside email address or direct me to another website.

It was only seven o'clock, but my body was threatening to shut down if I didn't immediately make up for last night's three-hour nap.

I plugged in my phone to charge and collapsed into bed.

That internal stirring had been steering me here all these years, to this atypical life. I couldn't have known this was where I belonged because, like Darren at Blake and natalia's, I wasn't ready to know. But now I was. And it was good.

When I woke the next morning, I checked my email again.

So That Happened

I had taken to praying to the onanistic gods exactly twice on the day of a meet.[1] Once in the morning; once two to three hours before playtime. Doing so allowed me to leave the house refreshed and relaxed so I would think with my brain, not my "head." On top of that, I had discovered my stamina peaked two to three hours between ejaculations because my libido had settled into a state of functional calm. This practice became religious. But on one impossible-to-forget occasion, I made the mistake of skipping synagogue.

Danielle and I had exchanged a brief email several months prior, but neither of us followed up. I'd occasionally see her online, but she hadn't built upon her single cert in four years of membership, which more than hinted that she wasn't active. That should have been a warning to me, but her profile pic displayed a curvaceous figure with a more-than-ample chest and shoulder-length chestnut hair that framed a sweet

---

1 I didn't know *onanistic* either. My editor suggested it, so I looked it up. Onanism is a synonym for "masturbation." Who knew, right? Way classier and more literary-sounding than jack-off or whack-off. Note to all you self-publishers—editors do play a role.

face. So I reached out and invited her to accompany me to Annie and Andy's party.

I never missed an opportunity to play with Annie. She was stunning. Latina, late thirties, petite, with defined abs. Her boob job may have been one size too big for her frame, but it was ideal for breast lovers. Best of all, Annie was one of the warmest and kindest people I knew. She welcomed everyone, even those she was meeting for the first time, with a tender embrace that couldn't help but put you at ease. Oh, and did I mention she was bisexual?

Andy was a dedicated voyeur. He delighted in watching Annie with other men, evidenced by his perpetual ear-to-ear grin. He was beyond gracious, not only because he encouraged men to indulge with his wife, but also because he called everyone "friend." "How are you, my friend?" "Enjoying yourself, my friend?" "Please, friend, enjoy my wife." Never applying an iota of pressure, Andy insisted everyone relax and partake of the refreshments he supplied at his own expense.

I suggested a meet 'n' greet to Danielle, and if everything clicked, we'd head out for a night of fun.

What I should've done was called it a night the instant Danielle scuttled into the bar in her elaborately designed and constructed excuse for footwear. I should've called it off, left, and never contacted her again. Nothing other than or less than that precise reaction should have occurred. And that is exactly what would have transpired had I not skipped my ablutions.[2]

I have an intense and deep-rooted aversion that borders on psychotic hatred for women who, in the supposed name of fashion, don pseudo footgear that defies all logic and common sense. Put simply, when shoes inhibit one's ability to walk to the point that one's gait re-

---

2 I have no idea if the Jewish faith believes in ablution. My bar mitzvah was forced upon me by my parents, and, other than *shalom*, *mazel tov*, and *Hanukah*, I can't remember a single Hebrew word. So, to the religious sticklers, just go with me on this one.

sembles that of a pterodactyl in need of a double hip replacement, shoes cease being shoes and become medieval torture devices. As I firmly believe one has the inalienable right to slog out a living as long as the environment and humankind are not at imminent risk, my ire does not lie with the architects of these pedal iron maidens, but rather with the consumer.

Don't get me wrong: I fully appreciate and highly value the visuals heels add to the overall carnal experience. However, I elect to forgo the added stimulation when the wearer of said footgear hasn't mastered balance and coordination in them. I still vividly recall the first time I took a kickball to the nuts. One fateful recess in second grade, the red rubber ball line-drove into my groin, turned my legs to Jell-O, and knotted up my diaphragm. If I close my eyes now, I can see the constellation of stars that engulfed my field of vision as I lay prostrate, staring up at the heavens. But that pain decades ago doesn't hold a candle to catching a stiletto in the scrotum. I'm not sure if there's a clinical phobia for fear of testicular agony, but if so, pencil that in to my medical history.

So when Danielle tripped toward me in a pair of overpriced, ridiculous heels that all but prohibited her ability to walk, my instincts screamed, pleaded, and begged me to slip out the back. But my full tank of pagan semen screamed louder.

As she approached, I noticed her profile pic wasn't wholly representational. Fifteen to twenty pounds heavier and a hard-lived ten years older, Danielle bore certain physical traits not accurately depicted in her profile. Namely, sagging jowls and a gravity-affected gut that draped over the front and sides of her jeans that were even tighter than her "shoes." The coup de grace was her aroma when I greeted her with a friendly hug. Holy God almighty! One part cheap perfume, eight parts body odor. In Danielle's defense, profiles aren't scratch 'n' sniff, but Lord have mercy.

My semen chimed in that I was no Brad Pitt, so who was I to judge?

I forged ahead with conversation in the hopes that her stellar personality would cajole me and my battered olfactory sense into forgiving her "truthy" online presentation.

"How was your week?" I asked.

Danielle paused five to six seconds as my question traveled some convoluted route down her ear canal and into her brain, where a belated chemical reaction transpired and somehow alchemized a response. "My week . . . yeah . . . it was . . . my week was . . . was . . . was good."

The only reasonable explanation for Danielle's unnaturally delayed response had to be severe brain trauma. Either that or her auditory system skipped tens of millions of years of Darwinian survival to be inherited directly from dinosaurs. Despite my having been pummeled over the head with multiple bloodred flags about moving forward with that night's plans, once again, my semen intervened and explained that Danielle's response was a totally reasonable, nervous reaction for a first meeting.

The bartender tossed a drink napkin in front of Danielle.

"Can I . . . I would like . . . like a . . . vodka."

"Just vodka?"

"On the . . . rocks."

"No mix?"

"I brought . . . I have . . . my own."

The bartender delivered a tumbler half-full of vodka on ice, which Danielle topped off with her personal stash of diet tonic. She took a hefty gulp, which seemed to produce an instantaneous calming effect.

"Thanks for meeting out here," she said with slightly more fluidity, lending credence to my semen's nerve theory. "I still can't drive."

I assumed she meant her car was in the shop or maybe her brain trauma imposed certain motor vehicular restrictions. Just to be sure, I followed the line of conversation. "Really? Why's that?"

"Oh. Just a DUI." She verbally shrugged off my question, as if I'd inquired about her recovery from a paper cut. "My last one was, like, a whole four years ago. But did the judge consider that? Of course not." Judges can be so persnickety like that. "I still drive to, like, work and the grocery store and stuff. I mean . . . I have to go places . . . you know?" She slugged back the rest of her drink and motioned the bartender for a refill.

Any normal, somewhat intelligent human in my position would have initiated any one of a million different exit strategies by now. But with my full tank of swimmers primed and ready, I still considered Annie and Andy's party a viable option.

"Oooh, are the Lakers playing?" Danielle's eyes had gravitated to a wall-mounted flat screen. "I *love* the Lakers."

I decided it wise to break from our stimulating conversation, but Danielle quickly proved me wrong. Every Laker possession was accompanied by her unrelenting, high-pitched "Come on, Lakers! Come on, Lakers!" Each Laker shot was punctuated with an eardrum-snapping "Hit it!" And every other moment, whether it involved dribbling, passing, even rehydrating during time-outs, had Danielle whooping, clapping, and bellowing. Tables sneered and fiercely muttered expletives under their breaths. I knew I was guilty by association, but there wasn't anything I could really do.[3]

After she drained her second cocktail and ordered a third, Danielle confided in me, "You know, I was thrown out of another bar because they said I cheered too loud."

"You don't say?" I feigned surprise.

During the second quarter, I plied Danielle with a fourth, fifth, and

---

3 I'm as much a sports fan as the next guy, but believe me when I say Danielle's conduct redefined the stereotypical, obnoxious superfan. To her credit, she hadn't smeared on body paint or fashioned some eyesore of a hat in honor of her team that blocked the view of dozens behind her, but she more than made up for that abhorrent accoutrement with her vocal performance. Holy hell, the decibel level she produced was rivaled only by tornado sirens, and her voice's timbre I can only describe as the spine-curdling sound produced by chalk made of sandpaper scratched against a blackboard by the bladed hand of Freddy Kruger. So, yeah, it was a tad hard to ignore.

sixth cocktail with the dying hope that I would unearth some gem of a personality. When halftime arrived, I suggested we leave to make the party on time. I paid the tab and we got in my car. I consulted my directions and realized the hotel was a little farther than I'd estimated. Like, thirty miles farther. I dreaded the prospect of forty miles of conversation with Laker Fan Numero Uno, so I joked, "Feel free to pass out."

I had just merged onto the 101 when Danielle started snoring. Though the alcohol had failed to transform her into a charmer, it had succeeded in wearing her out, a result for which I was grateful beyond words, especially since it lasted the entire forty-five minute trek east.

If you've never frequented a Residence Inn, be warned. It stands to reason that room 322 would be found on the third floor and in close proximity to rooms 321 and 323, right? Well, ye ol' Residence Inn finds such natural order too easy and predictable. Why not make locating your room a fun and memorable experience? Like, say, a scavenger hunt? One is well advised to carve out fifteen to twenty minutes to meander the maze of fourplexes. Expect to wander lost and double back on yourself time and time again, until the mad genius Residence Inn cartographers have broken whatever will you possess and finally grant you mercy by magically producing the suite for you. Oh, and if you have a sleepy, drunk female staggering in tow in the most poorly designed footwear in the history of fashion, tack on another ten minutes.

A decent layer of sweat had formed on my body from this endless sojourn (not to mention assisting Ms. Congeniality to her feet from two stumbles) when, finally, unit 322 appeared like an oasis. Why I hadn't considered 322 would be located next to unit 522, I couldn't tell you.

Annie hugged me and offered Danielle a welcoming hand, which was met with a cold, hesitant, dead fish of a handshake. We were introduced to the rest of the guests, to whom Danielle didn't extend a single ounce of cordiality, instead distancing herself on a bar stool in the far corner.

By this time, an inferno of hatred for Danielle was raging in my bowels. In retrospect, my ire was truly directed at myself, but it wouldn't have existed without the DUI Playmate of the Month. Since I had traveled all this way, I was resolved to enjoy myself. Danielle could do what she wanted for all I cared. I shoved a beer in her hand and went to meet the other guests.

"How are you, my friend? Are you ready to play?"

"Of course, Andy. Are you kidding me?"

"I'm happy to hear it, my friend. Annie is ready, too." Andy stared at me with a look that said, "Get to it!"

I heeded Andy's cue and found Annie. I began massaging her shoulders and kissing her neck and, in a matter of minutes, the two of us were in the master suite with a decent audience observing and growing aroused. I had just enjoyed a round of oral from Annie and was repositioning for some doggy when I heard it. The same sound that had followed me the forty miles here. I unwrapped a condom and tried to turn a deaf ear to the sound, but it was useless. Through the open bedroom door, across the living room, slouched against the wall and barely balancing on the bar stool was my date. Snoring.

"Everything okay, my friend?" Andy tried to preserve the momentum.

"Yeah. Fine." But when I went to put on the condom, all was not fine.

"Is okay to take a break, my friend. Victor would like to play with Annie."

Whether a break was okay or not, it was necessary. I excused myself to the restroom, where I tried to formulate a plan to extricate Danielle from the party. She didn't drive, so I couldn't just kick her out. I didn't know of a nearby bar, so shoving fifty bucks at her and telling her to go enjoy the rest of her diet tonic also wasn't an option. Briefly I entertained calling her a cab, but some quick math revealed that the fare back to the Valley would put me out a month's rent, which wouldn't be the end of the world, but I would despise myself for the two months it would take me to right my financial ship. The only workable solution I came up with was to try like crazy to ignore her, which was going to be one hell of a task.

I exited the bathroom to find Annie exploring one of tonight's female guests and concluded that ignoring Danielle might not be as hard as I thought. I joined the other men ringside, admiring the action and mentally and emotionally transcending to an oh-so-happy place. Within seconds, I was ready to jump back into the ring. But then:

"Is there any more beer?" the sandpaper voice screeched down my spine.

I turned to find Danielle behind me. Other than Andy, she was the only guest still fully dressed.

"Did you check the fridge?"

"Yeah. There wasn't any."

"Well, there's your answer then."

She stood there, terrified, trying to comprehend the seemingly incomprehensible fact that there was no more beer to imbibe. It was as if someone had just told her, "Sorry. We've run out of oxygen."

I had had more than enough.

"Go. Downstairs. Now," I commanded her under my breath. She knew I wasn't fucking around and immediately about-faced. I silently and inconspicuously removed myself, dressed, and located Andy.

"I'm sorry, but we're going to leave."

"Is too bad, my friend. We see you again soon?"

"Absolutely. Please apologize to Annie for me."

"Of course, my friend."

I grabbed Danielle, firmly "assisted" her to my car, where I ordered, not suggested, her to pass out. Whether she slept or not on the return trip I can't be certain, as my ears were deaf with rage. What I do know is not a single word was spoken between us. I pulled up to the bar, the crime scene at which tonight's debacle had begun, and more than nudged her out. I didn't even wait for the passenger door to close before I peeled off.

As penance for that night's royal fuckup, I shunned those onanistic gods for an entire week. That taught me.

Lesson 10:

Playtime

Playtime has arrived! But you're not yet in the clear. There are still plenty of ways for things to go awry. Granted, at this point things look better than good. But you have to clear a few more hurdles.

Location! Location! Location!

Even if you've offered your home, more times than not, first play with a swinger will be at a hotel. Understandably, everyone wants to feel safe, and although you've emailed, chatted, talked on the phone, and met in person, you're still very much strangers. Relinquishing home field advantage, many believe, isn't wise.

Guys, you're benefiting most from this experience, so expect to pay for the room.

The Final Interview

It's unrealistic to think you'll know every single thing about your playmate before playtime. So, in order to create a most enjoyable session of play for all involved, take a moment before the clothes come off to be crystal clear on everyone's dos and don'ts. Hopefully, you've discussed these issues at length during the courting process. If not, now's your last chance.

I realize a pointed inquiry into one's sexual proclivities seconds before play may feel awkward, but consider the alternative. Would you rather interrupt playtime to ask if she'd like you to cum on her stomach or face? Best to know that in advance, wouldn't you agree?

Here's an incomplete list of topics about which you'll want absolute clarity from your partner before play begins:

- Kissing
- Dirty talk
- Turn-ons
- Turn-offs
- Oral
- Spanking
- Hair pulling
- Favorite positions
- Condoms or bareback?
- Condom preference
- Desired new experiences
- Pictures or video allowed to be taken?
- Hard limits

- Anal sex
- Any specific fetishes

Again, this list is not by any means complete. Anything critically important to someone should be brought to everyone's attention.

A (Single) Man of Your Word

A recurring story I hear from women and couples involves men who were told dos and don'ts, yet still tried to impose their desires. If a woman is anti-anal, don't try to talk her into it in the heat of the moment. If a couple states that safe sex is mandatory, don't attempt to sneak in unprotected. Respect everyone's boundaries at all times, guys. No exceptions!

Cold Feet

It's understandably aggravating when, after spending months getting to know a couple, driving dozens of miles to a motel, and paying for the room, you're told they don't feel chemistry. But it happens.

Cold feet are an inconvenient and frustrating Lifestyle reality. Disappointment and annoyance at failed play is a normal human reaction, but Hulking out will do more harm than you realize. Remember, the Lifestyle is a ridiculously small and gossipy community. Annoy one couple and ten others hear about it. Lie to a single female and every one of her swinging friends will block your profile before your next log-in.

Compassion, on the other hand, creates a beneficial ripple effect. The sensitivity and understanding you display in the face of rejection will serve your cause. Lifestylers you never met will marvel about the kindhearted swinger about whom their friends raved. Single females will fight for your attention. Couples will seek you out. Single males will flock . . . Actually, it doesn't matter when it comes to single guys. They'll take what they can get. But impress everyone else with a reputation as a patient, understanding, and sensitive swinger and your profile views will skyrocket. You have no idea.

Another reason not to lose your cool is that just because you're denied play now doesn't mean you won't play later. Many planned meetings canceled on me at the eleventh hour were resumed at a later date.

The Certification

Athletes are taught to follow through with their motions; hitting a baseball, swinging a golf club, kicking a soccer ball. So it goes with playtime.

Treat after-play like you would the follow-up to a party. I'm not suggesting formal thank-you notes on personalized stationery, but expressing a little gratitude in a Lifestyle-appropriate manner goes a long way. The most suitable sign of appreciation in the Lifestyle is the cert, the swinger's version of the thank-you note. It expresses gratitude and, additionally, helps the recipient further his or her or their Lifestyle experience.

As I've said, another's testimony carries more weight than self-description. Certs also paint a more dynamic picture of one's personality and abilities. Submitting certs for others is just as important as receiving them. In addition to being courteous, they offer members the chance to enhance their profile.

And certs are often the gift that gives back. More times than not, certifying someone will inspire one in return. And if your gesture doesn't spur them to reciprocate, perhaps playtime wasn't as stellar as you thought and it's probably best to move on.

• • •

Getting through the gates of Swingland is great, but staying inside the fortress and remaining active is another challenge altogether. Doing so involves perpetuating the behavior that secured your first playdate, so you can impress others and expand your circle of swinging friends as far and wide as your libido desires.

Lesson 11:

Party Primer

Should you take the Lifestyle leap, you'll probably find yourself at a party at some point. Newbies reason, rightly or wrongly, that it's easier to secure play in a group setting. Many long-term swingers develop a taste for variety, and house or hotel parties are easy opportunities to satiate that desire. In addition, they are perfect settings in which to expand your circle of Lifestyle friends. So while the party setting might intimidate the newbie, after some time in the community, you'll find parties are great.

If you haven't gathered, though I've yet to host one, I've attended my fair share of house and hotel parties. I'm not averse to hosting; I just don't derive enjoyment from party planning. Too much responsibility for my taste. I contend that an affinity to host is coded in one's DNA or, in my case, genetically absent. That being said, I'm an ideal guest. I can be counted on to arrive promptly (if not a little early), contribute to the edible offerings (I award those whose efforts allow me to enjoy myself), and clean up after myself (and others, if need be).

Now, as this book has the potential to unleash droves of newbies onto the party scene, I feel a sense of responsibility to prepare the reader to properly attend.[1]

How to Be a Lifestyle Party Guest

Numbers-wise, there are far more guests than parties. Which is a very, very good thing. If the reverse were the case, parties would suck. Not much play to be had at a party of one, is there? Well, there is, just not with someone else. General Vanilla etiquette applies: Be polite, be kind, and respect the location. However, since sex is the reason everyone has gathered, there's additional protocol to observe.

Your goal. When attending a party, have the goal not just of enjoying yourself, but also of being invited back. This mind-set will inform your behavior and, hopefully, make an impression on the hosts and guests. I'm not suggesting you tie on an apron and wait hand and foot on everyone. However, if something other than the party itself isn't your endgame, your behavior will be infused with a positivity that will affect everything else.

Arrive on time. There's no such thing as "fashionably late" at a Lifestyle party. Latecomers delay playtime for everyone and, more times than not, interrupt the action in progress. Every swinger will tell you that nothing is more annoying than a tardy guest. When one shows after the stated arrival time, a guest enjoying himself has to stop what he's doing to open the door and admit the latecomer. And the latecomer not only puts out the guest who answers the door, he distracts everyone

---

1   NOTE: The contents of this lesson do not apply to Lifestyle clubs, as they are an entirely different beast. As noted in Lesson 9, due to the volume of guests they cater to, clubs make it a habit to be explicit with rules and manage expectations, either via website or over the phone. On the other hand, house and hotel parties exist in more of a gray area, as they offer a more intimate setting and aren't always held with regularity or even at the same location. So be sure to separate parties and clubs in your head.

else by forcing them to pause their fun to ensure the latecomer is a welcome guest. Not to mention, at a hotel party everything hits the skids for fear the knock is management having a look-see.

Don't come empty-handed. Someone has spent time and effort (and often their own money) executing a party at which you are, essentially, being spoon-fed sex. Bring something other than your libido to express your gratitude. I'm not talking Fabergé eggs. A bottle of decent wine. An appetizer. Often, I contribute a fruit plate. A single male who puts in the time to assemble a fruit platter makes women wonder with what else he takes his time. Also, a round of good, adult fun depletes energy. Dose up on refined sugar and you peak fast and crash harder, which prematurely ends playtime. Fruit is sweet but doesn't have the crash-and-burn effect of refined sugar. More important, though, it keeps the party going.

Bring condoms. Obviously this applies to the men, but perhaps not so obviously also to women and couples. Odds are you will be asked to contribute a "donation," but this isn't an all-inclusive deal you're buying into. Most times, house and hotel parties are BYOC. And even if they aren't, do you want to chance the integrity of condoms supplied by someone else?

Now, guys, one of you idiots never fails to "forget" to bring condoms. How a guy attending a sex party manages to "forget" condoms is unfathomable to me. So much so that I can surmise only three possible explanations for doing so: a thinly veiled ploy to have unprotected sex, a lame attempt to save money, or irrefutable proof of your moronic IQ. Whatever your reason(s), fellas, don't be this guy. Grow up, grab a box of rubbers, and don't make a scene.

Next, despite my vehement admonition, this situation will still arise (and with startling frequency). Imagine a party in full swing, everyone enjoying themselves, when Special Agent Johnny Utah asks the group at large, "Can I borrow a condom from somebody?" Before I speak to the proper response to such a moment, let me first have a word with Keanu the Über-Ignoramus. Let's get something straight here, Neo. First off, you're an idiot for not bringing your own supplies. Second, you're not "borrowing" a condom, as you best not be intending to return it. You're asking to be "given" or "supplied" a condom. Own up to your situation and be done with it.

Now, when Ted "Theodore" Logan here sounds his prophylactic SOS, the group reaction will be one of extreme annoyance. Everyone will marvel at how this chromosome-lacking homunculus has made it this far in life without killing himself. Within milliseconds of Bobo the Wonder Chimp's mayday call, a chorus of irritated grunts, put-out sighs, and heated exclamations of "Are you serious?" will reverberate off the walls. Unfortunately, though everyone other than Thomas Anderson is gnashing their molars to the gumline, the situation isn't going to resolve itself.

For the quickest response, I look to the single men. Guys, this situation is actually an opportunity. As much as you may want to yank aside Idiot Boy and lay into him about the valuable party etiquette you learned from some helpful, informative, and entertaining text, don't. You'll cause more of a scene than he already has. Rather, defend with a swift offense: Pack extra condoms. Before the group gets too bent out of shape and the sexy vibe is irretrievably lost, toss a rubber at Mentally Deficient and be done with it. Simple as that. You may not realize it, but that simple act just single-handedly saved the party. It averted worsening an already uncomfortable situation and allowed everyone to get back to the fun. Sure, you're out a buck and down a condom, but what could have mushroom-clouded into a party-stopping, potentially party-ending, dilemma, you quashed to barely a blip on the radar. Way to go, you! And the best part is, I guarantee you some female partygoer took note of your preparation, problem-solving ability, and call to action and mentally filed it away so she can later express her gratitude. Whether she hits you up anon or invites you to another party, you've earned yourself a cache of priceless brownie points. Of course, women and couples can do this as well, but I was throwing the guys a bone.

Bring a towel. Good hosts stock a hefty supply, but not always. And, mark my words, at hotel parties you'll find that even before play-time has commenced, the room-supplied stock will be soaked through and have morphed into a petri dish of everyone's personal nastiness. Bring a towel and avoid an off-putting unhygienic experience. Plus, doing so will lessen the host's load and put you in her good graces.

Shower beforehand. Show up in need of a hosing-off and you've landed yourself on everybody's no-play list. In addition to limiting play opportunities, there's no guarantee you can shower at the location. Perhaps there isn't a shower, just a tub. Also, if there's only one bathroom (as at most hotel parties), you're prohibiting others (mostly women) from relieving themselves. Talk about getting on someone's bad side. Finally, occupying the bathroom delays playtime for anyone who wants to freshen up before the festivities begin. Come clean and smelling fresh. That is all.

Bring ONLY what you need. Few things are more suspicious than a guest wheeling in a set of luggage to a sex party. Questions abound as to the baggage's contents. Also, suspicion added to the already awkward situation that is a sex party infuses a hefty dose of fear into the already fragile vibe. Guests wonder, how kinky this guy who towed in his Louis Vuitton collection is. Finally, logistically speaking, space is at a premium at a hotel party. Unless your life depends on a transportable dialysis machine, a modest-size gym bag is more than sufficient for your purposes.

Clean up after yourself. Use a condom? Throw it (and the wrapper) out. Borrow someone's lube? Recap it and return it to its proper owner. Have a few drinks or eats? Make sure the bottles, cans, plates, wrappers, and napkins make it to the trash can. One of the surest ways never to get invited back is to treat the location as your own personal dump.

A special word to the special ladies. Perhaps this flirts with being too graphic, but I feel a need to speak with the female ejaculators. First off, you're awesome. Really and truly, you are. I realize some of you are self-conscious about your unique ability. However, please know that I can't fully express the intense joy I experience when I assist one of you to climax in your own special way. It is really a warm, fuzzy feeling.

Having said that, guests appreciate a little forethought. Not everyone is aware of your talent, and, often, it's discovered too late. Though I and many others enjoy the squirter experience (warning: here comes the graphic part), not everyone appreciates being forced to play in its aftermath. I'm not asking you to announce your gift to the attendants at large, but since multiple people will be using the same play areas, it's a kind gesture to lay down a towel prior to play in an effort to keep the field in a more welcome and play-ready state. Was that couched gently enough?

All righty. I've laid out all you need to know and do to secure yourself a Lifestyle experience. I wish I had some final piece of wisdom to inspire you to get out there and give it a go. But, alas, I don't. All I can think to say is good luck.

Lesson 12:

When Fit Hits the Shan

Even the most carefully planned playtimes can go badly. The important thing to remember is what to do if things go awry.

What do you do if the male's profile pics were, at best, a few decades old? How about if the female you've been courting turns out to have a personality beyond bland? Or if the husband and wife who assured you they were in a deeply loving marriage begin snapping at each other to the point you're Googling a divorce attorney for them?

Extricating yourself from an in-person meet is trickier than rejecting over email. Sure, you could excuse yourself to the bathroom, then dash out the back exit, but even unsavory swingers run in social circles, and in high-tailing it, you risk building a bad reputation.

There are plenty of tactful rejections. "I don't feel the chemistry" or "I'm not comfortable playing right now" are a few. You can even play the "no play" card I discussed earlier. While you may prefer to give them a piece of your mind, it's best not to cause a scene. Unfortunately, not everyone can take a hint, and sometimes you'll need to state your disinterest in no uncertain terms.

Worst-case scenario is things get rocky during playtime. Maybe hubby wasn't completely honest with the "straight" label. Perhaps the woman isn't as sexually adventurous as she led you to believe. Frustrations can arise at inopportune moments, and making a graceful exit can be akin to pulling off a Houdini-esque escape. At these times, you may want to run for the hills. However, again, there are better ways.

For example, excuse yourself to the bathroom. Once calm, return and voice your discomfort. If the situation occurred owing to a misunderstanding, resume playtime. However, if the impasse can't be overcome, feel free to leave. Either way, a composed response is better than an emotional storm-out.

Case in point: I lucked into a spontaneous meet with a single female. We agreed to sushi and conversation and, if we clicked, we'd play at my place, which we did. Early on, I placed my mouth around one of her nipples and inhaled a Rapunzel-length hair that whip-cracked the back of my throat and triggered my gag reflex. Rather than demand she undergo an immediate chest wax, I composed myself and avoided her upper torso for the rest of playtime. My measured response preserved playtime and protected her feelings. Granted, I would have rather she'd taken a moment to perform some strategic plucking, but it wasn't like she had a dick.[1] Though we never met again (my decision), to my knowledge she never badmouthed me to others, which I have to believe played in my favor.

In extreme cases, a graceful exit may not be possible. As long as you've tried your best, do what you need to do to stay true to yourself.

One final word on crappy swing experiences: At the risk of sounding sentimental, bad experiences don't have to be *all* bad. I've found that my smattering of memorable-for-the-wrong-reasons encounters

---

1 Perspective really is everything.

made me appreciate the good ones that much more. Not to mention, the less-than-perfect times make great fodder for stories.

If it's any consolation, no one escapes the Lifestyle unscathed. In fact, a subpar experience is an initiation of sorts. While not the ideal homecoming, bad play is a sign you've officially arrived.

The Morning After

Student Became Teacher Becomes Student

No matter how tempted, how curious, how much I might be jonesing for play, I long ago vowed to avoid newbies. The few times I did manage to navigate their questions, indecision, and wavering and actually made it to playtime, it all ended disastrously anyway.

How could I forget that first-time couple, the husband of which relied on a few too many alcoholic beverages to soothe his nerves, which rendered him incapable of performing and caused him to projectile vomit his liquid courage, bringing a speedy end to the night before the fun truly began.

While I can't estimate with any level of certainty the newbie flake factor, I'd wager it's well north of 90 percent. But even with my anti-newbie stance, Tony and Nicole's profile stood out.

Sure, Nicole had a firecracker of a body, but it was their couples profile that drew me in. It was nothing fancy. They simply took the time to explain who they were and what they sought, which resulted in a profile more genuine than I'd come across in some time. My interest grew when they displayed impeccable senses of humor over email and chat.[1] Courting had entered its third week when Nicole suggested a video chat. Unfortunately, I've never been technologically savvy, a personality flaw Nicole graciously forgave moments before a window opened on my monitor offering a view of her and Tony lying in bed. Until that instant I'd yet to see their faces, perhaps because I wanted to live in ignorant bliss as long as possible before reality crushed my hopes. However, my fantasy wasn't dashed. In fact, it improved. Nicole had a cute smile laced with a devilish sexiness, and long, dark curls that framed an innocent face and bright eyes. Peeking into the frame was Tony, whose ruggedness was offset by a thick shock of salt-and-pepper hair.

Meet tonight? IMed Nicole.

Tad late for sunday? Besides, they lived in Thousand Oaks, a hefty jaunt from West LA, a distance I preferred not to traverse for a pair of unproven, inexperienced newbies.

Tony snatched the keyboard from Nicole, typed, *this change your mind?* then lifted Nicole's shirt.[2]

Address please, I responded.

I arrived at the Starbucks near their home to find they'd already appropriated an outside table isolated from the others. Tony and Nicole might have been newbies, but it was evident they had innate Lifestyle smarts. Remaining private while in public is an art swingers develop over time with experience. Just because our way of life carries a highly secretive component doesn't mean we don't eat out, grab a drink, or convene at our friendly neighborhood coffeehouse. We do. Moreover, we do so in full exposure of Vanilla folk (pun fully intended). But part of our awareness allows us to talk freely about sex even in the company of non-Lifestylers without drawing unwanted attention. Strategic seating is one such method.

---

1   Don't misunderstand; I hadn't grown tired discussing fantasies and trading pics. Does anyone, really? But make me laugh and I'm smitten. Keep me laughing—as did Tony and Nicole   and I'm yours.

2   I'll leave this visual to your imagination. But, suffice to say, more than just my interest grew.

Tony and Nicole proved just as funny in person, though Nicole was visibly nervous, a reaction I understood. Not only were they newbies, but their threesome fantasy was, at best, a few months old, newborn status in Lifestyle years. Then faced with the materialization of such a fresh fantasy, Nicole had more than a lot to process.

I promised her that despite the connotation of her "enticement" over video chat that convinced me to an impromptu meet, I didn't hold any expectations. We could chat and call it a night, I assured her, which seemed to give her some relief.

As I'd done at every other meet-up, we swapped stories. Tony lamented that every couple they'd contacted went bust. Never did he think it'd be this hard to find a compatible couple, which was why they had started considering single males. They'd gotten to know one other male, who'd flaked, which Nicole took personally. I assured her that that schmuck's behavior in no way reflected on her. Swingers flake. Plus, I added, I had just driven thirty miles on a Sunday night to a remote Starbucks on the spur of the moment to meet her. That had to count for something.

Nicole smiled.

I asked about their reasons for wanting to experiment with the Lifestyle. Tony said they'd tried role-play and toys, but that didn't satisfy. They asked about my experience. I shared a few stories, then recounted head-butting the ceiling fan at Theo and Arianna's, which sent them into hysterics. After they caught their breath, Tony admitted he'd been intimidated by my number of certs, but after hearing my story he was sure my abilities were comparable to his. I promised him I was no threat.

On that high note, I excused myself to the restroom to give Tony and Nicole a chance to confer. We'd covered a lot of ground in very little time. Web chat to meet 'n' greet to potential play was normally a progression that took me a couple weeks, minimum. With Tony and Nicole, in less than two hours, I detected that they had found themselves in uncharted waters and quite possibly felt lost at sea. But what they didn't realize was that my killing time in the restroom was just as much for my benefit as it was theirs. Never had courting clicked so well, so easily, and so quickly. And with a pair of unmarried newbies, no less: the couple demographic *least* likely not only to be in the Lifestyle, but also to actually participate. And they were good-looking. And smart. And funny. And sexy. Nicole, I mean. Well, I'm sure Tony was sexy, too, in his own right, but that's never been my thing. In any event, I marveled at how I had somehow engineered this absurd situation. Had I finally stumbled upon some magic courting formula? Had my six years of experience subconsciously coalesced into an actual technique? Or was this simply written in the stars?

I traced the chronology of events: the initial, nonpushy, nonthreatening contact; the honest, respectful email exchanges; the witty online banter; the (almost daily) open and honest communication; the flirting; listening to and heeding my instincts when advised to nudge courting to the next stage; Tony and Nicole feeling comfortable enough to suggest a spontaneous meet. Through it all I couldn't isolate a single difference in how I'd interacted with Tony and Nicole from how I had with all other potential playmates. In the end, I found no explanation for this unexpected success. I simply had to ride the wave and see onto what shore I washed up.

Then it dawned on me that I was getting worked up in the restroom of a Starbucks, a setting that didn't feel appropriate for the magnitude of my epiphany. So I washed my hands—I had to "sell" my absence, after all—and returned to Tony and Nicole, to whom I joked, "Well, that was your chance to escape. You're stuck with me now." They exchanged a knowing glance before Tony suggested we partake of the hot tub at their complex, which we did, then climbed into bed, Nicole lying naked between me and Tony.

"So how does this work?" she stuttered.

"How would you like it to work?" I responded calmly in an effort to relax her.

Due to what must have been an endless stream of images defiling her imagination, Nicole couldn't form a single word. She did, however, muster a nervous laugh. Tony took the reins and casually informed me that "Nicole's an amazing kisser."

I took Tony's hint and began making out with Nicole. In no time, she was leading the action and then began bragging that Tony and I couldn't possibly have the stamina to wear her out. Truly, it was more of a gauntlet thrown down than a snub of our manliness. Needlessly, Tony asked if I was up for making Nicole eat her words and, like a tag team of veteran lotharios, we rose to the challenge.

By two in the morning, we were overworked, overheated, and on the precipice of physical exhaustion, so we agreed to declare the contest a draw. Then, after a quick rehydration, I drove leisurely home, emailed work that I was taking a sick day, and blacked out in bed.

Inspired by the unexpected awesomeness of the Tony and Nicole experience, I rekindled communication with another newbie couple whom I'd been courting for some time. Ozzie and Anita were a young couple with two kids, both with learning disabilities. Family matters made scheduling a bitch, to say the least. Over the course of more than a year, we'd planned to meet at least four times, each of which they were forced to cancel at the eleventh hour due to some emergency involving their children. I understood—family must come first—but was still disappointed.

For the fifth attempt, Ozzie and Anita requested a quiet location in my area and promised, if we clicked, we'd head to my place. The whole day I was prepared for them to cancel. I even sent Ozzie a text a few hours before the designated time to assure him that I'd understand if they couldn't make it. I was eager to meet, but not if they were distracted by family matters. Ozzie replied that they appreciated my concern, but all was fine and they'd see me shortly.

As I expected, Anita was sultry, petite, svelte yet curvy: a naughty Tinkerbell. She was Spanish and, though she'd lived in the States more than a decade, still carried a thick accent. Ozzie was tall with a personal trainer's body. Personality-wise, he was a tad bland and reserved, but friendly enough.

It took us a good ten minutes to come to terms with the fact that this meet was really happening. More than a year of emailing and failed meets to reach this moment. All of us admitted we had harbored much doubt it'd ever come to pass. Turned out they'd emailed with other males, but I was the only one patient and understanding enough to endure the rescheduling so they could have their first Lifestyle experience. I told them I was honored and also that there was no pressure from me for play. If they were on the fence, I understood.

"We should tell him," Ozzie told Anita, who nodded her consent.

Their cryptic exchange made me nervous.

"You know our children are learning disabled," Ozzie began. "Well, so am I. Asperger's."

He explained how overstimulation affected him and how it was the reason they requested a quiet meeting place.

"All this is to say, if we play, it'll probably just be you and Anita. I'll only participate if I feel extremely comfortable. I just don't want you to feel it was anything you did, if I just watch."

"I appreciate it. Thanks for telling me."

Not well versed in mental disorders, I wasn't sure if the situation was now one wherein I'd be taking advantage of another. I mean, sure, I wanted to play with Anita. But not if it meant exploiting Ozzie. So, for the rest of cocktails, I debated whether play with Anita was morally defensible and, in the end, decided to let Ozzie and Anita determine matters. They decided we'd play.

During play, Anita frequently stole glances at Ozzie, who reclined on the couch beside my bed, to make sure he was all right. And he was.

So much so, in fact, that mid-play he approached Anita, who was on all fours performing some impressive oral on me, and joined. He kept his shirt and shorts on and didn't appear at ease, but he participated, which, even in the heat of play, struck me as quite a big deal.

Ozzie finished in a matter of minutes and excused himself to clean up; Anita and I wrapped up shortly thereafter. Before they left, Anita whispered to me how happy she was that Ozzie felt comfortable enough around me to take part. Now, I have no training whatsoever in the fields of psychology, therapy, or medicine. Other than the required prerequisites at my liberal arts college (inaudible) years ago, I have virtually no exposure to the subjects. However, the satisfaction I felt after receiving Anita's thank-you is what I imagine sustains a person through years of graduate and doctoral study, mountains of student loans, and grueling exams and licensing tests. In my case, after Anita shared her feelings, I didn't know what else to say except, "You're welcome."

It was that transcendent experience that, two years later, spurred me to send that first email to the profile that I knew, just *knew*, was a fake.

I was performing my daily scan of online members in search of new profiles when I happened across NewFem4Fun the same day her profile was posted. One glance at her only pic and I knew I didn't need to waste my time. To refer to NewFem as a golden, rainbow unicorn would be insulting. This prize filly was smelted from the purest titanium, had flawless eyes that made the Hope Diamond look like a shard of cubic zirconia, wielded a blinding, bejeweled horn, and flew upon a neon rainbow that gushed forth from the very loins of Aphrodite her goddess self. But even if her divinely anointed beauty was actually being offered up on the site, she was a free member without a single cert, and everyone knows the formula to deducing a fake isn't rocket science: *One profile pic + Free member status + No certs = El Fake-O.*

Within days, like every other fake profile, NewFem's would be flagged by members, deleted by monitors shortly thereafter, and the registrant's email address permanently blacklisted.

NewFem had to be fake. That was the only explanation as to why a woman of her caliber would join the site. A pic collector, possibly a promoter for some other sex-centric dot-com, must have uploaded some random pic of a leggy and lithe body that showed a hint of golden blond hair that draped over a dual horizon of perfect breast before the head was cropped out. There just couldn't be any other rational explanation.

But day after day, I spied NewFem online. I kept waiting for the ax to fall, but after she'd survived a week, I decided to skim her self-description, which began:

> *Newly curious single female in search of friend to explore the kinkier*
> *side of life. I'm not in any rush and am not interested in anyone who*
> *is. To be honest, I'm not sure if this is really for me, but I'm willing to*
> *give it a shot.*

Spammers don't waste time crafting a believable profile, as their life expectancy on any site is a fraction of that of ejaculated sperm. Their strategy is to slap together something just comprehensible enough that satisfies the minimum-word-count requirement, along with a pic (the real reason anyone views a profile), to ensure it'll pass basic security filters and post. Once part of the community, they rattle off as many emails as possible to any and every member in hopes of maybe, just maybe, convincing a handful of desperate, frustrated hornballs to click through to their site. As NewFem's profile appeared to have had some thought and effort put into its creation, at least by my first read, I figured it couldn't hurt to toss out an email. After all, her profile didn't ask for an outside email or phone number—two more indicators of fake/spammer status—so I did. And she responded. And, after a few days of back-and-forth, emailed me some personal pics to prove her authenticity.

Mid-twenties, blond, and blessed with the chest of a woman of much larger stature, Kirsten could have been a centerfold. No joke. Whereas I once had a girlfriend whose fake tits caused men to crane their necks when she walked by, Kirsten snapped vertebrae.

Kirsten was also very cautious. She was in no rush to meet anybody, much less play. She was clear that if she connected with a compatible guy, and if her gut gave her the green light, she'd meet. But playtime would only be the result of a long courtship, as she had to feel extremely comfortable.

At first, Kirsten's need for a sense of extreme comfort before considering play felt like a regression to the emotional morass of certain girlfriends long past. Especially with her need to have all her questions answered (repeatedly) and her uncertainty labeled as "normal" and "understandable" (again, repeatedly). But once she opened up about her reasons for seeking Lifestyle experiences, my hesitations over plunging back into the quagmire of my past evaporated. Kirsten didn't withhold any detail, not one single adjective, when she painted the deliciously graphic and divinely explicit pictures of her fantasies. My mind experienced every detail in Technicolor, Cinemascope, HD, 3-D, and Dolby 5-point-whatever surround sound effects.[3] She shared her deepest, most secret curiosities, which were the stuff wet dreams are made of. Day after day, we engaged in historic IM sessions while she toiled away in her cubicle at an escrow company. For good measure, we threw in some epic phone sex. And Kirsten quickly put me to shame. She was a mega-beast with the dirty talk. Nothing, and I mean *nothing*, was off limits with her. Try to embarrass her with some extreme suggestion miles past what you thought was the line in the

---

3   James Cameron, eat your CGI'd heart out!

sand and she'd retort with a sincerely contemplative "Hm. Add that to the to-do list."

My God . . .

After a month of some of the most intense give-and-take I'd ever experienced, Kirsten and I decided to meet. She reiterated that play probably wasn't in the cards (again the need for extreme comfort). Her rationale was bolstered by the sudden celebrity status showered upon her by site members. Any single female is the Holy Grail of the Life-style, but factor in Kirsten's undeniable allure and everyone was clamor-ing to sip from the Chalice of Kirsten.

Though not a stranger to attention, Kirsten hadn't expected the level of adulation thrust upon her the instant she joined the site. Be-sieged by dozens of daily emails and IM requests, she was overwhelmed by the sheer volume of interest. She wanted some good adult fun, but what she got was a Beatles welcome that scared the bejesus out of her. Somehow through that deluge of attention she felt a connection be-tween us that she deemed worthy of a face-to-face.

I prepped for play while not expecting it. I'd kill myself if Kirsten ended up wanting to play and I wasn't ready. We met at a cocktail bar halfway between our respective corners of the city. Everything was friendly and fun, nowhere near the level of sexual intensity we'd reached over chat, and, as expected, there was some nervousness on her part. This was her first in-person meet, after all. Not to mention, the courting progressed much faster than either of us had anticipated it would.

Even though she'd explicitly stated that we probably wouldn't play, I couldn't get the heated chat sessions out of my head and soon found myself pressuring her. I'd never pressured before, but I did with Kirsten. After only thirty minutes, I walked Kirsten to her car and forced a kiss on her. With my libido in overdrive from the drinks, I was convinced all she needed was a little push and we'd be headed back to my place. While she kissed me back, she upheld her no-play rule and drove off.

A few days later, I hit her up on chat and apologized for my behavior. She was kind to accept. But I knew I'd blown it. She was spooked. And I couldn't remember ever feeling that terrible. A month later, I caught Kirsten online and we briefly chatted. She revealed that she'd found a great guy on the same site. I congratulated her. She deserved him.

My mistake with Kirsten remains the most regrettable of my swinging life. And while I subscribe to the notion that regret is a waste, as what's been done cannot be undone, I'd be lying if I said I still don't wish for a do-over of that day.

I learned my vast bulk of Lifestyle smarts from those more experienced. Email etiquette, meet 'n' greet protocol, playtime tricks, you name it. Without veterans of every level of ability, I'd be more clueless today than when I started out. But newbies taught me my most valuable lesson: As much as I think I know, I'll always be learning. And I'm grateful for it.

When It Rains

The Lifestyle can be a heartbreaking existence of wasted energy, aborted hope, and effort for naught. It takes Kevlar skin and a Chicago Cubs fan's constitution to repeatedly brush off the disappointment and keep at it with the hope that someday, one day, you'll secure that one experience that makes all that blind sacrifice worth the suffering. And, once in a lifetime, that experience lasts nine days.

SATURDAY

An Evite reminder chastised me for not having RSVPed for Shelly's GB. Brian, Shelly's hubby, had reserved a penthouse suite and was corralling a group of guys to massage Shelly as a prelude to the festivities. It wasn't because of Brian or Shelly that I hadn't yet RSVPed. Shelly was a sexy BBW who gave great head and was as kind a soul as could be. Brian, as well, was great fun to be around. Not to mention extraordinarily gracious to share his wife. The reason I hadn't RSVPed was Brian had sent out the invite a month in advance and I never confirmed that far in advance. It's not all that uncommon to plan a month out, but I didn't know what could happen over the course of a month. I could have taken a shine to a new fetish, been invited on a Lifestyle cruise, maybe even found "the one." Okay, probably not that last one, but the point is, you never know. Shelly's party was the following Saturday at 5 P.M.

SUNDAY

As I clicked attend for Shelly's GB, it dawned on me that Kitty's GB was the same day. I did some quick mental math and calculated that with some careful time management and creative travel planning I could work them both in. Problem solved.

MONDAY

An unsolicited email from a couple informed me about a party they were hosting Friday night in the Valley. Based on the couple's profile, and their mass of certs, Louis and Terri were highly active in the community. They were mid-twenties, Hispanic. On the thick side with a goatee, Louis had a cool, laid-back air about him. Terri was a compact BBW with a ginormous chest on which, from what I observed in their pics, Louis loved to suck.

Louis informed me that some regulars were going to gather at a Van Nuys bar Tuesday night, if I wanted to join. Not a bad suggestion. I promised Louis I'd do my best to stop by. Reason I couldn't confirm was that I'd been emailing with Rob and Taylor for a few weeks, and they'd asked to get drinks Tuesday night. If all went well, they said, we'd play Friday.

Rob and Taylor were in their late forties but looked much younger. Rob had a football player frame with a barrel chest, salt-and-pepper hair, and a boyish grin. Taylor was Cali girl all the way: strawberry blond, with a perky chest and a mischievous smile. In one pic she was sex incarnate with an extremely low-cut, short black dress with fishnets. They seemed a fun, loving couple with a penchant for rough sex, dirty talk, and some strap-on play (I made a mental note to get some clarification on that last one; didn't want any awkward misunderstandings). The only drawback was they had just one cert and it only attested to their authenticity. No feedback on performance, experience, or personality. Certainly one cert is better than none, but theirs was generic at best, so my comfort was minimal.

I suggested an earlier time to meet to Rob and Taylor. That way I could do drinks with them then join Louis and Terri's group. They accepted.

TUESDAY

I arrived at the Mexican restaurant as Rob and Taylor were finishing dinner.[1] They appeared the stereotypical suburban loving couple out for a casual weeknight dinner—not the raucous, sex-addicted duo their profile depicted them as. Hair pulled into a ponytail, Taylor wore a powder-blue sweater, jeans, and sneakers. Rob was in a button-down and slacks. They could've come straight from a PTA meeting. Rob greeted me with a residual Texas twang. Taylor, as I guessed, was Cali born and bred.

The usual chat—Where you from? How's the site treating you? What brought you to the Lifestyle?—soon became more personal as we quickly reached a level of comfort. Turned out they weren't married and had kids from prior relationships, though I'd have never guessed Taylor was a mom. Even with the sweater and jeans, it was clear she had quite the body.

---

1   I know, I know. The cliché Los Angeles Mexican restaurant meet-up. But there are just so darn many of them, it's convenient. Plus, who doesn't love all-you-can-eat chips and salsa?

Rob told me about the time he took Taylor to her first strip club. He bought her a lap dance and the dancer allowed Taylor to touch her. The men at the club were so engrossed with Taylor's lap dance that the stage performer ended with few tips. I relayed how I injured myself during sex and had to get an arthrogram, which caused Rob to shoot beer out of his nose.

The forty-five minutes couldn't have gone better. So much so that Rob insisted on picking up the tab even after my protests. I hugged Taylor (incidentally, she smelled phenomenal), and Rob confirmed Friday's playdate as he shook my hand. I offered up my place and they said they'd let me know.

I headed to Louis and Terri's gathering, where everyone was keeping to themselves. I wasn't sure if most were newbies or just leery of exposure at a Vanilla bar. Thankfully, the drinks took effect and a moderately decent time was had. No one blew me away, but then again, I couldn't stop thinking about Taylor the Dream MILF. Everyone was nice enough, so I decided to give this Friday's party a shot should Rob and Taylor flake. I said my goodbyes and was the first to leave.

WEDNESDAY

Before heading into the office, I emailed Rob and Taylor that I had enjoyed last night and looked forward to Friday (a little reminder to head off flakiness never hurt).

Later in the day, Rob responded:

> Be warned: Taylor is quite the handful. She can't get it rough
> and hard enough. Be sure to slap her ass, pull her hair, and
> don't worry about being too firm with a hand around her
> neck. Just dominate her. Oh, she also loves, loves, LOVES
> being told what to do. And don't be afraid of offending ei-

ther of us. I affectionately refer to her as my fuck slut as she
adores it. Only nos: farm animals and potty games, LOL.

I'd heard the same bragging way too often from husbands/boy-
friends. And virtually every time, the woman's insatiable libido was
vastly embellished. The men weren't liars, just in love. The truth was,
it was their love that was insatiable, not their woman's sexual appetite.

My knee-jerk reaction was to give Rob's "warning" as much credence as I had the others. However, after replaying drinks with them—
Taylor quiet but focused; confident, not arrogant—I determined there
was a better than good chance that was the calm before Hurricane Taylor. I could very well have been walking into a Category 4, even 5. The
warning signs were there.

Rob's email ended: *We need to tire her out before I leave for business
in Texas on Saturday.*

I joked: *Sounds great!! I'll find some Viagra!!! LOL.*

Rob: *I would if I were you.*

No LOL. No j/k. No :-) or ;-).

He was serious.

Rob: *7PM, Friday, your place. Rest up!*

I was officially worried. First off because my gut was screaming to
take Rob at his word, a reaction it had never had before, and, second,
because my weekend had shaped up amazingly:

Thursday: Deena
    Friday: Rob and Taylor
Saturday: 1 p.m. — Alternate for Kitty's GB
        5 p.m. — Brian and Shelly's party
        8 p.m. — Mindy's GB (with a caveat that I might not make
            it)
Sunday: Perhaps Deena again

That schedule made me the envy of all single men, but the downside was I was sensing performance anxiety. With no frame of reference for this jam-packed itinerary, I hadn't a clue how I would fare. I needed insurance, so I went where all overly sexed, anxiety-ridden men seek help: Craigslist.

Why the hell is Viagra prescription-only? If ever a drug benefited mankind, it is Viagra. Were it readily available, not only would humanity exist more peacefully, happily, and satisfied, but slap on a tax and the nation's debt would disappear overnight. Granted, there would be a better than average chance the global population would spiral out of control within a couple years, but at least every nation would be in the black for a change.[2]

Before I tried my luck with the CL "vendor" pool, I considered concocting some story for my internist about job stress inducing erectile dysfunction, but I knew she'd prescribe a battery of tests to determine whether stress or some more serious physical malady was to blame. The downside to having a well-educated, practiced, and ethical doctor is cockamamie stories fall on deaf ears. If I made an appointment, I'd be looking at a small fortune in copays, deductibles, and unnecessary tests, all for a reliable stiffy. I was none too keen on voluntarily becoming a lab rat, nor did I have the time for medical shenanigans before Sexapalooza kicked off, so I stuck to CL.

A quick search revealed three vendors in my area, all of whom scaled their prices based on the number of pills purchased. One to nine pills: $10 each. Ten to twenty pills: $9 each. A full bottle (30 blue dia-

---

2   It occurs to me that this is my first mention of drugs. I should clarify that I don't hold anything against recreational drug use, as long as it doesn't hurt anyone else. The simple fact is, I've never enjoyed drugs. I spent a week in high school smoking marijuana and found all it did was make me lazy and hungry, both qualities I could easily achieve without drugs. In any event, like everywhere else, drugs do exist in the Lifestyle. Posts that mention "party and play" refer to such. So, yes, there are swingers who mix drugs and sex. If that's your thing, have at it; if not, you can just as easily avoid it. Now, back to my suspect drug purchase.

monds) was $180 and delivered free of charge. The Domino's business model lived on!

I immediately spotted an error in the pricing model. Nine pills x $10/pill = $90. At the same time, 10 pills x $9/pill = $90. I could exploit this mathematical loophole to stretch my dollar, but this slip-up did nothing for my confidence in the legitimacy of my potential suppliers or the safety of their product. But I figured a few emails couldn't hurt.

After I clicked send on the last one, I started to worry. I'd seen *To Catch a Predator*. Could there possibly be a black-market Viagra version? I envisioned myself in a neon orange jumpsuit handcuffed and leg-shackled as the judge arraigned me on purchase/possession of a controlled substance. When the substance in question was identified as Viagra, the gallery would erupt in laughter. I doubted Viagra carried any street cred in the pen, so I'd have to join a gang and race to put on as much muscle as possible in order to survive.

In an attempt to pacify my quickly spiraling out of control dementia, I did some research and discovered there are two kinds of Viagra: Pfizer Viagra and generic Viagra. The former is a patented, prescription-only, FDA-approved medication that comes in 25mg, 50mg, and 100mg doses. The other is a knock-off usually manufactured by foreign countries, then illegally mailed into the country. The Pfizer site warned against generic, partially, I'm sure, to steer more business to itself, but also because who knew what ingredients composed the unregulated pills? At best, an innocuous placebo; at worst, cyanide.

I was staring down the barrel of a four-day sexfest where I'd have to perform who knew how many times, so for the good of my weekend and the preservation of my health I decided only to consider Pfizer.

CLKing was first to respond. He was in Pasadena and claimed to have Pfizer 100mg for $12 a pill (apparently, the online prices were just a marketing ploy to drum up interest). Before I tapped into my Jewish roots to play some haggling hardball, I decided to wait until I heard from CLKing's competition. Perhaps they'd undercut his pricing.

Dude64 asked how many pills I wanted. I responded: *100mg Pfizer, 6 pills. NOT GENERIC.* I had no idea why I said six other than it felt right. He emailed a phone number.

Should I call from my cell or work? If I chose work and he was a psycho he could cost me my job. But I also didn't want a potential sociopath in possession of my cell number. In the end, I turned off my cell's caller ID and dialed. My call was rejected, as the person didn't accept calls from private numbers. I emailed Dude64, who confirmed that he didn't accept blocked numbers. Didn't those sting operations block their phone numbers, too? If so, didn't that mean that if Dude64 didn't accept them either, then he wasn't a cop? It sounded good enough to me, so I unblocked my caller ID and redialed.

Carl was his name. As online prescription drug shopping was new territory for me, I didn't know the questions to ask or the red flags to look for. The only thing I could figure to ask was if his pills were Pfizer, not generic, which Carl had already made clear via email they were. But I figured I needed to ask something, so I asked him again and he confirmed they were. The entire call felt not unlike working up the gumption to ask a woman out on a date. The conversational rhythm was awkward and funky and a discomfort permeated the vibe. After more than a few lengthy, uncomfortable pauses, I figured Carl sounded as normal as a Viagra dealer could sound (though I had no frame of reference upon which to base this conclusion), so I confirmed my six-pill order. He said I could pick them up downtown. I told him I was at work and would prefer to get them later that night. He said he had a Passover Seder on the west side and wouldn't be free until after 11 P.M. The fact Carl was a practicing Jew comforted me. He couldn't be dangerous if he sported a yarmulke, observed high holy days, and refused to skip Seder for business, right?

I told Carl 11 P.M. would be fine. He promised to call me after Seder and drop off the pills on his way home.

The instant I hung up, I decided I didn't want Rabbi Boner knowing where I lived. It was two thirty. I could make it to the ATM, then downtown by three forty-five. I called Carl back. He said it was fine for me to pick up my order as long as I made it before sundown, which I took as confirmation that Seder wasn't just a line to instill a sense of comfort in clients.

So I was ditching work to buy Viagra from some devout Jew on CL. What had become of my life? Then again, I couldn't believe I'd scheduled six playdates in four days. Yeah, life had definitely taken a hard left from its normal run.

I pulled into the alley at three forty-three and laughed at how fucking cliché the whole scenario was. Middle-class white boy ventures into dangerous inner city to feed his addiction. Albeit the addiction was slightly different than the cliché.

A rap on my window snapped me out of my mental tangent. Carl was schlumpy, late forties, and wore baggy, beat-up khakis, a flannel, and crooked glasses that made him look more English professor than drug dealer. I rolled down my window and Carl handed me a Saran-wrapped sextet of blue pills, which I inspected.

100mg. Pfizer. Said so right on the pills.

I handed him the money.

"Shalom," he said as I drove off.

Honestly.

THURSDAY

All day I vacillated between complete disbelief that I had summoned the courage to make yesterday's purchase and total doubt over my sanity. Every free moment I scrutinized the pills for counterfeit signs as described on Viagra.com. Blue, film-coated, rounded-diamond shaped. "Pfizer" debossed on one side, "VGR 100" on the other. I even locked my office door to watch the online video that outlined various counterfeiting methods, which only succeeded in terrifying me with the possibility that I had purchased six tabs of rat poison dyed with sky-blue ink toner and bound with gypsum. But other than my method of acquisition, I couldn't find anything dubious. In the end, it boiled down to whether or not I trusted Rabbi Carl.

I decided to perform a trial run with Deena that night. We'd played regularly for several months, so if Rabbi Carl did me dirty I could reasonably count on Deena to call 911 instead of a cab to anonymously drop me at the emergency room.

Deena made me dinner, after which I excused myself to the bathroom, where I uttered a small prayer and ingested a pill. I had thirty minutes before the magic was supposed to kick in or possibly seconds before the life was snatched from me, so I prolonged foreplay. And then . . .

Mazel tov, Rabbi Carl!

Deena and I went a second round before I headed home with an overwhelming feeling of confidence that I was prepared for my weekend.

FRIDAY

I left work early to tidy up for Rob and Taylor, who arrived right at 7 P.M. Taylor wore the black dress and fishnets from her picture and looked fucking amazing. Gone was the PTA mom; in her place had materialized a visage of carnality. We had barely closed the door before Taylor was rubbing her body all over mine and whipping her tongue around my mouth.

"I take it you wouldn't care for drink?" I asked as I came up for air.

Rob laughed at my suggestion that Taylor needed to be coaxed with liquid courage.

We headed to my bedroom and Category 6 unleashed itself so savagely that I didn't need daddy's little helper. Hurricane Taylor did whatever she wanted with Rob and me, mostly at the same time, and we struggled to keep up. Rob definitely wasn't kidding.

It was an amazing night, easily ranking in my top three. I must have lost fifteen pounds in water weight from the workout. By far, Taylor was my favorite EVER.

When they left three hours later, I collapsed on my thoroughly used and decently sweat-dampened bed to catch my breath. Not long after, I passed out.

SATURDAY

As I suspected, no one flaked on Kitty, so I was bumped. A petite Asian who referred to herself proudly as a slut, Kitty never failed to command a big turnout. It was just as well, because I needed more rest after Taylor. When I woke, I still couldn't believe the night I'd had with her. Truly unreal.

I finally rolled out of bed just before eleven and cleaned up from the previous night's blowout. At four I packed my gym bag: towel, condoms, bottle of lube, extra pair of underwear, deodorant, toothbrush, toothpaste. Before I left, I wrote a cert for Rob and Taylor:

I can't express in words the wonder that is T. But I'll give it a shot. Sexy, sultry, gorgeous, and the ultimate pleaser, T redefined sex for me. Making this life-changing event possible, and to whom I'm forever grateful, is R, a cool, laid-back, generous man I can't help but believe the women adore. T & R, I can't thank you enough. If anyone is lucky enough to meet this couple, drop everything to make it happen.

No traffic, so I made it to the hotel in Norwalk thirty minutes early. I parked, answered some emails, and perused new profiles before I headed to the penthouse, where Brian greeted me in his patented Hawaiian shirt. I knew some of the guests—Raymond and Sienna and Gil—so there was no need for awkward pleasantries.

Apparently Shelly's GB had ballooned to an orgy (no complaints from me). We were waiting on four more, Brian informed me, so I should help myself to the hors d'oeuvres.

Twenty minutes later, the final two couples arrived and Brian wasted no time unfolding a massage table in the middle of the living area. Shelly hopped up naked and a few guys assumed masseuse duty. I was more than fine hanging back, affording the eager beavers ample room to play. There was plenty to go around.

Brian was in the same state of mind. He reclined in a lounger with an unobstructed view of Shelly. My only complaint about Shelly has been that she telegraphs. For example, with three sets of hands kneading her skin, she moaned too loud to be believable. Her performance was obviously for Brian, who possessed some sort of massage fetish. But she didn't have to be so melodramatic.

Thankfully, things soon moved to the bedroom. Never known for his patience or tact or stamina, Raymond leapt on Shelly and got off in a matter of minutes. I tagged in and took my time to make sure Shelly was paid more attention, though it wasn't easy. As she did during the massage, Shelly telegraphed. Her face contorted in forced expressions that were way over the top and distracting. I had to mentally detach in order to stay hard and decided it best to end round one before things got too soft.

I finished and rolled off. I rinsed off the latex smell, wrapped a towel around my waist, and cooled down in the living area, where one of the wives was on her knees fluffing a pair of guys. She was fully dressed with her more than ample tits out so each fluffee could play with one. I relaxed on the nearby couch and partook of some veggies and dip while I watched her work. When her patients were sufficiently primed, she spanked them each on the ass and sent them back into the bedroom. She then turned to me and asked if I was interested in her services.

"Recuperating," I politely declined.

"No help speeding recovery?"

"You're not playing?"

"My time of the month."

"In that case, sure."

She scooted over on her knees and opened my towel.

"I'm Monica," she told me then set to work before I could introduce myself.

She was good. Very good. I saw why she had to send the other guys to the bedroom. I'd have happily sat there all day.

There was a knock at the door. Without breaking stride, Monica switched to manual with one hand and opened the door with her other to let in a mid-forties couple with whom I had played at a party some months back. If memory served, Bart and Debra. And memory definitely served, with the recollection that Debra's oral skills placed a close second to Monica's.

"Everyone's in the bedroom," Monica informed them. Debra shot me a wink before she and Bart disappeared into the back. "Well, soldier," commented Monica, "time for you to head back into the fray."

She was right. The little guy was back at full attention.

I thanked Monica, then headed once more into battle. For good measure, I popped a blue diamond, as I hated the thought of possibly insulting with a subpar performance.

In the ten minutes I was absent, the action had heated up. Everyone was playing. On the bed. In chairs. On the floor. Against the wall. Moans even echoed from the shower. Before my eyes adjusted to the dim light, a hand grabbed my forearm. It pulled me to Debra, who was being undressed by Bart. She kissed me. I spied some open space on the bed and led Debra to it. She was passionate and amazing, just like I remembered. Out of the corner of my eye, I glanced at the bedside clock: seven seventeen. I'd have to leave by seven thirty in order to make it to Mindy's GB in time. I finished my fun, cleaned up, dressed, and slipped out without disrupting the vibe.

While my GPS loaded directions to Mindy's party, I found Rob and Taylor had left me a cert:

What a truly amazing gentleman! We had an awesome time; this man was friendly, polite, articulate, and fun! R enjoyed seeing T loved and pleasured so much by this young man. He seemed to know what she wanted and when without her asking! We definitely will get together again; T wants more and more of this awesome guy!

So kind it made me smile.

I got a text from Mariah asking if I was free to accompany her last minute to an on-premises club. I was more inclined for some fun with Mariah than with Mindy, so I texted Mariah to send me the address, then emailed Mindy's host with my regrets. Since I was a soft confirm, I wasn't worried about the last minute no-show. I grabbed a sandwich on the way and, thirty minutes later, parked down the street from Larry and Helen's in Covina.

I'd never been a fan of clubs, but I'd always been a fan of Mariah. She'd been here one time before, but she left after twenty minutes because, she said, the single guys creeped her out. She wanted to give it one more shot, which is why I agreed to be her "date."

I texted her that I'd arrived and she came out in a robe to meet me. She said the place had a pool, a hot tub, a group room, a couple of private rooms, and even things she called "pods." We entered and she helped me get my complimentary robe, which wasn't a bad touch. We went to the pool and adjacent hot tub, where a dozen or so couples and a smattering of single men were skinny-dipping.

It wasn't the most hygienic of settings—the water had a thin film on its surface of what I presumed was lube—but it was blazingly hot out, even at dusk, so I grinned and bore it.

A few couples introduced themselves, but Mariah wasn't feeling them. In fact, she said, she wasn't taken by any of the guests. I told her I wasn't chomping at the bit to play myself, so we could just relax if she wanted. She admitted she was horny and asked if I wanted to explore a pod. I didn't know from a pod, but she was calling the shots, so I followed her lead.

We headed into the garden area, which was really more of a sub-urban jungle, to find four wooden structures that were a cross between utility sheds and sweat lodges for little people. They didn't have doors, just curtains. Moaning emanated from the first two, so Mariah pulled back the curtain on the third and summoned me in.

Inside was a short, narrow hallway with four makeshift cubby spaces, two on each side. Carpentered inside each cubby was a twin-size bedlike space with a foam pad on top. Think tour bus architecture with summer camp decor and no budget whatsoever.

Mariah yanked me into a cubby and closed the curtain. Immediately we started sweating, as not only was the summer clime atrocious in the Inland Empire, but we had zero circulation in a space barely big enough for one medium-size human. We made do as our excessive sweat and the residual lube from the pool alchemized into an oil slick and made sex more like baby oil wrestling.

Soon we were in doggy, and I caught something out of the corner of my eye: a guy peeking into the space with eyes bugged and tongue leering, jerking himself hard with one hand and gripping an unwrapped condom with the other. Worse, he was staring at *me*. I knew I didn't interest him sexually; he was just hoping I'd finish up so he could tap in. But even if I wasn't fucking full steam courtesy of modern medicine, Bro hadn't a chance with Mariah.

"Wanna cool off in the pool?" I asked Mariah in hopes of making a smooth egress from Sir Perv.

"Sure."

I glimpsed Creepy Guy watch us leave, disappointed.

"What's that you said about the guys creeping you out?" I asked Mariah.

As neither Mariah nor I were really feeling things, we called it a night when the barbecue started.

SUNDAY

I woke up rock hard (Viagra ain't no joke) and forgot what I had scheduled for the day. I checked email and texts and remembered I had tentatively scheduled another meet with Deena.

I showered, checked my profile. A few responses from some newbies. A couple of rejections. The usual.

Deena texted: *Helluva weekend. Gonna lie low 2day.*

I responded: *Me too.*

I needed the rest.

Full Circle

The hand with the meteoric diamond clenched the headboard to keep the rest of its body from black-holing into red-kimonoed Bob.[1] Bob, whose mass pancaked his portion of mattress to the frame, which caused our section to plummet toward him at a steep angle.

"Did I choose well, honey?" Bob asked his wife, his honey. Sierra was her name, a fact I'd learned moments before the three of us commandeered one of the private rooms.

"OhgodohgodOhGodOHGOD," Sierra crescendoed as I fucked her doggy-style.

I was staving off Bob's gravitational pull with only a mattress spring burrowing into my knee. I hoped I wouldn't sever anything important, as I knew from experience that nothing puts a damper on a night of erotic revelry like a little medical emergency. Just to be safe, I repositioned to surer footing without breaking stride.

Bob mimed for me to spank Sierra. I did, but she didn't so much as

---

1 Yes, the same Bob from the opening chapter. We've covered a significant amount of ground, so you may have forgotten him. Thought I'd play it safe.

acknowledge my act. Okay, perhaps there were some acts I'd never quite get the hang of. (Sorry, Melissa.) Bob mimed for me to do it harder. I unleashed a firm, authoritative spank and Sierra let out a long, guttural moan and began bucking against me.

I felt her ramp up to orgasm. She had a viselike grip that pulled me with her like a runaway train tows a flailing caboose. I controlled my stamina long enough for Sierra to reach a mighty climax, after which Bob flashed me a thumbs-up. To him, he was letting me know I'd done him proud; to me, though, it was confirmation that I'd completed my quest. That simple motion, the flick of Bob's thumb, his show of approval, was the permission I needed to finally exorcise the crushing weight of personal shame over my sexual inadequacy that I'd carried with me for so long. And in doing so I followed Sierra's lead and finished up playtime.

I collapsed on top of Sierra, who collapsed onto the bed. My cheek melted into her back and I heard her staccato heartbeat flit through the tinny ring in my ears. The muffled thumping blended with her inhaling, exhaling, inhaling and lulled me off somewhere peaceful and warm and home.

When my hearing was restored and the carnal notes drifting in from the rest of the house brought me back to the moment, I opened my eyes to see Bob staring down at me. I was still on top of Sierra, so gravity was shifted ninety degrees and the kimonoed Bob looked like a 'roided-out Buddha cratered into a mattressed wall.

"That was amazing," the Buddha whispered to me.

Thank you, he mouthed.

Like I said, I'm fucking hubby, too.

I grabbed a bottle of water from the nightstand and left Sierra and Bob to some private one-on-one time.

In the bathroom, I freshened up, gargled some mouthwash. I glanced in the mirror and saw that I inhabited the same body of the

one who was once convinced he was destined for cloistered life. However, the sad, lost, desperate eyes through which that two-pump chump
viewed the world were not staring back. In their place were two focused
orbs that radiated calm, unwavering confidence, and unshakable know-
ingness. I knew it was unshakable as I shook my head, then looked
again in the mirror to see that same, unyielding mojo. Nowhere in my
eyes was there even a residual trace of the frenzied fear and implacable
worry that had been their lifeblood. This man in the mirror, I didn't
fully recognize him, but I liked him. I most certainly did.

I popped a mint, wrapped a towel around my waist, and proceeded
down the candlelit hall. I passed the closed door behind which I heard
Sierra and Bob enjoying each other and stopped at the threshold to the
group area, where I surveyed the sea of intertwined bodies and limbs
that occupied every inch of floor space, undulating in synchronized
rhythm. It was a work of art. All those people with their individual
lives, their singular journeys through life, every one of them unique and
different, yet bound in communal ecstasy. Not to mention it was one
hell of a sexy sight.

Then I saw the Kid.

Across the sea of flesh, on the other side of the room, directly across
from me. Fully dressed, he wore the hallmark newbie expression—the
one of surreal wonder that says the mind can't process what the eyes see.
That same look of awe kids have on Christmas morning. Like first-time
parents have witnessing birth. Or believers meeting their god.

I watched him mentally wrestle to reconcile the world he'd always
known with this new one he'd always thought was a myth. An entirely
new outlook on life and its limitless possibilities washed over him like a
kinky baptism, and he knew life for him would never, *ever* be the same.
That part of him that couldn't stop wondering if he would have been
better off not coming finally gave up asking, "What if I hadn't taken
the red pill?" because it didn't matter. What's done cannot be undone.

I wondered what had brought him here. Did he have that same inner stirring that I had? Was he on some sort of quest? Or was his presence merely a fluke? We all have our own reasons and experiences that informed and guided us here, but ultimately we stay because we belong.

Aware that he was in his most fragile, malleable state, I wanted to grab him by the arm, pull him out of earshot, and lecture him about all those dead-end searches. The countless emails to profiles and posts. The chatting. The texting. The fruitless pic swaps. The phone calls from private numbers. The meet 'n' greets. The fakes and flakes.

And flakes.

And flakes.

The Kid needed to know about the motels, hotels, and secluded public locales he'd miraculously bypassed to land on that night's guest list. All the chasing and searching he should have endured before earning an invitation to a party of that caliber. The hoping, the praying. The never-ending, soul-crushing, suicide-inducing rejection. Most important, I wanted to ensure he wouldn't fuck shit up. He needed to know his presence was a privilege easily revoked. How one false move, one inappropriate comment, one unwelcome advance would land him in exile for life. For his preservation, and more important for mine, it was imperative I snap him out of his euphoric state and set him straight.

Then I felt a hand slide down my back and under my towel.

"I hope you saved some for me," Rose whispered in my ear.

Hmm, I thought. Why not let him enjoy his bliss a little longer . . .

Lesson 13:

Downtime

Curious readers, did you get the uncensored glimpse into the Lifestyle I promised? Was there enough debauchery for those just interested in sex? And for those in search of a knowledgeable guide, are you now armed with enough information to give it a go? I hope I delivered on all counts. However, if I came up short, I pray you find solace in knowing that I tried my best.

I'm sure some of the swinger stereotypes I railed against shone through. But I bet there was a fair amount you didn't know—flip-flops?—or perhaps hadn't even considered—The Break?—and that's good. If you knew everything, life would be one hell of a boring ride. Not to mention exhausting. Which brings me to my final lesson.

The Lifestyle takes a toll. Searching, emailing, scheduling, rescheduling, re-rescheduling . . . It can feel like more than a full-time job. I'm not complaining, just saying. I also want to say that the dedication necessary to become part of and to remain active in the Lifestyle makes breaks from the grind unavoidable. At times you just have to take a breather. Either that or risk physical collapse. Seriously. Though the

Lifestyle can provide an ever-evolving chronology of new and exciting fun, everyone has, at some point, needed time away.

For me, it's cyclical. Search, play, rest, repeat. And with every passing year, the time spent searching becomes less, play occurs more frequently, and rest periods last longer and longer. (Though I'm sure the needed rest has more to do with the progression of age than with the intensity and frequency of play. Father Time is a merciless bastard that way.)

Downtime for me is also when many questions bubble to the surface. What am I doing? Where am I heading? What is the Lifestyle endgame for me? What happens when I discover the limits of Swingland and, God forbid, when the fantasies run out? *Do* they run out? Is my quest finite or boundless? And, without fail, the Big One: Will I forever remain a single male in this community?

Since I began this whole swing thing, I have dated. But so far no one's clicked. At least not longer than a few weeks. And just as I knew during those torturous years when I floundered in relationship turmoil, before I even knew from the Lifestyle, I'm well aware my dating issues lie squarely and solely on me. It's been more than some time since I exercised the social muscles required to date without the foregone conclusion that sex was on the agenda. Sure, I've done plenty of emailing, chatting, texting, but in the Vanilla world, my version of all that comes *after* the finish line. I have to relearn how to run the race. And the thought of relearning that at which I royally sucked brings up a volcanic surge of anxiety and trepidation. The same dread that had me avoiding sex for fear of embarrassment. And the same terror that previously boomeranged me with a vengeance from my Vanilla homecoming back to playtime.

The fact is, I'm uncomfortable outside the Lifestyle. But for some time I've felt another internal stirring, an inner turning of the tide.

Dare I say it, a desire for a relationship. Granted, it's been a glacially slow shifting, but it's insuppressible and, frankly, not one I particularly want to stop.

Acts as simple as holding the hand of that special someone, her resting her head on my shoulder, or both of us just silently enjoying dinner palpably raise the temperature of my skin. In a good way. As ridiculous as that may sound, knowing what you do about my colorful past, the thought of a relationship—not just sex—fills me with a different sense of life. Again, in a good way.

However, I'm faced with the dilemma that I don't fit perfectly into either the Lifestyle or Vanilla world. I don't always have the energy (or stomach) for play, or the stomach (or energy) for the regular world. I want parts of both, but all of neither. For some mystical, seemingly unattainable hybrid reality is what I yearn. And, frankly, I often doubt its existence. But, then again, this was how I once viewed sex—as some far-off, hidden land populated by divinely anointed, nonhuman superbeings and look at me now. Not to brag, but I can hold my own.

I want to live in Swingland *and* the Vanilla world. I want the whispered nothings and the threesomes, the house parties and the honeymoon, a pseudo family inside the Lifestyle and a blood-related one out. But, in my mind, it's always been one or the other. For years I've been unable to reconcile a peaceful coexistence. Whether that's reality or just a mental block, I haven't fully figured out. But I feel my outlook changing. After all, the couples I've met and continue to meet in the Lifestyle make it work. Admittedly, it just may take me a tad longer. If you hadn't picked up on this during your read, I tend to be a slow learner when it comes to the social side of life.

But until I come to terms with everything, I'm beyond grateful to have a community in which I can seek refuge. A world I understand and whose rules, protocols, and customs have become second nature to me. After all these years, it can't help but feel like home and its people like family (in a nonincestuous way, of course). Invariably and thankfully, each time I return to my little sanctuary, I am welcomed with a warm, familiar embrace I can't express in words. Nor do I really want to. And that's probably a good thing.[1]

---

1 Perhaps this last lesson was really for me. But I'm sure there were a few nuggets in there you can use. If not, well, after all I've shared, I think I've earned one chapter just for me, don't you?

Little Black Book

Bonus Lesson:

So You Wanna Host . . .

There are probably some DIYers who've been taking notes. Those who insist on blazing their own trail rather than following the herd. I commend you. As does the community. For without you, our playtime opportunities would be measurably fewer.

However, for newbies who want to jump right in and host a party, doing so isn't simple. A good host doesn't slap together a guest list, rent any old space, and order everyone to get busy. The host bears great responsibility and is looked to with lofty expectations. Hosts hold high office in the Lifestyle. They create experiences, propagate ethics, and often are the make-or-break influence for guests (mostly for newbies).

In a very literal sense, hosts are the most visible Lifestyle ambassadors. When supplying an inaugural swing experience for someone, whether explicitly or by example, hosts set the behavioral tone, future expectations, and a frame of reference by which one views the Lifestyle. Give newbies a less than pleasurable time and odds are you've decided for them, possibly quite erroneously, that our little subculture isn't their cup of tea. But cultivate a safe, welcoming, and unintimidating environment for a first-timer, and you've given a newbie all she needs to decide for herself if the Lifestyle is right for her. And if she does join our clan, the hospitable experience you created will have encouraged her to carry on the mission of community betterment. Good job, you!

As well, experienced swingers place a significant amount of trust in hosts. Veteran Lifestylers have faith that hosts will architect realistic experiences for newbies and, despite any guest's individual level of experience, will uphold our ethos of understanding, respect, and discretion. When it comes to hosts, practiced Lifestylers expect a certain quality of experience, which includes a safe, friendly, welcoming environment; a decently vetted guest list; an acceptably clean facility; and logistically sound planning.

True, hosts bear quite a bit of responsibility. But they also hold the keys to the kingdom and, with them, a VIP all-access pass to a fantasyland of sex. I'd say the pros outweigh the cons in this arrangement.

So, in light of the fact that I may have inspired some readers to try their hand at hosting, let me offer some guidance.

How to Host a House Party

A house party host has one goal: to serve the party's purpose. Are you organizing a specific experience for a particular individual (GB, DP, wife share) or facilitating an event to focus on many (orgy)? Is there a theme other than just sex? Are you focusing on a fetish or welcoming varied tastes and predilections? Ask yourself the Passover question: "Why is this party different from all other parties?"[1]

Once a host answers these questions and countless others that will

---

1   Okay, so maybe my fellow Jews don't ask that exact question on Pesach. But it does illustrate my point quite effectively, wouldn't you agree?

define party parameters, she has drawn the general guidelines that will inform all decisions ahead of her, the honest answers to which will ensure the best overall experience for her guests.

Here are some of the basic questions hosts must answer when planning parties:

- **How big should my guest list be?** More often than not, *your* house will be the party locale, which means you probably don't want to be the recipient of a citation for a zoning infraction. I'm assuming you don't reside at a nightclub where you'll want a line fifty deep waiting behind a velvet rope in clear public view to prove to the world that your house is the place to be. Let your home's architecture dictate the size of your guest list. The *Brady Bunch* dwelling and the *John & Kate Plus 8* compound excluded, homes aren't built barracks-style. Two dozen swingers on a queen-size bed require a keen sense of geometry that puts a crimp in enjoying the moment. Invite a good number of guests without maxing out capacity. Lastly, since this is your home, it's best to make sure you know everyone on the list or, at the very least, have those guests you don't know referred by a trusted source.

  A question of prime importance to ask when assembling your guest list is . . .

- **Should I adhere to a gender ratio?** Unless you're facilitating a specific scenario such as a same-sex experience, aspire to an even gender ratio, meaning an equal (or as close to equal as possible) number of men and women. That way you avoid having an inordinate number of guests without partners waiting for an opening (pun fully intended).

An example of why gender ratio is an important factor at a party:

Well into my time in the community, I was contacted by a couple who hosted monthly get-togethers with different themes: Orgy Night, Couples Only, and BBW Appreciators are a few examples. The couple, a husband and wife, complimented my certs, suggested I'd be a good fit for their gatherings, and invited me to the upcoming Orgy Night. I accepted, drove forty miles to the house, and walked into a living room of, I kid you not, thirty men and *two* women. Now there's nothing wrong with a heavily lopsided gender imbalance. Sometimes that's what the host is going for. But, in my case, I wasn't sold a sausagefest experience. On top of the bait and switch played on me, guests weren't invited with consideration paid to, well, anything. Ages, sizes, personalities, even degrees of cleanliness were not criteria when the hosts were handing out invites. It was simply a numbers game to them, and a poorly played one at that. If not for the two wives in silk robes, the slapdash assemblage of disparate guests could have easily been waiting at a bus stop. The chemistry was that nonexistent. Needless to say, I didn't stay.

However, one thing the hosts of this ill-fated gathering did well was answer . . .

- **How do I disseminate information?** It's important your guests know the party particulars in advance. Date, time, location, theme (if any), donation amount (if any), what to bring (BYOC, BYOB), etc. . . . Email is best. It's fast, simple, convenient, and, unless the bone-headed recipient deletes your message, not easily forgotten or misplaced.

Sending a text isn't a good idea, as the day of your gathering you're going to be hit with an onslaught of texts from guests running late or flaking or claiming they didn't receive your previous text with the deets. Do you really want to tend to a cell blowing up like an EKG machine attached to a victim of cardiac arrest? Hell no! This is playtime!

One last word on disseminating information: Do so in advance of the party, but not *too* far in advance. People forget. Ideally, send a tickler email a week in advance, then one with all the pertinent info the day before. That way your guests can't claim ignorance.

- **When should my party start?** There isn't a prime time to start a party. Some are daytime, others at night, still others kick off in the wee hours. Whenever you decide, impose an arrival cutoff time. That way playtime isn't interrupted by Keanu, the lobotomized latecomer.

- **How do I handle parking?** Hotels have parking lots. My guess is your 'hood does not. A cul-de-sac that looks like the Burning Man campgrounds alerts neighbors to your soirée. Take it from me: it's no fun when Deputy McBonerkiller ends the fun prematurely. In your email listing the party specifics, ask guests to park a block or two away. It's a minor inconvenience compared to the embarrassment of public exposure.

- **Where should my guests play?** You don't need me to tell you that you won't like the sight of your unprotected couches after a swing function. To preempt such issues, don't blow your savings at Serta or vacuum seal everything in plastic. Just purchase some affordable sleeping pads and fitted sheets. Guests will appreciate their skin being saved from rug burns, and you'll appreciate not having to refurnish your house.

- **Should I have refreshments?** To avoid being eaten out of house and home, as well as to show some class, provide snacks and drinks. Don't lay out an all-you-can-eat smorgasbord, but a few options are appreciated. If finances are an issue, implement potluck or a nominal donation. You're offering up your place, after all; a little reciprocation isn't out of line.

- **How do I prepare my home?** Clean, vacuum, dust, lay out some air fresheners. Launder sheets and closet your prized linens. Take out the trash and place waste bins near play areas so that guests may conveniently dispose of "personal" detritus. Ensure sinks and toilets are functioning properly and reliably (don't risk a mid-party clog), hand soap and towels are in plain view, and extra rolls of toilet paper are within arm's reach. Lastly, lock up valuables and post signs on rooms you don't want guests to enter. A house party that reverts back to a home after the fun is always best.

- **Have pets?** Even if they love people, board them or keep them separate from the fun. It's a little awkward when you're trying to pleasure someone and Fluffy is rolling around trying to grab your attention for a belly rub.

- **Lastly, what about smoking?** Let everyone know the house rules or designate an area where people can cop their nicotine fix. Also, with today's cannabis laws becoming laxer by the toke, you may want to let your drug policy be known.

A WINNING HOUSE PARTY

MILF Jessica's GB was held at Leo's house in Whittier. I arrived at 2 P.M., as instructed, to find there were already a few guys watching porn in the den. I said the requisite hellos and, as Jessica had yet to arrive, found a place on the couch to wait with everybody else. Not a lot of conversation, but it was friendly, nonetheless. More guys showed and it looked as though there was going to be a decent number of guests, which boded well for the experience Jessica wanted.

While we waited, Leo went to the porch and retrieved a plastic tarp. The massive kind onto which one piles leaves, then drags to the curb for pickup. One of the guys inquired as to what Leo was doing. Jessica was a squirter, Leo said. "Huge squirter" was his exact phrasing—with a heavy, melodramatic emphasis placed on "huge." Having planted that mysterious, emphatically pronounced adjective in our heads that made us all envision a tsunami the force of which would knock our planet off its axis, Leo proceeded to his bedroom, where he draped the tarp over his mattress. We all expressed to one another how Leo's action was excessive and, frankly, pretty funny, but from the unseen master bedroom, Leo's disembodied voice chastised us, "Laugh now, but you'll see."

The guest of honor arrived twenty minutes late with hubby in tow. Jessica was considerably older than the pic that had been circulated over email. She had the leathery skin of a decades-old chain smoker with a tanning booth addiction. Though I was less than keen on the wee bit of license Jessica had taken with her pic, I'd driven all the way to Whittier and she warmly greeted each guest with a hug, a kiss on the cheek, and a sincere thank-you for participating and excusing her tardiness. She seemed a good person, so I stayed.

There were ten guys plus hubby, and, after hubby mixed Jessica a drink, he laid out the rules: condoms for penetration, no anal, she likes it rough. Everyone understood, so we relocated to Leo's bedroom, where his queen bed was indeed wrapped in the tarp.

I looked to Jessica, frightened about her reaction to Leo's preparation, but she didn't bat an eyelash. If anything, she seemed relieved. Perhaps Leo was right; we'd soon see.

Jessica got down to business and tended to anyone who wanted her to. Kevin had the most energy of the bunch and led the charge. He was also the first to unleash what I can only describe as the torrent of Jessica. I'd never (and still haven't) seen anything like it. The geyser she produced was so large in volume and powerful in force that it pushed Kevin out of her, deflected off his abdomen, and sprayed his face with an impressive sheen. All of us froze in astonishment, but Kevin howled in enjoyment, shook his head back and forth like a dog shaking off the rain, and proceeded to perform oral on Jessica so she'd anoint him with an encore directly on his mug.

My initial thought was that Jessica had somehow hidden a water balloon inside her. But the gushers came every other minute, and they weren't decreasing in volume or strength. One by one, we voiced our sincere apologies to Leo for doubting his judgment and thanked him for preparing us.

I tapped in when Jessica was lying facedown on the bed. I lay before her so she could service me while another guest enjoyed her from behind. I must say, Jessica's oral skills were impressive. Not the best I've ever experienced, but definitely up there. You could tell she took immense pride in her abilities.

After an hour of play, Jessica took a smoke break, during which the rest of us killed time by swapping stories. Kevin talked about some woman he'd met on CL who was a total bitch to him and kept mouthing off and doing coke. But he still played with her, and, in the end, she admitted it was all an act to get Kevin to grudge-fuck her. She turned out to be actually super nice.

Jessica returned and knelt on the floor to blow three guys at once who, after a few minutes, bent her over the bed and positioned towels under their feet to secure traction in the face of Jessica's floodgates having been ripped off their hinges. Jessica kept gushing, so we took turns mopping the hardwood to guard against anyone slipping or getting injured.

Everyone was polite and did their utmost to give Jessica the group experience she sought. A week later, Jessica sent a mass email to the group thanking us for the experience.

Leo was a good host. He organized a gathering with a specific goal for a particular individual. It served Jessica's desires, upheld guests' expectations, and went off without a hitch. Granted, the tarp was slightly jolting, but it proved necessary. The party wasn't the most high concept event or the most intricate production, and needn't have been. Leo had a goal and he achieved it, masterfully so.

How to Host a Hotel Party

While there's a lot of crossover between house and hotel party planning, the hotel party has some additional considerations that must be addressed. Remember, you're not on your home turf, a situation that must be handled accordingly.

- **Your venue:** The Four Seasons may be the pinnacle of luxury, but it isn't suitable for an orgy. Similarly, guests will be none too pleased with the Bates Motel. A standard room at a three-star establishment is fine, not to mention economical. Also, you'll want to choose a hotel with easy access. A cabin in the Poconos may ensure unparalleled privacy, but will paying guests want to strap on the snow chains to make the journey? Luckily, many reputable hotels are located right off major freeways. Reserve a room at one of those.

- **Your guest list:** Just as house size influences the number of guests, let room size limit the number of invitations you extend. An economy room offers different capacity than the presidential penthouse. Popular is great, but fifty horny adults in a budget suite isn't logistically wise. Also, unless your event demands otherwise, you want to strive for an even gender ratio even more than a house party host. Remember, these are "paying" guests; you don't want them getting irritated having to wait to play.

    A major difference between the house and hotel party guest list is how each treats the flake factor. I've well established the flakiness of swingers. But because a house party host knows her guests or had them referred by reliable sources, she has a much lower flake factor. The hotel party host, though, tends to invite more non-vouched-for guests. Remember, she has to cover her expenses. And it's these unknown, unproven guests who are most apt to flake and, by doing so, set off a detrimental chain reaction. Flakes disrupt the gender ratio, which adversely affects playtime, which leads to fewer returning guests and, ultimately, less feasibility of future parties. The most immediate effect for the host, however, is too many flakes decreases the amount of donations collected that were supposed to cover expenses.

    To guard against flakes, a hotel party host should pad the guest list. If she judges ten the ideal attendance, she should invite twelve or thirteen. That way, should a few guests flake, she'll have it covered. But should everyone show, she's only slightly over her ideal number, so the room won't be uncomfortably jam-packed. Make sure not to overpad; having too many guests risks irritating everyone by cramming too many into too little space. Also, if you have to turn away last-minute arrivals due to overcrowding, you'll have upset them, too. A safe guesstimate of flakes is 10 to 20 percent of the guest list. Plan accordingly.

- **Room location:** You're on another's private property, which means you don't want to draw attention to yourself or your adult-themed party. Doing so will end the fun before it begins. Don't tell management you're hosting an orgy, but a little white lie that you're a light sleeper secures a room out of the way.

- **Advance info:** You won't have the room number until you check in, which may be the day of the party. As such, be sure to let your guests know the approximate time you'll email that information. However, because it'll be such short notice, you may have to get your guests' cell numbers so you can text the room number. Earlier, I mentioned having been communicated the room number by way of a piece of paper the host had placed on his windshield. This method worked just fine. What I'm saying is, make sure to have a plan to let everyone know which room, as reception may grow suspicious of visitor after visitor asking to be directed to the gang bang.

You may also want to scout out secondary entrances to help your guests avoid front desk exposure. It doesn't take a trained eye to spot pheromone-spouting men and sluttishly clad women scurrying to the elevator, trying to draw as little attention as possible.

- **Arrival times:** Small groups arriving five minutes apart are less conspicuous than a platoon of twenty marching through the lobby. It takes a little planning to schedule everyone's arrival times, but it's well worth avoiding detection. Also, you may want to enforce a strict cutoff time. This ensures punctuality and avoids inconvenient interruptions.

A HOTEL PARTY FOR THE AGES

Fullerton was a bit of a drive, but I got to the hotel just before arrival time. I pulled into a parking space and saw Brian and Shelly getting out of the car beside me. For discretionary reasons, I didn't acknowledge them, headed inside, and took the elevator up to the room. When I got out, I saw Tim, Raymond, and deaf Asian Katy waiting in the hall. Tim said Lissandra and her hubby needed a few more minutes to prepare. We waited as more attendees arrived and joined us in the hall. Ten minutes later, and just before our little group grew to suspicious size, we were invited in to the corner suite.

Lissandra was just as attractive in person as she appeared in her pics, and her husband, Marty, had a refined elegance. They looked the perfect *Ozzie and Harriet* suburban couple. Both wearing festive Christmas sweaters, they greeted each of us and welcomed us into the room they'd decked out in full-on holiday decorations, complete with platters of homemade brownies and cookies, which Lissandra made us promise to eat. I saw the raised, heart-shaped Jacuzzi filling with thick bubbles to one side and a king-size bed on the other. A couch and a few sofa chairs furnished the rest of the space. The awkwardness that always begins these events was quickly dissolved by Lissandra's bubbly personality, helped by the fact most of us already knew one another, having met at other parties.

More guests arrived, bringing our total to three women and twelve guys, a gender imbalance we were told to expect, as ladies' night was the subtheme. Lissandra was getting antsy and told Marty to start. Marty asked for everyone's attention. We quieted down and he gave a speech:

"Welcome, everyone. I'm so glad all of you could make it. Some of you we know, some of you we don't. Either way, we regard you as friends and we hope to see you again in the future. Lissy and I are very excited to see everyone and we know this will be a fun time had by all. So, Merry Christmas and let's get naked."

A formal speech was a little weird, but the weirdness washed away when play began. Lissandra quickly became occupied as she was by far the most attractive of the women. Also, the email said she was a three-hole slut, so, of course the guys beelined for her. I opted not to be part of her first platoon and instead hung back. I did, however, take Shelly up on her offer for some head as I knew her talents intimately. I watched Lissandra tend to two guys at once while Marty snapped no-face pics (no faces except for Lissandra's).

There was too much activity to write about everything in detail and, frankly, I'd rather let my memory savor this one. But I have to share what happened upon Tina's arrival. Tina came with her boyfriend and another guy, all of whom looked shell-shocked by the volume of action they walked in on. They eased their way into the room and saw Lissandra in a Santa hat on all fours with Asian Katy beneath her eating her out while Tim doggied Lissandra from behind and she sucked Brian's cock. A true challenge of positional acumen. Lissandra spied Tina and her jarred state and, ever the gracious hostess, popped Brian's cock out of her mouth and bade the new arrivals, "Try the fudge. I made it myself." Then she resumed sucking off Brian. Totally hilarious!

The party was a hit and everyone asked to be invited back next year.

Lissandra and Marty went the whole nine yards. Corner suite, holiday decorations, homemade fudge. Most hotel parties aren't nearly as elaborate. And they needn't be. What Lissandra and Marty's guests remember most is the fun, not the attention they paid to prep. Sure, it felt nice walking into the spacious, decorated room with a Jacuzzi and an impressive spread of food. But when play began, all that faded away.

What I hope you take away from Lissandra and Marty's party is the tone they set. Under all the bells and whistles, they hosted a warm, well-planned, and discreet hotel party. Perhaps Marty's speech wasn't the norm, but it didn't leave anyone confused about their intentions. Everyone felt more than safe enjoying a sexy holiday celebration.

• • •

There's no secret recipe to success when it comes to party planning. Even the most meticulously executed event can flop. But Wayne Gretzky said, "You miss one hundred percent of the shots you don't take." I support you in taking your shot at hosting. Just do so with common sense and logistical forethought. Oh, and don't hesitate to throw an invite my way.

Acknowledgments

William Callahan, who came out of nowhere, worked in record time, and over-delivered at every turn.

Matthew Benjamin, who believed and who labored to mold the story to readable form.

Matthew Kelty, who suffered early, semi-coherent drafts, yet never left me in want of support, encouragement, and, most important, honest critique.

Polly Watson, who made me sound gooder than I be.

Josh Karpf, who ensured my words looked their best and who korrekted [*sic*] scores of late-stage changes.

The teams at Touchstone, Simon & Schuster, and InkWell, all of whom calmly and patiently shepherded this first-time scribe through the marathon maze of publication.

Shane Harris, who did the same.

Sophie Vershbow, who was ever so sweetly scandalized.

Tyson Cornell and Julia Callahan of Rare Bird Lit, who hit the ground running.

Acknowledgments

David Forrer, who assumed responsibility.

Dad, who told me to be whatever I wanted in life, but said the greatest gift I could give him would be *not* becoming a lawyer. And Joan for not objecting.

Mom, who assured me erections were normal and who, I'm certain, never foresaw one of her progeny committing this sentence (or this book) to print.

Tom, Cheryl, and Ramona, none of whom saw this coming.

Kerry, who listens to me blather on about everything and nothing.

Inna, worth every copay.

Matthew Specktor, much-appreciated advisor.

Mark Sarvas, ditto.

Tank, trusted confidant.

Chris, of enviable prowess.

Seb, who makes me "suffer for good."

And, finally, to those who spotted your cameo, thank you not only for being part of my quest, but also for enduring the rockier stages of my evolution. It wasn't easy for me, so I can't imagine how it was for you. I don't know many of your last names—perhaps even your real first ones—but I know *you*, which is what truly matters. Should my recollection of events differ from yours, please know it wasn't intentional. In Googling quotes about memory, I found that Tennessee Williams wrote, "Memory takes a lot of poetic license. It omits some details; others are exaggerated, according to the emotional value of the articles it touches, for memory is seated predominantly in the heart." Which is where each of you—even those of you lucky enough to have escaped the final edit—reside.

Glossary

The following are common Lifestyle acronyms, sexual positions, and terminology.

Acronyms

BAC—Big Asian Cock
BBBJ—Bareback Blow Job
BBC—Big Black Cock
BBW—Big Beautiful Woman
BDSM—Bondage Domination and Sadomasochism
BJ—Blow Job
BLC—Big Latin Cock
BWC—Big White Cock
BYOC—Bring Your Own Condoms
CL—Craigslist
DA—Double Anal, where the anus is penetrated by two penises
D/D Free or DDF—Drug and Disease Free
DP—Double Penetration. Two men penetrate a female simultaneously: one vaginally, one anally
DPP or DV—Double Pussy Penetration or Double Vaginal
GB—Gang Bang. Group sex, with attention focused on a single female
LTR—Long-Term Relationship

Glossary

MBF—Married Black Female
MBM—Married Black Male
MLF—Married Latin Female
MLM—Married Latin Male
MWC—Married White Couple
MWF—Married White Female
MWM—Married White Male (Not to be confused with MFM)
MFM vs. MMF—MFM is a threesome situation where the female is the center of attention and there is no bi action between males. MMF leaves open the possibility of bi action between males.
MFMF—Two men and two women engaged in sexual relations. Usually two couples.
NSA—No Strings Attached. Synonym for casual sex.
SAF—Single Asian Female
SAM—Single Asian Male
SBF—Single Black Female
SBM—Single Black Male
SLF—Single Latin Female
SLM—Single Latin Male
SWF—Single White Female
SWM—Single White Male

Positions

69—Two participants simultaneously perform oral sex on each other, stomach-to-stomach, with each person's head pointing toward the other person's feet.
Prone/Missionary—Female lies on her back and the male is on top, facing her.
Cowgirl—Female straddles the male's hips, facing him.
Doggy—Female on hands and knees with the male on his knees behind her.
Piledriver—Female on shoulders with her legs thrown back over head with the male standing, penetrating the vagina from above.
Public Displays of Affection (also PDA)—Physical acts such as hugging, kissing, holding hands, and petting that are done in full view of others.
Reverse Cowgirl—Female straddles the male's hips, facing away from him.
Sidesaddle—Female lies on her side while male penetrates straight-on (as in missionary position).
Spoon—Male and female lying on their sides, facing the same direction, one behind the other.
Standing 69—Simultaneous oral sex between two participants where one stands and holds the other upside down.

Standing Doggy—Female standing, bent at the waist, with male behind her.
Standing Missionary —Both participants are standing upright, facing each other.
Standing Reverse Cowgirl —Male stands and holds female in front of him facing away from him, with female not touching the ground, and male penetrates her.

Terminology

Alternative (also Alt)—A subculture of the Lifestyle that connotes BDSM.
Anal Sex (also Anal)—Insertion of penis into the anus.
Analingus—Oral sex performed on the anus.
Ankle/Wrist Restraints—Sexual tools that bind a participant's ankles or wrists.
Ass-to-Mouth (also A2M)—Anal sex followed by fellatio.
Autofellatio—Sexual act in which a male participant performs fellatio on himself.
Ball Gag—A tool used mostly in BDSM that consists of a ball-in-mouth gag restraint, possibly harnessed to the head.
BDSM (Bondage/Domination/Sadism/Masochism)—A specific type of sex that centers on erotic, but not necessarily sexual, activity.
Bi-curious—One who is sexually interested in the same gender, but hasn't experienced it.
Bi-friendly—One who isn't bisexual or bi-curious, but who doesn't object to the concept of bisexuality.
Bisexuality (also Bi)—Sexual orientation where the individual has sex with both genders.
Bit Gag—A tool used mostly in BDSM that consists of a bar running through the mouth, possibly harnessed to the head.
Blowbang—A gathering of multiple men, usually at least four, and only one woman, wherein the men are serviced by the woman only orally.
Bukkake—A fetish, having a Japanese origin, in which a group of men ejaculate onto a woman.
Butt Plug—A sexual tool usually made of plastic, latex, or glass, which is inserted into the anus.
Candids—More revealing pictures, nude or partially nude.
Certification (also Cert)—An online testimonial many websites use so members can authenticate other members and/or render a performance review.
Collar—A sexual garment (usually leather and associated with the BDSM lifestyle) like those worn by dogs and cats. Typically denotes a submissive in a BDSM relationship. The terms *collared* and *owned* mean a submissive is in a committed relationship.
Corset—A piece of lingerie usually worn by a female.

Glossary

Cougar—An older woman who sexually pursues younger men.

Creampie—The result of a man ejaculating inside a woman's vagina or anus.

Crop—A tool used in BDSM that is almost identical to the whip used by jockeys on racehorses.

Cross-dressing—When a man dresses up in women's clothing or a woman dresses up in men's clothing.

Cunnilingus—Oral sex performed on the female.

Daddy/Mommy—The dominant member of a couple.

Deep-Throating—A type of fellatio that takes the erect penis deep into the mouth.

Dominant (also Dom or Domme)—Someone who enjoys dominating sexually.

Domination—A sexual behavior characterized by generally brutal, punishing acts.

Donation—A monetary contribution required for attendance at certain Lifestyle gatherings. They are customary at swing clubs, for most hotel parties, and occasionally at house parties. Single females often aren't required to donate. Couples usually pay a moderate amount, single males the highest.

Exhibitionism—Erotic behavior, sexual or not, that takes place in a publicly visible area. Such behavior includes, but isn't limited to, flashing, oral sex, and intercourse.

Facial—When a male ejaculates on the female's face.

Fellatio (also Blow Job)—Oral sex performed on a penis.

Fetishes—An erotic act of a sexual nature for which one holds a particular affinity. Examples are BDSM, spanking, hair pulling.

Fingercuffing—A tamer version of DP in which a recipient is simultaneously penetrated vaginally or anally while performing fellatio on another male.

Fishnet—A type of stocking, usually worn by a female, where the weave of the material has more space between threads.

Fisting—A sexual act in which all five fingers and hand are inserted in the vagina or anus.

Flake—One who commits to an in-person meet but doesn't show.

Flashing—A central component of exhibitionism in which the flasher reveals his or her sexual organs to onlookers in a public setting.

Flogging—An erotic act, normally in BDSM, in which one participant whips another with a flogger, a specific kind of whip that is characterized by a hard handle and many leather tresses.

Fluffer—A female who makes a male's penis erect, usually with her mouth or hands, in preparation for sex with another.

Foot Worship—A fetish that involves fascination with feet.

Footing—A sexual act in which some or all of one's foot is inserted into a vagina or anus.

Gagging—Fellatio performed to the point where the performer coughs and drools excessively.

Gag—A sexual tool used to inhibit use of one's mouth. Examples are bit or ball gags.

Gang Bang—A sexual act in which a minimum of four men have simultaneous sex with the same woman.

Garter Belt—A garment worn around the waist that holds up stockings.

Glory Hole—A hole in a wall through which a male inserts his penis and has it anonymously pleasured. Normally found in adult bookstores or theaters.

Grinding—A sexual act where one rubs his or her genitalia against another's.

Group Sex—Similar to Orgy, but more specific in that everyone engages in sexual acts.

Hair Pulling—An erotic act where one's hair is pulled by another, normally during sex.

Hall Pass—Figurative permission that one half of a committed couple grants to the other half that allows the other to engage in sexual relations outside of the committed relationship.

Hand Job—A sexual act in which one person pleasures another by use of his/her hand.

Hard Swap—A sexual situation in which couples trade spouses to engage in sexual relations. Considered a step up from Soft Swap.

Hotel Party—A Lifestyle gathering at a rented location, usually a hotel suite. More intimate than a club, but more informal than a house party. Donations are usually required to cover expenses.

House Party—A Lifestyle gathering at a residential location. More intimate than clubs and hotel parties due to the location being the home of the hosts, which requires trust and discretion. As most guests are friends or vouched for, donations aren't usually requested.

Leash—An erotic tool, usually in BDSM, that attaches to a collar.

Lifestyle—A global community whose members (swingers) engage in sexual relations as recreational or social activity.

Lifestyle Club—A Lifestyle gathering held at a private residence that is run in a businesslike manner. Donations almost always required.

Meet 'n' Greet—Informal gathering of swingers during which everyone susses out the others in hopes of determining the presence of sexual chemistry. The meet 'n' greet immediately precedes playtime.

Mutual Masturbation—Sexual act in which at least two adults masturbate together.

Newbie—Inexperienced swinger.

Nipple Clamps—Sexual tool, usually in BDSM, that attaches to the nipples.

One-on-One—Lifestyle encounter between two individuals who are not in a relationship. Usually a single male/female and another single male/female. Occasionally a single will meet with half of a couple; however, this experience requires a Hall Pass.

Oral Sex—A sexual act in which one uses his/her mouth to stimulate another's genitalia.

Orgy—A group sexual act that involves six or more participants, at least two of which are females. If there is only one female, the act is considered a Gang Bang.

Paddle—A sexual tool, usually in BDSM, that is characterized by a flat, firm design usually made from leather.

Playtime—Informal term for sexual relations between swingers.

Reverse Gang Bang—A sexual act in which a minimum of four women simultaneously engage in intercourse with the same man.

Role-play—Sexual relations couched in a scenario such as Teacher/Student, Cop/Suspect.

Rough Sex—A more aggressive form of sex that may include hitting, punching, slapping, etc.

Sex Swing—A bondage toy suspended from a ceiling that holds a participant for sex acts.

Slut—Endearing slang for one who enjoys sex and engages in it frequently.

Soft Swap—A sexual situation in which couples trade spouses and partake in kissing and petting, but not intercourse.

Spanking—An erotic act whereby one participant strikes the buttocks of another with at least a moderate amount of force.

Strap-on—A sexual tool worn about the waist, normally by a female, which has a dildo mounted on it to simulate an erect penis.

Submissive (also sub)—One who likes to be dominated sexually.

Swinger—One in the Lifestyle.

Sybian—A motorized toy that resembles a saddle with a dildo coming out of the top.

Threesome—A Lifestyle encounter with three participants. Usually a couple plays with a single male or female. However, three singles may participate as well.

Triple Penetration (also Airtight)—A sexual act wherein there occurs simultaneous penetration of the mouth, vagina, and anus by penises.

Unicorn—Slang for a single female active in the Lifestyle.

Vanilla—*Lifestyle slang.* NOT of or in the Lifestyle.

Voyeurism—A type of fetish in which one watches others engaged in sexual acts.

Whipping—An erotic act whereby one participant strikes another with a whip, usually on the buttocks.

About the Author

Daniel Stern is a screenwriter who placed in the top four of Project Greenlight, was a Sundance Lab screenwriting finalist, and produced the independent feature films *This Is a Business* and *Half-Dragon Sanchez*. He has a B.A. from Wake Forest University and an M.F.A. from the Actors Studio Drama School. Currently, he lives in Los Angeles.

Author Certs

"Sexy, sensual, responsive . . . if you pass him up, well, good—because then he will have more time to get together with us!"

"A workout AND dessert! Intoxicating   "

"The evening was off to a great start and ended with a bang, actually a few bangs."

"He started with a sweet languorous tenderness that soon rose to a burning passionate climax. He brought me there over and over again."

"Dangerous is this man's middle name!"

". . . took the time, patience, and effort to get to know us and was never pushy or in a rush; he's polite, respectful, and fun."

"He conquered me like Napoléon conquered France . . ."